Women, Football and E
Histories, Equity and Exp

Preface

International Football Institute

The International Football Institute (IFI) is a partnership between the University of Central Lancashire (UCLan) and the National Football Museum to advance football research and its application. IFI was launched by Malcolm McVicar, Vice Chancellor of UCLan, in November 2003.

IFI has four aims: to adopt a multi-disciplinary approach to research; to engage in football-related knowledge transfer; to disseminate its work to the widest possible audience, locally, nationally and internationally; and to enhance the reputation of UCLan and the National Football Museum.

IFI brings together two organizations with outstanding expertise in relation to the study of football. UCLan, one of the UK's largest universities, has a critical mass of scholars undertaking research aspects of football from a wide range of perspectives, from history and sociology, economics and business studies, to science and coaching. The National Football Museum, which explores the history of English football, has a particular international significance, as England was the birthplace of the modern game, and the Museum is also the permanent home of the FIFA Museum Collection. The Museum holds the world's finest collections of football memorabilia, totalling over 30,000 items, including the collections of the English Football Association and the English Football League. The National Football Museum is at Deepdale Stadium, Preston, the world's oldest football league ground which is still in use today, where football has been played since 1878, and which is less than one mile from the Preston campus of UCLan.

In June 2005, IFI held its second international academic conference, entitled 'Women, Football and Europe', which attracted over 70 delegates from around the world. The conference was led by myself, Dr. Jessica Macbeth, Dr. Jonathan Magee, Jackie Day (all of IFI) and Kate Potter (David Taylor Partnership) and this volume brings together many of the papers presented at this conference. IFI is very grateful to Dr. Jayne Caudwell, Dr. Katie Liston and Professor Sheila Scraton for their contributions as members of the Conference Editorial Board and their work as co-editors of this volume. With regard to the Vancouver Protocol and the order of Editor order of this volume, Jonathan Magee is listed as first Editor to reflect his substantial contribution in the preparation of the manuscript for publication.

Kevin Moore
Director
International Football Institute
www.uclan.ac.uk/ifi

Museum Director
National Football Museum
www.nationalfootballmuseum.com

International Football Institute Series

Jonathan Magee, Jayne Caudwell,
Katie Liston, Sheila Scraton (eds.)

Women, Football and Europe: Histories, Equity and Experiences

Meyer & Meyer Sport

Editors of the
International Football Institute Series:

Graham Baldwin, Kevin Moore and Jonathan Magee

British Library Cataloguing in Publication Data
A catalogue record for this book is available from the British Library

Jonathan Magee, Jayne Caudwell, Katie Liston, Sheila Scraton (eds.)
Women, Football and Europe
Oxford: Meyer & Meyer Sport (UK) Ltd., 2007
ISBN: 978-1-84126-225-3

Aachen, Adelaide, Auckland, Budapest, Graz, Indianapolis, Johannesburg, New York, Olten (CH), Oxford, Singapore, Toronto
Member of the World
Sport Publishers' Association (WSPA)
www.w-s-p-a.org
Printed and bound by: CPI Wöhrmann Print Service
ISBN: 978-1-84126-225-3
E-Mail: verlag@m-m-sports.com
www.m-m-sports.com

CONTENTS

ACKNOWLEDGEMENTS

Thanks are due to Dr. Graham Baldwin (Chair, Strategy Group of the International Football Institute) for his support in the production of this book and to Suella Catterson, Emma Kelly and Gail Simpson (Catering and Conference Services, UCLan) for their help in organising IFI Conference 2005 'Women, Football and Europe'. We are grateful to all the presenters and participants at that conference for their support and responses to versions of the chapters contained in this volume.

And finally, we are grateful to Myrene McFee for book-making and index-compiling skills.

Jonathan Magee, Jayne Caudwell, Katie Liston and Sheila Scraton.
January 2007

ABOUT THE CONTRIBUTORS

Jayne Caudwell is senior lecturer in the sociology of sport and leisure cultures at University of Brighton. She is course leader for the degree in the *Sociology of Sport and Leisure* and teaches social and cultural analysis of sport and leisure at undergraduate and post graduate level. She previously worked at Leeds Metropolitan University and the University of Wolverhampton. Her main research interests are gender, sexuality and football cultures and recent publications include Caudwell, J. (ed) (2006) *Sport, Sexualities and Queer/Theory* (London: Routledge), Caudwell, J. (2003) 'Sporting Gender: Women's Footballing Bodies as Sites/Sights for the [Re]Articulation of Sex, Gender and Desire', *Sociology of Sport Journal* 20: pp. 371–386, and Scraton, S., Caudwell, J. and Holland, S. (2005) '"Bend it like Patel": Centring "race", ethnicity and gender in feminist analysis of women's football in England', *International Review for the Sociology of Sport,* 40/1: pp. 71–88. Jayne has played national league football for Wolverhampton Wanderers and Huddersfield Town and has played for, and managed, Hackney Women's FC. Also, she gained her referees qualification and preliminary coaching qualification in the early 1990s.

Ruth Jeanes is a full time Research Associate at the Institute of Youth Sport at Loughborough University, working on evaluations of national initiatives aimed at increasing physical activity participation in young people. She is also currently undertaking a part-time PhD examining the construction of gender identity amongst young female footballers. Her particular research interests are gender, youth sport, and developing research methods to improve communication with young people involved in research. Ruth is a Football Association Level 1 Coach and is involved with coaching junior girls teams at local level.

Tess Kay is Senior Research Fellow in the Institute of Youth Sport at Loughborough University. She is a social scientist with extensive experience of academic and policy-related research in the areas of sport and leisure studies. Her main research interests are in sport, leisure and social structure; sport, leisure and the family; and sport, leisure and gender. Tess has undertaken contract research for the Football Association and has recently completed a study of black and minority ethnic representation for Leicestershire and Rutland County FA (with Steven Bradbury). She is

Managing Editor of *Leisure Studies* journal and a member of the *World Leisure* Editorial Advisory Board. Recent publications include *Sport and Social Exclusion* (with M.F.Collins, Routledge) and 'The Family Factor in Sport' research review for Sport England. She is the supervisor of doctoral studies by Ruth Jeanes on girls' experience of football, and by Jo Welford on women's experience of the male football structure.

Colin King is Project Manager of the Martin Shaw King Trust, focusing on addressing structural inequalities in coaching, management and administration and capacity building of Black and Minority Ethnic communities. He is also a Lecturer at Westminster University in Race, gender, youth and transition. Colin has 20 years of managing social work provisions in mental health and child protection and has been delivering coach education and working to enhance the social and political position of black people in the structures of sport for the last 15 years. His main research interests are institutionalised racism in coaching, management and administration, misdiagnosis in schizophrenia and mental illness and racism, and child protection and race. Colin's main pulications are King, C. (2004) *Offside Racism. Playing the White Man* (Berg: London and New York) and King, C. and Wagg, S. (2004) "'Play the White man': Identifying institutional racism in professional football" in S. Wagg (ed) *British Football and Social Exclusion*. (Routledge London and New York). Colin also possesses the UEFA A Coaching License and is a Level 1 FA Educator and Child Protection Tutor.

Katie Liston is Senior Lecturer in Sociology at the Department of Sport and Exercise Sciences, University of Chester and Programme leader for the MSc degree in the Sociology of Sport and Exercise. She is also co-director of the Chester Centre for Research into Sport and Society which is a teaching and research centre for postgraduate students (www.chester.ac.uk/ccrss). Prior to this, she worked at University College Dublin for a number of years where she combined her teaching and research interests with national and international sports representation in Gaelic games, athletics, rugby union and football. In the latter, she has attained national club titles, a number of senior international caps and she has participated in the UEFA Women's Cup. Her main research interests lie in sociology generally and the sociology of sport in particular, and recent publications have included studies of pain and injury, women's football, gender relations in sport, and the sociology of sport in Ireland.

Ramon Llopis Goig researches in the Department of Sociology and Social Anthropology at the University of Valencia (Spain) and teaches Sociology of Sport, Social Research Methods, and Multivariate Data Analysis. His substantive research interests include gender issues, racism, national identity, mass media, consumption and globalization in sport, with a particular emphasis on football. He has been involved in recent research comparing football cultures in England and Spain, and he is co-author (with John Williams) of *Groove Armada* (London, Mainstream Publishing, 2006). He has published extensively in academic journals, as well as contributing chapters to several books. His most recent article is *Football Clubs and National Teams: The Ethnoterritorial Dimension of Spanish Football* (Revista Internacional de Sociologìa, 2006). He is currently working on a monograph on *Sociology of Football in Spain*, and a collection entitled *Postnational Football: Identity Transformations of the Global Game in Europe and Latin America* (Barcelona, Anthropos, forthcoming).

Jessica Macbeth is Lecturer in Sports Studies in the Department of Tourism and Leisure Management at the University of Central Lancashire. She was previously Research Fellow at the International Football Institute and was a member of the Editorial Board for the IFI Conference 2005: Women, Football and Europe. Prior to joining uclan Jess was a PhD student in the Department of Sports Studies at the University of Stirling. Her main research interests include sport and socialisation, sports subcultures and various issues relating to women's football and disability football. Recent publications include Macbeth, J. (2006, forthcoming) 'Becoming a Footballer: Socialisation Experiences of Women Footballers in Scotland', *Football Studies*, 9(1) and Macbeth, J. and Magee, J. (2006) '"Captain England? Maybe one day I will": Career paths of elite partially sighted footballers', *Sport in Society* Volume 9(3): pp. 444–462. Jess is a devoted fan of Port Vale FC.

Jonathan Magee is Chair of the Operational Group at the International Football Institute and is also a Senior Lecturer in the Division of Sport and Leisure at the University of Central Lancashire. His research interests in football include labour migration, economy, and identity and politics in Northern Ireland. Jonathan was Co-Editor (with Alan Bairner and Alan Tomlinson, Meyer and Meyer Sport, 2005) of *The Bountiful Game: Football Identities and Finance* which was an outcome of the IFI Conference 2004

'European Football: Influence, Change and Development'. As a football player he was capped by Northern Ireland at every level to Under 21, represented Northern Ireland, Ireland and Britain in international university tournaments, participated in the 1991, 1993 and 1995 World Student Games, and also played in the European Cup Winners' Cup. Jonathan is a UEFA 'A' Licensed coach and Staff Coach at the Centre of Excellence at Preston North End FC.

Laurence Prudhomme-Poncet works as a physical education and sport teacher in a secondary school in Lyon and successfully defended her doctoral thesis on the history of women's football in France in 2002. As an Associate Researcher at the *Centre de Recherche et d'Innovation sur le Sport* (Université LYON I, France), she worked on the history of women in sports, in particularly ball games. Her main publications are Prudhomme-Poncet, L. (2003) *Histoire du football féminin au XXe siècle*, (Paris: L'Harmattan), Prudhomme-Poncet, L. (2003) 'Mixité et non mixité: l'exemple du football féminin', revue *CLIO, Histoire, Femmes et Sociétés,* No. 18, and Prudhomme-Poncet, L. (2002) 'Femmes de foot', revue *Panoramiques*, No. 61. In Lyon, she played for Caluire Sporting Club from 1981 to 1995, for the University team from 1990 to 1993 and also coached a girls team between 1989 and 1991.

Aarti Ratna is a Lecturer at the Carnegie Faculty of Sport and Education, Leeds Metropolitan University. Her interest in sport, 'race' and the politics of identity and difference is explored through her doctorate study, which she is currently completing at the Chelsea School, University of Brighton. The thesis is specifically about British Asian females and their experiences of playing football.' She has spoken about her PhD research at a number of international conferences about sport, sociology and social policy. Aarti also works for the English Football Association as a Racial Equality Tutor and in the past she has sat on workshop panels for the anti-racism football organisation '*Kick It Out*'.

Sheila Scraton is Professor of Leisure and Feminist Studies at Leeds Metropolitan University and is currently Pro-Vice-Chancellor (Research). She has extensive experience teaching on undergraduate and postgraduate pathways in leisure and sport studies and was the founder of the Gender network across the University. Her major research interests include cross-national qualitative work on women and sport; sport, ethnicity and gender; women and football; older women and leisure; gender and physical education; leisure and feminist theory. She has published extensively in leisure and sport studies, is a member of the Advisory Boards of *Leisure Studies*, the *Journal of Sport and Social Issues* and *Sport, Education and Society* and was a panel member for Unit 69, RAE 2001 (Sports-related Subjects) and is Deputy Chair of Unit 46, RAE 2008 (Sports-related Studies). She is a life long supporter of Liverpool FC (mens) and now follows the women's game whenever possible.

Bente Ovèdie Skogvang is Associate Professor in the Department of Health and Sport Studies, Institute of Sport Science, Hedmark University College, Elverum, Norway. Previously Bente was a Research Fellow and Research Assistant at the Norwegian School of Sport Studies in Oslo and. Bente has recently completed her doctorate "Toppfotball — et felt I forandring" ['Elite football — a field of changes'] at the Norwegian School of Sport Studies. Bente co-authored Skogvang, B., Peiterson, B. and Stanley-Kehl, K. (2000) Soccer Today (Wadswort's physical education series. Wadsworth Thomson Learning, Belmont, USA) and presented a paper, 'Transfer of African Football Players to Europe and the Media' at the World Congress in Sociology, Durban, 2006. Bente has also been Director of Serieforeningen for kvinnefotball and has a long personal history with women's football which includes referring the 1996 Olympic Games Women's Final and being a member the Executive Board in the Norwegian Football Association from 1996–2002.

Susanna Soler-Prat has a degree in Physical Education and a degree in History and has been an Assistant Professor in INEFC (Physical Education and Sport Studies Centre) in Barcelona since 2003. Susanna's areas of expertise in teaching include multiculturalism and gender in PE and sport, and women and sport, sport history and performance sport and sociology. Her main research interests are on values, particularly gender relations in PE, and women's elite sport. She is presently conducting a PhD on Gender relations in Physical Education. Susanna's publications include Puig, N. & Soler, S. (2003) *Women and Sport in Spain*. Susanna has played 5-a-side football since 1993 and was selected by the Catalan national team from 1996 until 2004 when they were sub-champions of the Spanish National

Championship in 1998, 1999 and 2004. She also coached the Catalan Junior National 5-a-side squad from 1999 to 2002.

Jo Welford is currently completing a PhD at Loughborough University, provisionally entitled 'Discourses of Difference: The Experiences of Female Footballers in the UK'. This is an in-depth study of the experiences of women involved in various football roles, playing and non-playing, exploring the tensions they face through being involved in a sport closely associated both structurally and culturally with men and masculinity. Main research interests include women and football, the application of feminist post-structuralism, youth sport provisions and values, and the structural links between male and female sport. She has also been involved with various research projects for the Institute of Youth Sport, and currently plays football and sits on the committee for Loughborough Students WFC.

INTRODUCTION

Jayne Caudwell, Katie Liston, Jonathan Magee and Sheila Scraton

In England, according to the Football Association, "football is now the number one participation sport for women and girls, with over 100,000 playing regular football in England. This wide participation base, in addition to the clear health, education and social benefits, is good news for today's grassroots and future England teams" (www.thefa.com/Euro2005/NewandFeatures/Postings/2005/06/Euro2005_EnglandPlayersReception.htm). This statement was made in the context of a celebration reception at the Houses of Parliament for the England team and the tournament organisers of the 2005 UEFA Women's Championships. The selection of England to host the 6th UEFA Women's Championships was in part recognition of the growth and development of football for girls and women in England (with the north-west of the country particularly vibrant) but also significant in that the tournament was held for the first time in the self-proclaimed 'home of football'.

Eight nations (Denmark, England, Finland, France, Germany, Italy, Norway and Sweden) competed across five venues in the north-west of the country throughout June 2005 and there was major disappointment in the England camp that England's efforts were not rewarded by qualifying for the latter stages. As it was, Germany defeated Norway in the final at Blackburn Rovers's Ewood Park ground to record their fourth tournament victory. Without the tournament this publication — and the companion volume (Magee, Baldwin and Kelly, 2007) — would not exist as it is a collection that has emerged from presentations delivered at the International Football

Institute Conference 2005, 'Women, Football and Europe', hosted by the University of Central Lancashire (UCLan) in Preston, England. The conference was held during the tournament in conjunction with Sport England as part of the Euro 2005 Legacy Programme and had the backing of UEFA, the European Governing Body. The conference provided a forum that recognised not only the emergence of women's football as a popular pastime but also the importance, depth and variety of emerging scholarly activity. What is contained in this volume is a collection of papers that have been themed around issues of history, experiences and equity in women's football.

Keynote speakers at the conference included Karen Espelund (Chair of UEFA Women's Football Committee), Kelly Simmons (Head of Football Development, Football Association), Jean Williams (author of *A Game for Rough Girls: A history of women's football in Britain*), Gail Newsham (author of *In a League of Their Own! The Dick, Kerr Ladies Football Team*), Sue Lopez MBE (former England international and Head of Women's Football at Southampton FC and Director of Centre of Excellence) and Sir Trevor Brooking (Director of Football Development, Football Association). uclan was a poignant choice of locations in which to host the first ever academic conference dedicated to women's football, as the famous Dick, Kerr Ladies team of the early to mid twentieth century was based in Preston. Indeed the Conference dinner was a celebratory evening dedicated to the Dick, Kerr Ladies team, with former team members in attendance.

Much of the research on women's football today has been driven by the competitive successes and the related increasing public profile of national teams such as those of the U.S.A, Germany and Norway. However, it is easy to forget that women have been playing football since the late nineteenth century. Section One takes as its point of departure the historical emergence and development of what has come to be known as 'women's football' in various European countries. This section builds upon existing historical literature on women's football in Europe, much of which has, perhaps unsurprisingly, focused on Dick, Kerr's Ladies. Indeed, readers will note Prudhomme's reference to the competitive outings between Dick, Kerr's Ladies and a French women's football team in the early 1900s. That being said, we know relatively little in comparative terms about the emergence and development of women's football beyond Britain. Thus, the contributions in Section One are an important step in this regard because they add to the fund of social and historical knowledge about women's football. In Section One, Macbeth, Prudhomme and Skogvang offer us hitherto unavailable access to empirical data on the similarities and differences in the development of women's football in different areas of Western Europe. Taken together, the three socio-historical investigations of women's football in Scotland, France and Norway provide an important foundation for researchers in this field of study to extend further the parameters of comparative research *within* and *across* national boundaries.

As Macbeth notes at the outset of Chapter One, in spite of various cultural and social differences some striking similarities have emerged in international socio-historical investigations of women's football, the most noteworthy being that "it [women's football] has generally been marginalised and treated as subordinate in relation to dominant sports cultures" (p. 3). This is nowhere more evident than in Scotland where Scottish football culture is dominated by men at all levels, including the level of ideology. Whilst the more pessimistic readers amongst us might despair at Macbeth's account of the ways in which women's football in Scotland has, at different stages of its development, been suppressed by the dominant sports culture such that women's football was considered an anathema at one point in time, she argues that the resilience of advocates of women's football contributed strongly to the emergence of an enduring, organized and modern sport in the twentieth century. Indeed she suggests that, "by 1921, women's football in Scotland had, arguably, reached a peak in popularity and this was reflected in the organization of international and domestic matches that attracted significant numbers of spectators" (p. 12). Not unlike existing accounts of women's football in England (see, Lopez, 1997 and Williams, 2003, for example) the changing social climate in Scotland in the early to mid twentieth century reflected a narrower acceptance of women's football as the charitable role of women's football became less relevant in the context of social reorganization. Of particular significance here, Macbeth argues, was the reaction of the Scottish Football Association to UEFA's 1970 motion to recognize women's football. In contrast to other FA's such as Sweden, West Germany and Denmark, the Scottish FA chose to receive the motion as a recommendation rather than an expectation thereby delaying the eventual recognition of the Scottish Women's Football Association established in 1971. That being said, rapid transformations have taken place since then such that Macbeth has concerns about the potential skill drain resulting from female Scottish players 'plying their trade abroad'.

Prudhomme's examination of the development of women's football in France in the twentieth century — a process that is described as "a chaotic development ... (with) a complete interruption in the middle of the twentieth century" (p. 27) — raises a number of important issues. In Chapter Two, readers will note with interest Prudhomme's claim that, because of World War One, teachers, doctors and other professionals did not include women's football in their public support for physical education programmes for women. Undoubtedly, this has parallels in other countries. But the particular form in which this was expressed in France in the early twentieth century meant that the opposition of the national athletics federation (Union des Societes FranÁaises des Sports Athletiques) to women's football was rebutted somewhat by the formation of the Federation des Societes Feminines Sportives de France (FSFSF) in January 1918. The FSFSF established the first official women's football championship in 1919 which was played under adapted playing rules including smaller field dimensions and shorter playing time. In Prudhomme's words, "the game was thus referred to as *edulcore, denicotinise* which when translated means 'sweetened, sanitized" and "*adouci, adapte, feminise* which means softened, adapted, more feminine" (p. 30). However, the expansion of women's football was relatively stagnant in the inter-war years (as was the case with women's rugby union in France) such that the FSFSF withdrew its support for these two sports and concentrated its efforts on other more acceptable sports. Nonetheless, and as we have seen elsewhere in Europe, a 'new age' for women's football in France (post 1965) saw the game move from being a sideshow to official recognition by the national men's federation in 1970. Notwithstanding these developments, Prudhomme concludes the discussion with a cautious note about the potential condemnation of women's football to relative anonymity in the sporting media and, related to this, the knock-on effect for the delayed professionalisation of the women's game.

Section One concludes with Skogvang's discussion in Chapter Three of the history of women's football in Norway. Supporters of international women's football will be more than familiar with the competitive successes of the Norwegian team in the past decade or so but less familiar, perhaps, with the historical trajectory of women's football in that country from a 'show game' to a national and international success story. Indeed Skogvang argues that:

> as in other countries, the journey for women's football in Norway involves 'show matches', a ban by the game's authorities and subsequent struggle for acceptance and integration into the Norwegian Football Association (NFA) before popularity and acceptance was achieved. (p. 41)

Skogvang's personal involvement in Norwegian women's football from the early 1970s on as a player and an international referee contributes to an insightful and entertaining discussion of what appear to have been tense social relations between advocates of women's football and the Norwegian Football Association in the 1930s. Thus, it may surprise readers to learn that, in spite of the recent international success of female Norwegian footballers both individually and collectively, earlier formal public support for women's football "was intermittent and sporadic ... Consequently women's football remained under-developed and under-supported until the late 1960s and early 1970s" (p. 44).

One reason for the subsequent successes of Norway in international women's football was the impact of the women's movement in Norway in the 1970s and the establishment of the Gender Equality Council. These broader social changes, which were occurring relatively independently of sport and women's football in particular, contributed to a more open social climate in Norway which enabled the women's game to diffuse steadily, though not without its detractors, throughout the country. There was the view, for example, that football would become, in Norwegian terms, a 'frøkensport' or a 'sport for wimps' if women were to be formally recognised by the Norwegian Football Association. Skogvang points to the leading role played by pioneers of the women's game in the face of this opposition and the consequent establishment in 1975 of an NFA Women's Committee. Since then, Norway has been involved in European and international competition and often with great sporting success. Alongside this success on the field of play, and perhaps of more interest here, Skogvang's discussion also highlights the social success of women's football off the field of play and the ways in which the Norwegian model of integrated development can offer many lessons for others.

Equity is the focus of Section Two of this publication, and remains a key concern for those involved in debate surrounding women, gender and sport. For the past three decades sports feminists have rallied for equal opportunity for women to participate. The idea of equal rights and a just system, in sport, has propelled a liberal feminist agenda that has been successful on many fronts. Football can now be described as a sport in which women are treated fairly. Participation rates, opportunities to train, compete, coach, manage and officiate have increased significantly. The numbers of women currently involved in football is a result of changes in the infrastructure of the game.

In recent times, it is the governing body, the Football Association, which has instigated moves toward gender equity. For example, the *Football For All* campaign "is about fairness" and "recognising inequalities exist and taking steps to address them" (www.thefa.com/TheFA/EthicsAndSports Equity). The FA has an Ethics and Sports Equity Department, an Ethics and Sports Equity manager, and an Ethics and Sports Equity strategy. Racial equality, homophobia, disability football, social inclusion and women's football are areas that are specifically addressed. The concern for equity in football has also fuelled research and writing by those studying the game. Academics, practitioners and policy-makers have helped expose inequality, injustice and the processes and practices that marginalise and exclude players, coaches, managers and officials. In this publication we explore equity as it relates to race, ethnicity and racism, sexuality, homophobia and, to some extent, gay pride.

For some time now, the FA has been involved in tackling racism and continues to work towards achieving racial equality in the game. Initiatives include: financially supporting the *Kick it Out* campaign; achieving Sporting Equals Racial Equality Charter; initiating Report Racism project; forging links with the Commission for Racial Equality, *The Voice* and *Eastern Eye* newspapers; and encouraging county, national and international footballing organisations to act against racism. It can be argued that within many of these campaigns 'race' is understood in relation to the experiences of Black men. Through a focus on professional men's football and professional male players the aim to "unite against racism" (www.thefa.com) is in danger of ignoring the diverse experiences of 'race' and ethnicity, and of course gender.

In Colin King's chapter, discussion highlights the complexities of 'race', racism and gender. King, known for his work on Black players' experiences of professional football in Britain, reflects on gender relations within the institutions of football and the Black community. King continues to develop his arguments surrounding whiteness, again adopting Franz Fanon's concept of the 'white mask', and extends previous analysis through a consideration of how whiteness impacts on Black women's experiences of football management. King outlines the ways a Black woman manager negotiates the culture of the White man, and argues that the negotiations are similar, in some ways, to how Black male players have experienced the professional game. In addition, he considers how Black masculinity can function to deny Black women equality. Drawing on anecdotes and personal experiences as a Black man working in football in South London, King considers previously omitted nuances of 'race' and racism, to expose the gendered experiences of Black women. Such detail is often ignored in official policy.

It can be argued that ideas surrounding 'race', racism and ethnicity are founded on a socially constructed, and therefore artificial, racial binary of Black and White. Such a construct has, in the past, occluded discussion of the diversity of 'race' and racism. More recently, Asian ethnicity has come to the fore. The FA now celebrate *Asians in Football*, and the National Anti-Racism Week of Action in Football (13th-25th Oct. 2005) included reference to "black, Asian and other ethnic minorities" (www.thefa.com/TheFA/EthicsAndSportsEquity/RacialEquality/Postings). Links have been made with men's teams such as Sporting Bengal United, Sporting Khalsa and Guru Nanak FC. Professional clubs, such as Leicester City, Charlton Athletic, Leeds United, and West Ham have helped raise public awareness of opportunities for Asian boys and men in football. One of the few initiatives concerning girls and women that has been supported by the FA is the British Muslim women's team attendance at Islamic events (www.thefa.com/TheFA/EthicsAndSportsEquity/Racial Equality/Postings).

As King made clear in his chapter, attempts to achieve equity in football often forget the particular experiences of women. A focus on equity and *Asians in Football* must remain mindful that girls and women might share some experiences of racism with boys and men, however, 'race', racism and ethnicity are gendered and it is important to explore the detail. In her chapter, Aarti Ratna provides a valuable example of how young women players experience racism, ethnicity and gender in football contexts in England. She draws on doctoral research, in particular interview research findings, to analyse how the research participants (19 British-Asian players) give meaning to comments and practices that mark them as 'other'. Ratna identifies racist comments and practices: however, her discussion goes beyond documenting this important evidence. Ratna's analysis of the different ways the players give meaning to racism is significant because it demonstrates the power of whiteness and the conditions some players must negotiate to participate. Her findings make links with King's analysis of whiteness and provides us with detail previously missing, and possibly ignored, from work on gender and equity.

Similar to recent engagement with Asianness, equity and football, the FA has been slow to address issues surrounding sexuality and fairness. The Ethics and Sports Equity Strategy does state that homophobia is punishable with sanctions, which include banning perpetrators. The policy continues to be developed and the recent homophobia summit (2005) aimed to provide a forum for the FA to produce clear guidelines on anti-homophobia. As with previous attempts to address inequality the FA have a habit of co-opting professional men's clubs, in this case Coventry City, Manchester City, and Manchester United. Such an approach raises public awareness: however, the male context tends to promote a focus on men and boys. If due care is not taken, women's and girls' experiences might be understood as the same as men's, or, be annexed as less important. Lesbianism and bisexuality, for women, have never been criminalised and a possible consequence is that women's sexuality is not stigmatised in the same way men's sexuality is in British society. However, this does not necessarily add up to a reduction in homophobic behaviour towards women and girls. In her chapter, Jayne Caudwell charts some of the incidents of homophobia experienced by members of a lesbian-identified football team. The chapter demonstrates the different responses to lesbianism in the game and highlights how the treatment of homophobia has changed since the club's inception, some 20 years ago. What emerges from the account is that women at the club, regardless of sexuality, have been and continue to be active in challenging homophobia. It appears that an 'out and proud' sensibility has helped determine an intolerance for homophobic behaviour. Such local gay pride enables a contestation of inequality and has gone some way towards ensuring fairness. The case study suggests that despite lack of formal [equity] policy, lesbian players and in this case a lesbian-identified team have played-on.

Equity in football, for women, is related to the history of the game and to past and present gender relations. Histories and gender relations are further complicated by other social relations to power. In Section Two we have considered 'race' and ethnicity and homophobia and sexuality. We have not addressed [dis]ability and acknowledge that there is a pressing need for research on women, gender, [dis]ability and football.

When considering the chapters in Section Three it is worth noting Ramazanoglu and Holland's (2002: p. 124) suggestion that:

> Experiences and how they feel, remain central to understanding similarities and diversity in gendered lives, and to investigation of inequalities, injustices and institutional power.

Throughout this book we are seeking to understand and learn more about women's complex relationship with football, a game that has been shown to have strong historical roots as a male sport inherently linked to dominant notions of masculinity. Yet, as more and more girls and women get involved with the game it has become increasingly important to find out more about how they *experience* the game. Feminist research in particular has argued that it is important to explore the connections between ideas, experience and reality — to find out how people "live in real bodies, in real relationships, in a real world" (Ramazanoglu and Holland, 2002: p. 134). The final section of the book focuses on research that begins to explore the experiences of different women and their relationships to football as young people, adults, players, teachers and fans. By focusing on women's experiences, these chapters provide us with knowledge and information that moves beyond the confines of statistical surveys on participation rates to a deeper understanding of the material, lived experiences of playing and watching football.

An important theoretical development over the past decade has been the recognition that women are not an homogenous group but that their differences must be recognised and understood. All the chapters in Section Three identify the complex and often contradictory network of gendered experiences that can be a part of playing and/or spectating football; a game that traditionally has been male defined, controlled and dominated. Jeannes and Kay draw on both feminist cultural studies and postmodernism in their analysis of the experiences of 13 girls aged 10 or 11 years in an after-school football club. Their gendered analysis concludes that football can be just one of many spaces that can support the construction of alternative identities that challenge dominant discourses of 'acceptable' femininity. However, this is by no means total nor straightforward, and the girls also conformed to more traditional notions of femininity, especially through their appearance. As in the work by Flintoff and Scraton (2001), it is clear that there is a complex network of behaviours that interweave activities of compliance and resistance. We should not think of girls and young women as inactive players in the reproduction of the gendered game of football. There seems to be plenty of evidence to suggest that these girls have an accurate awareness of the reality of men's control in the broader world of football, whilst still not always connecting this world to their own more micro experiences.

Soler-Prat provides further qualitative data on girls in school by focusing on the gendered experiences of girls and boys in mixed sex physical education (PE) sessions in a school in Spain. Whilst the cultural and geographical location is significantly different, the research identifies a contradictory and complex network of beliefs, ideological positions and actions similar to the findings of UK based research. Once more there is little evidence of a shift in the structural relations of gender, produced and reproduced in the football sessions. However, there are identified spaces of resistance to traditional gender relations, initiated by both teachers and students. The early experiences that girls have of playing football have been shown, in previous research, to be crucial to their continued participation as adults (Caudwell, 1999; Scraton, Fastings, Pfister, and Bunuel 1999). Although there are now a number of important initiatives being developed in the UK and across Europe to increase the opportunities for girls to play, we still have little knowledge of how they experience these initiatives and whether gender relations continue to be reproduced or are challenged in the coaching context.

A major strength of the 'Women, Football and Europe' conference was the bringing together of researchers from across Europe, who all had an interest and involvement in women's football. However, it is interesting to see, across the collection, the similarities of experiences as well as the differences related to specific cultural and national contexts. All four chapters that research experiences identify the significance of understanding 'space' in relation to women's football. Welford and Kay identify footballing space as gendered and identify the persistence of material and ideological barriers that continue to impact on girls' and women's experiences of playing. However, they also identify the significance of the particular space in which their research was located; an English university space. This specific space affords not only opportunities to play and develop high level skills, but also the establishment of strong social networks that help the players to create their own football 'space'. Having a 'space of one's own' was also highly significant in the work of Llopis Goig, who provides a fascinating introduction to the experiences of women football supporters in Spanish peñas (supporters clubs). Yet again, there is evidence that women 'choose' to create their own football space and that, in this case, they clearly see this space as a space for liberation from an extremely gendered community of football supporters.

What we hope this collection demonstrates is the importance of digging beneath the surface of statistics that paint a rosy picture of increased participation by women in football. It is important to recognise, from researching qualitative experiences, that these figures of increased participation, whilst an important and significant development, can mask the complexities that continue to impact both positively and negatively on girls and women who quite obviously 'love to play and watch football'.

References

Caudwell, J. (1999) 'Women's football in the United Kingdom: Theorising gender and unpacking the butch lesbian image', *Journal of Sport and Social Issues*, Vol. 23, No. 4: pp. 390–402.

Flintoff, A. and Scraton, S. (2001) 'Stepping into active leisure? Young women's experiences of active lifestyles and their experiences of school PE', *Sport, Education and Society* Vol. 6, No. 1: pp. 5–21.

Lopez, S. (1997) *Women on the ball: A guide to women's football*. London: Scarlet Press.

Magee, J. Baldwin, G. and Kelly, G. (eds) (2007) *Women, Football and Europe: Contemporary Perspectives*. Oxford, UK: Meyer and Meyer Sport.

Ramazanoglu, C. and Holland, J. (2002) *Feminist ethodology: Challenges and choices*. London, Sage.

Scraton, S., Fastings, K., Pfister, G. and Bunuel, A. (1999) 'It's still a man's game? The experience of top-level European women footballers', *International Review for the Sociology of Sport*, Vol. 34, No. 2: pp. 99–111.

Williams, J. (2003) *A game for rough girls? A history of women's football in England*. London: Routledge.

www.thefa.com/Euro2005/NewandFeatures/Postings/2005/06/Euro2005_England PlayersReception.htm (accessed, 29 March 2006)

www.thefa.com/TheFA/EthicsAndSportsEquity

www.thefa.com/TheFA/EthicsAndSportsEquity/RacialEquality/Postings

SECTION ONE: HISTORIES

Women's Football in Scotland: An Historical Overview

Jessica Macbeth

International Football Institute, University of Central Lancashire

Introduction

The history of women's football has received due attention in an emerging body of research (Williamson, 1991; Newsham, 1997; Hong and Mangan, 2003; Williams, 2003a). A prominent theme emerging from international histories of women's football is that, in spite of differing social and cultural contexts in which the game has developed across different societies, it has generally been marginalised and treated as subordinate in relation to dominant sports cultures.

Women's football in Scotland is notable only by its relative absence from such research. Commentaries on football in Scottish society give some explanation: for example, Bairner (2000: p. 102) argues that "hegemonic masculinity ... has surrounded football in Scotland for so long" and it is an integral characteristic of Scottish football culture. And, of the limited research on women's football specifically, it has been noted that social attitudes to women in sport, the onset of the First World War, changes in women's place in Scottish society, the influence of the Scottish media, and the role of the Scottish Football Association (SFA), are among a number of factors that have combined to mould the historical development of women's football in Scotland (Macbeth, 2002; 2004).

This chapter has evolved from historical and sociological research on women's football in contemporary Scottish society (Macbeth, 2004). The dual focus of that study — historical and sociological processes — was important, as Sugden and Tomlinson (1999: p. 387) stress:

> It is vital to give research into contemporary phenomena a dynamic historical dimension — to identify and connect the key institutional developments and critical moments of individual and collective action which underpin the area of social interaction under scrutiny and help to frame its contemporary form and suggest its legacy.

In order to do more than just offer a description of a series of (sometimes unrelated) events, this historical account aims to contextualise the emergence and development of women's football in Scotland within the wider Scottish context. In particular, it explores how women's football has, at different stages of its development, been suppressed and incorporated by the dominant sports culture and sports-related institutions in Scottish society. In doing so, this chapter will demonstrate how the development of women's football has been "constitutively inserted into the struggles, the forms of compliance and opposition, social reproduction and transformation, associated with changing patterns of social development" in Scotland (Gruneau, 1981: p. 10, cited in Donnelly, 2000: p. 84).

Methods

The historical data presented in this chapter were collected from a combination of primary and secondary sources. Consultation of existing international research on the history of women's football generated some primary information on the history of the game in Scotland. Indeed, various volumes of the *Domestic Annals of Scotland and The New Statistical Account of Scotland* revealed evidence of women's involvement in football in Scotland from as early as the seventeenth century. Systematic searches of archives and newspapers were also conducted at the Mitchell Library (Glasgow) and references to women's football during the late nineteenth and early twentieth centuries were located in the *Scottish Athletic Journal, Scottish Sport, Stirling Observer and The Herald*. The minutes of SFA meetings (held in the Scottish Football Museum (SFM) archives provided an insight into the SFA's attitudes towards women's football in the early twentieth century. Additional material held at the SFM included sports journals and newspaper articles on women's football from the late 1800s and transcripts of oral history interviews with past players from the 1970s. Having systematically gathered and analysed this data, the remainder of this chapter is devoted to the results of this. It is structured around an historical overview of women's football in Scotland that focuses on the following: the social origins of the game since the seventeenth century; the development of organised women's football; the emergence of an institutionalised and codified game; the measures that inhibited the development of the women's game in the twentieth century; and, the gradual incorporation of women's football into the contemporary structures of Scottish football.

Traditions and fads: women's football in Scotland from the seventeenth to the twentieth centuries

It is difficult to pin-point the exact moment in time when various sports took on their modern codified forms, and women's football in Scotland is a case in point. Williamson (1991) suggests that the origins of women's football can be seen in early eighteenth century Scotland. However, there is also some evidence to indicate that women participated in traditional forms of folk football in Scotland as early as the mid-seventeenth century. For example, church registers from Carstairs in Lanarkshire imply that, in the 1620s, women may have been involved in folk football and other activities, all of which are noted in the church register since such behaviour on a Sunday was considered a breach of the Sabbath. In Chambers words, "in August 1628, the minister of Carstairs regretted to the presbytery of Lanark the breach of the Sabbath 'by the insolent behaviour of men and women in footballing, dancing, and barley-breaks'" (1858: p. 488). It is currently unclear whether both men and women took equal part in all of these activities, but research on folk forms of football in the UK suggest that there was little or no differentiation between men and women, and between participants and spectators (Elias and Dunning, 1986).

In Scotland, women took part in various other 'amusements' and games, and minutes of the kirk-session of January 18th 1656 in the United Parishes of Wandell and Lamingtoune (Lanarkshire) state that "the utmost decorum and good fellowship are strictly observed" (Hope, 1845: p. 823). Having said that, the participation of men and women in folk football, particularly on Fasting's eve, was regarded as less civilised. In Hope's words:

> The sessione considering ane superstitious and abominable custone yt hes continued still in this paroche. That men and women uses promiscuously to play at the foot-ball upon Fasting's

> even; and also considering what evill and sadde consequences hes followed y^{re} upon, viz. Uncleannesse, drunkennes, and fighting, they doe unanimously discharge and inhibite the s^{d} old superstitious and abominable practise. And hereby macks and ordaines, that whatsoever persone or persones shall contravein this present acte, they shall be censured with the censure of the kirk. And the minister be desyred to publish y^{re} present acte out of pulpitt y^{o} next Lord's day, that none pretende ignorance. (Hope, 1845: p. 823)

Dunning and Sheard (2005: p. 20) also argue that "'football' and other popular games were banned on more than thirty occasions" between 1314 and 1667 in England and Scotland. There are also references to annual games of folk football between teams of married and single women during the eighteenth century in Scottish locations such as Inverness (Williamson, 1991: p. 1), Musselburgh and Inveresk (Fittis, 1891: pp. 155/164). According to Dunning and Sheard (2005: p. 22), in the UK "it was common to have a 'match at football' annually on a Saint's day or 'holy day'" and "Shrovetide, it seems, was the favourite occasion for engaging in such pastimes". And, as Dr Alexander Carlyle (1795: p. 19), the Minister for Inveresk noted, such annual traditions of folk football matches were not exclusive to men:

> As they [women] do the work of men, their manners are masculine, and their strength and activity is equal to their work. Their amusements are of the masculine kind. On holidays they frequently play at golf; and on Shrove Tuesday there is a standing match at football, between the married and unmarried women, in which the former are always victors.

It is not known how long these and other traditions lasted in Scotland and there is insufficient evidence to suggest that these events constituted anything more than participation in an annual tradition at that time. Having said that, existing historical evidence implies that Scottish women may have participated in folk football before their counterparts in England or elsewhere in Britain and the Republic of Ireland, though this tentative hypothesis undoubtedly requires further empirical verification.

Historical accounts of the development of women's football in other European countries seem to concur that women played football (or its folk variants) in Britain prior to its diffusion further afield. Research suggests, for example, that women's football emerged in Denmark, Germany, Norway, Sweden and France during the late nineteenth and early twentieth centuries (Brus and Trangbaek, 2003; Pfister, 2003; Fasting, 2003; Hjelm and Olofsson, 2003; Newsham, 1997). Whilst this historical research is in its incipient stages, the evidence that has emerged thus far does not challenge the adequacy of records indicating that Scottish women played football prior to their female counterparts elsewhere. Furthermore, whilst Williamson (1991) may have been correct in arguing that the origins of women's football can be found in Scotland, it could be the case (as is tentatively indicated here) that women's football emerged much earlier than he had anticipated.

In the late nineteenth century, there was an increase in the numbers of football matches involving women teams in Scotland (Williamson, 1991; McCuaig, 2000a). In other European countries, there is evidence of similar developments at this time, for example, there are "various descriptions of football-playing women ... from the end of the nineteenth and the beginning of the twentieth centuries" in Denmark (Brus and Trangbaek, 2003: p. 97). Matches in Scotland took a number of forms, including travelling women's teams (generally from England) playing either Scottish men's or women's teams. There was also an unofficial Scotland vs. England 'international' in Edinburgh in May, 1881 which represented "an innovation in football playing" (*Glasgow News*, 9th May, 1881). However, interestingly the match report also stated that:

> in the interests of public morals, [we must] protest against the institution of an exhibition which can hardly be called decent, and which is evidently got up to draw the shillings of the crowd ... Football is not a game for women; and the spectacle of a score of girls careering about a field in knickerbockers is not to be defended on any ground of public utility. (*Glasgow News*, 9th May, 1881)

Reaction to this match (one example of which is evident above) was "a sign of things to come" in terms of the narrower acceptance of the problematic association between women and traditionally male-associated sports such as football in Scotland. The first women's match that was played within

Scottish FA guidelines at Shawfields Ground, Glasgow in 1892 generated a negative response from the Scottish press who had, then, an almost exclusive role in portraying women's football to the wider society. *Scottish Sport* described this match as a "feeble imitation of our glorious winter game" and stated that:

> after witnessing how utterly unfitted the female anatomy is for the game, a rough section of the crowd invaded the pitch, surrounding the girls in a most insulting fashion ... it was the most degrading spectacle we have ever witnessed in connection with football, and we never want to see it faintly repeated ... we do not say that a little of modified football exercise, taken in private, would not have a beneficial effect to most girls, but we draw the line at public performances, which are nothing short of immodest. (*Scottish Sport*, cited in McCuaig, 2000b: p. 6)

Indeed, reference to the female anatomy being 'utterly unfitted' for football was typical of dominant medical opinion throughout the United Kingdom during the Victorian era (Hargreaves, 1994). Using feminist ideas, we could also interpret the term "our glorious winter game" as a reference to the accepted (and presumed) ownership of football by men in Scotland, though few records about the emergence of Scottish women's teams exist which could challenge this claim. In the late nineteenth century, English women's teams toured around Scotland and match reports and public reaction in the Scottish press around that time consolidated wider societal views regarding the perceived inappropriateness of football for women. Indeed, it seems that the emergence of a female football culture was considered anathema to the dominant (male) sports culture and the wider patriarchal society that existed in Scotland at this time.

Some women footballers exhibited resilience to negative reactions typified in the above accounts and several 'Ladies' football teams were known to have traveled around Scotland during the 1890s. These included the British Ladies Football Club who arranged a tour of Scotland in 1895 "under the banner of women's rights" (McCuaig, 2000b: p. 6) and Mrs. Graham's team of Original Lady Footballers who toured in Scotland from around 1894. The latter visited Stirling on Saturday June 27th 1896 and played at King's Park Football Club against eleven gentlemen from

Bathgate. The *Stirling Observer* treated the game as something of a novelty. In their words:

> as far as football was concerned the proceedings were farcical, the ladies making little attempt to play the game seriously, and the other side took matters very easily ... If they return to Stirling, which is not likely, the attendance will not be so large as it was on Saturday. (*Stirling Observer*, 4th July 1896)

This novel description of women's football became even more apparent over time in that many people involved formally in the football establishment disapproved of women's participation. In 1902, this culminated in a warning by the Council of the SFA to its member clubs not to play charitable matches against "ladies teams" (Williamson, 1991: p. 5). This warning appears to have been carried out with immediate effect. McCuaig (2000a) argues that this was evidence of a reaction, by the dominant male footballing culture, to the perceived threat of women's increasing participation (and presence) in football. Whilst the SFA's warning represented a potential threat to the further development of women's football in Scotland, at the same time women's football began to emerge elsewhere in Europe during the early twentieth century. For example, Fasting (2003: p. 150) suggests that, in Norway, "exhibition games often took place between a women's team and a team of untrained men" during the early 1900s. However, she argues that women did not decide "to play the game seriously" for many years after the Norwegian Football Association was founded in 1902.

In summary, the available historical evidence indicates that women took part in football games in Scotland from the seventeenth century to the late nineteenth century. This participation mainly took the form of annual folk traditions and, later, games between English touring teams and men's and women's teams in Scotland. However, this evidence is limited, thus we are unable to ascertain more detailed information about Scottish women's teams that took part in these competitive matches in the late nineteenth century. It could be argued, then, that women's participation in football prior to the early twentieth century represented traditions and fads. These were to be replaced in the twentieth century, by a more enduring, organised, and modern sport.

The development of organised women's football in Scotland around World War One

A more enduring stage of growth in the women's game occurred during and after the First World War and amongst working-class factory women in particular. As was seen elsewhere, the onset of the First World War led to Scottish women being grafted into the workplace and this, in turn, contributed to the relative disintegration of stringent Victorian principles. Indeed, we could say that the emergence of women's football in Scotland at this time was primarily related to raising money for war charities, boosting camaraderie and maintaining fitness amongst the emerging female workforce. This group of females acted as a partial solution to historically specific structural conditions in which females fulfilled workers' roles in the absence of males who were drafted into (or signed up voluntarily for) the British army.

Between 1914 and 1918, there was an increase in the numbers of spectators who watched women's football games and this was recorded in Scottish press coverage at this time. The charity matches also attracted greater press coverage in quantitative terms though this quantitative increase did not necessarily improve the quality of this coverage. Taken together, women's football in Scotland evolved to what has arguably been a peak in its development in the period just after World War One (Macbeth, 2002). In Scotland, as in the UK, this was reflected in the emergence of workplace teams and Williams (2003a: p. 31) suggests that, in the UK:

> The expansion of women's football organised by workers after 1914, sometimes on the initiative of welfare supervisors, was more pronounced in Britain than anywhere else: teams included Cardiff, Llanelli, Newport and Swansea in Wales, Aberdeen, Edinburgh, Glasgow, Renfrew, Rutherglen in Scotland and Belfast, plus English sides like Bennets of London and Dick, Kerr's of Lancashire.

The onset and consequences of the war contributed to the entry of significant numbers of women (often in their thousands) into employment in Scotland and the majority of the female workforce worked in the munitions industry (Lynch, 1992: p. 423/424). In a similar development to the emergence of the Dick, Kerr's Ladies team from a munitions factory in Preston (Newsham, 1997), women's football teams were also established within or by, and were associated with, factory workers in Scotland. For example, McCuaig (2000b: pp. 7–8) reveals that "one of the more significant teams [was] formed from the workforce of Beardmore's Forge in the East End of Glasgow" where the management pursued an active outdoor recreation policy. In the absence of a male workforce during the First World War, local women were assisted to form a football team at the Forge in order to raise funds for war charities and these developments were also paralleled in Europe at this time. In Sweden several women's football teams were formed in late 1910s and early 1920s and they "primarily played against 'gubblag' or old-boys' sides" (Hjelm and Olofsson, 2003: p. 182). Similarly, women's football in France was sufficiently popular in the early 1920s such that the *Fédération des Sociétés Féminines de France* accepted an invitation from the Dick, Kerr's Ladies' to send a representative team to play in matches for British war charities (Newsham, 1997). And, in the UK, Melling (1999: p. 59) suggested that, "from the First World War until 1921, women's infiltration into male traditional spheres [such as manual labour and football] was endorsed as part of the war effort".

McCuaig (2000b: p. 10) argues that these developments contributed, in part, to the expansion of women's football in various regions in Scotland. Taken together, these culminated in the participation of a representative Scottish women's team in international fixtures against England in 1920 and 1921. Reports indicate that the English side won both matches by 22–0 and 9–0 respectively. Whilst these defeats were convincing in and of themsleves, McCuaig (2000b: p. 10) suggests that:

> ... women's football in Scotland was flourishing. Following this second international, Dick, Kerr's conducted a tour of Scotland that attracted huge support. They played five matches — in Edinburgh, Kilmarnock, Aberdeen, Dundee and Dumfries — and attracted a total of 70,000 spectators. The 'Ladies' tour of 1921 illustrates the strength of women's football across the major towns and cities in Scotland.

However, where McCuaig (2000b) interprets the total spectatorship as an indication of the popularity and the continued flourishing of women's football in Scotland, Williamson (1991) proposes a competing interpretation. He suggests that there was a lack of organisation and a relatively slow growth in the diffusion of the game in Scotland. Evidence for his claim comes from the increased demands of war-related work which, according to him, meant that women did not have sufficient time to plan the structured development of women's football (Williamson, 1991: p. 23). One possible explanation for these two competing claims might be that the focus of Williamson's work — the emergence of women's football in England — led him to compare, less favourably, the 'slower' and more disorganised development of the game in Scotland with a more structured developmental pattern in England. However, by 1921, women's football in Scotland had, arguably, reached a peak in popularity and this was reflected in the organisation of international and domestic matches that attracted significant numbers of spectators (Macbeth, 2002). Thus, during and after World War One, women's football was associated, primarily, with charitable functions and, as such, the game did not represent a serious challenge or threat to the dominant sport culture in Scotland. Over the next fifty years or so, the women's game struggled to maintain such a high profile and the SFA and the Scottish media were instrumental in denying the women's game the opportunity to thrive in the post-World War One era.

"Measures to prevent women footballers": women's football in a residual state

Given the focus of existing research (see, for example, Williamson, 1991; Lopez, 1997; Newsham, 1997; Williams, 2003a) on the English FA's resolution to ban FA-affiliated clubs from allowing their grounds to be used for women's matches, it will not be a surprise to readers of this chapter to note that the SFA also formalised this resolution. As a result, women's teams in Scotland were similarly denied access to SFA-affiliated football grounds. Indeed, the formalization of this resolution was supported in the Scottish press. For example, a piece entitled "Measures to prevent women footballers" in *The Herald* (6th December, 1921) offered support for this and printed sections of the resolution. Similarly, Scottish Sport (6th December, 1921) focused on the medical justifications for the adoption of this resolution "as they considered the game unsuitable for females". For this reason, the action of the SFA "would appear to have a good deal of support".

By this time, women's football had been more widely accepted in the UK for almost a decade, providing that the emphasis was on the fund-raising functions it served. However, the cessation of war activities marked a shift in this wider public support. As I stated earlier, Melling (1999: pp.

59–60) argues that in the UK, "from the First World War until 1921 women's infiltration into male traditional spheres was endorsed as part of the war effort". However, from 1921 "the development of a state agenda for a return to pre-war forms" of social organization, and "attacks from the media, educationalists, sections of the medical profession and the FA suggest that ladies' football was high on this agenda". The situation for women's football in Scotland was no different. The SFA's imposition of the ban was considered justifiable by sections of Scottish society, and this was also reinforced by the Scottish press. Overall, the changing social climate reflected a narrower acceptance of women's football in Scotland because the charitable role of women's football was less relevant in the context of social reorganization after the war.

Little is known (or formally recorded) about women's football in Scotland in the ten years following the 1921 resolution. However, what is evident is that, despite attempts to arrange women's football matches, the SFA adhered to the 1921 resolution. Minutes of SFA meetings demonstrate the following:

> Ladies' Football
>
> Recommended — Aberdeen F.C. be informed: — this Association does not approve of clubs arranging or sponsoring or letting grounds for Ladies' football matches. (23rd January 1924)

The SFA issued similar instructions to Raith Rovers FC later that year and to Queen of the South FC in March 1925 (SFA meeting minutes, June 25th 1924 and March 11th 1925). The lack of evidence relating to women's matches during this decade and the prohibitive position of the SFA suggest that attempts to organise women's matches at SFA-affiliated grounds were relatively unsuccessful. The continued reiteration of the SFA's position by them means we can only surmise that, some Scottish men's clubs were either more sympathetic towards women's football than the SFA, or were keen to raise revenue from the use of their facilities by women at that time. Indeed, there is some evidence that women's football teams existed throughout the 1920s and Caley Ladies FC of Inverness appear in a history of Inverness Caledonian FC (c. 1926, Ruth Shuttleworth Collection, SFM). Thus, there may have been co-operation then between men's and women's teams but further research is needed to verify this claim.

In the 1930s, there were several noteworthy events including a match between Dick, Kerr's Ladies and the Rest of Britain in 1936, in which two Scottish footballers, Miss McNeil and Miss McMonin, were invited to play (McCuaig, 2000a: p. 2). The organisation of this event suggests that the game reflected a relatively high degree of public interest. It also seems that the Edinburgh Ladies were the ascendant women's team in Scotland in the late 1930s. Indeed, according to McCuaig, following their establishment in May 1937, they became a dominant force. In her words:

> Indeed, after only four months their match record was unprecedented — played 20, won 18, lost 1, drawn 1, one game including a recent victory over the team who had beaten them. Significantly, the team averaged a consistent gate of 5,000 at a time when supporter levels were declining in general under the strain of the economic depression of the 1930s. (McCuaig, 2000b: p. 13)

Here, McCuaig does not specify where these matches were played in order to accommodate such attendances, but it is clear that a sufficient number of women's teams existed in Scotland to provide opposition for the Edinburgh Ladies.

The women's game seems to have continued in a relatively residual state throughout the 1940s and 1950s though McCuaig (2000b: p. 14) argues that "women remained committed to playing the game in Scotland". However, they struggled to regain the heights of popularity attained during and after the First World War and, as the following minutes suggest, the SFA's continuing adherence to the 1921 resolution remained a key feature of relations between the sexes in football at this time:

> Ladies' Football (Item 40) (Executive and General Purposes Committee)
>
> On attention being drawn to the fact that in certain areas ladies' football is being permitted on grounds of clubs within the jurisdiction of this Association, the Secretary was instructed to reiterate the previous decision of the Association that such matches cannot be permitted or in any way encouraged. (SFA minutes, September 14th 1949)

In line with the findings of research on the history of women's football elsewhere, developments in the women's game from the 1960s onwards tend to feature more prominently in public records, and thus in research on women's football more generally. In the 1960s, the changing social conditions of "politics and cultural politics of feminism" meant that women's participation in the public sphere generally, and in women's sport in particular, was to a greater or lesser degree a feminist issue (Polley, 1998: p. 93). In Scotland, there is evidence of an increase in the numbers of women's teams who competed against each other throughout the 1960s. Indeed, Williams (2003a: p. 37) identifies the names of Scottish teams associated with various workplaces including "the Cambuslang Hooverettes, Johnstone Red Rockets, Johnie Walker and Fife Dynamites, Holyrood Bumbees, Tayside Toppers, Aberdeen Prima Donnas and the Glasgow Gay Eleven (based at the Gay's biscuit factory)". Stewarton and Thistle from Kilmarnock also formed in 1961 at the request of the Provost in order to raise funds for the Freedom from Hunger Campaign and they achieved some competitive success throughout the 1970s (Lopez, 1997).

The hosting by, and sporting success of England in the men's World Cup in 1966 is thought to have provided some stimulus for the participation of more women in football in England (Dunning, 1999), although Williams (2003b: pp. 118–119) argues that this is unlikely to have been "a major agent of change for most women players ... not least because football for women became popular at around this time in other countries". In the Norwegian context, Fasting (2003: p. 131) argues that the second wave of feminism and discussions about equal rights, human rights and women's rights were "important concepts in the debates about women's position in society in general" in the 1960s and 1970s, all of which had implications for women's participation in sport. It was within this social context that the first formal women's football league was organised in Glasgow in 1968. This league accommodated the then Scottish champions, Cambuslang Hooverettes, who made a name for themselves south of the border by reaching the final of the 1970 Deal International Tournament (Lopez, 1997). The ability of the Scottish champions to compete at that time against the best teams in England suggests that the standard of women's football in Scotland had improved throughout the 1960s (Macbeth, 2002). Although it might have appeared that the women's game was threatened with extinction in the mid-twentieth century, we can conclude that the people involved in women's football in Scotland demonstrated some resilience, and women's football survived in a residual state despite an "extended period of criticism and marginalisation" (Donnelly, 1993: p. 128).

The related residual status of women's football in the international context was due, in part, to the continued implementation of a ban by some national FA's. This ban was lifted in the 1970s in the UK. Existing research (see, for example, Lopez, 1997; Williams, 2003a) points to increasing pressure from UEFA as an important stepping stone in the rescinding of this ban in the UK and the social related development of women's football in the twentieth century. However, the attitude of the SFA continued to constrain the development of women's football in Scotland during the early 1970s. Following initial correspondence from UEFA in 1970, the SFA outlined clearly, and on numerous occasions, their opposition to women's football. In their words:

> There was submitted correspondence with UEFA, who enquired as to Association's attitude towards women's football, and with the Women's Football Association, who sought recognition, in Scotland. The committee were unanimous in their refusal. (SFA meeting, September 7th 1970)[1]
> Women's Football (Item 76, E. & G. P. Committee)

> There was submitted a letter from the Women's Football Association, requesting reconsideration of the Association's attitude towards women's football. The committee adhered to their original decision. (SFA meeting, November 11th 1970)
> Women's Football (Item 153. Executive and General Purposes Committee)

> The contents of a letter received from UEFA were noted. (SFA meeting minutes December 15th 1970)

From this, it is clear that the SFA was opposed to the official recognition of women's football. In particular, the final minute of December 15th 1970 implies that, although the contents of a letter from UEFA were noted, they were not discussed in any detail, presumably for the reasons outlined in the previous minute, that is, that the committee adhered to its original decision noted in September 1970.

The SFA's opposition was reinforced further in 1971 when "UEFA passed a motion which ended in a vote of 39–1, in favour of member countries taking control of women's football (Scotland was the odd one out) and this became an official UEFA recommendation by November of that year" (Lopez, 1997: p. 59). In contrast to other European FAs[2] the SFA took UEFA's motion as a recommendation rather than an expectation and they remained committed in their opposition towards women's football for several more years. However, there was some cause for optimism in the early 1970s despite the SFA's position. The Scottish Women's Football Association (SWFA) was officially inaugurated in 1971 and six teams registered for competition — Aberdeen, Edinburgh Dynamos, Westthorn United, Motherwell AEI, Dundee Strikers, and Stewarton and Thistle — and one of the more renowned Scottish players at that time, Elsie Cook, was made Honorary Secretary (Cook, 2000). The first official Scotland vs. England international match was played at Ravenscraig Stadium in Greenock in 1972. In order to comply with the then 51–year old SFA resolution, the Ravenscraig Stadium at Greenock was used as it was a non-SFA venue and "the officials at the match were provided by the Scottish Football Referees Association as opposed to the SFA" (Cook, 2000). At this time, Scottish women's teams were allowed to take part in the English Women's Football Association (WFA) Cup and two Scottish teams reached the WFA finals in 1972 and 1973. Taken together, these events were a stepping stone for the growing acceptance of women's football in Scotland in the latter decades of the twentieth century. We could say that they were also evidence of the gradual incorporation of women's football into the dominant football culture in Scotland at this time, though this is not to deny that there was strong resistance to this.

"It was agreed to give recognition to women's football": the gradual incorporation of the women's game into the dominant football culture

The issue of the continued adoption of the ban by the SFA was raised again in 1973. This is evident in further correspondence from UEFA in 1973 but SFA minutes do not offer much by way of evidence that the contents of the letter were discussed in any great detail by the SFA's Executive and General Purposes Committee.[3] On balance, UEFA's letter is likely to have contained further recommendations that the SFA offer official recognition to women's football because, a little over one year later, the SFA formally recognised the

Scottish WFA in August 1974.[4] In response to this, the SFA sent official correspondence to the Secretary of the SWFA on September 2nd 1974 requesting that, "in the circumstances, I would appreciate your sending me a copy of your Constitution and Rules for inspection" (c. September 1974, SFM Collection). Shortly after official recognition was granted by the SFA, the first official match was held at the grounds of an SFA-affiliated club, Celtic Park, between the Scottish Ladies' International side and a Scottish Select side in September 1974. The match was played, as McCuaig (2000b: p. 14) describes, "in recognition of the decision to endorse women's football" and was intended as a "'curtain-raiser' to the men's European Cup First Round first leg tie against T. P. S. Turka". Indeed, the formal affiliation of this and other women's associations with their respective national FA's represented a widening acceptance of women's football more generally in the latter part of the twentieth century.

This widening acceptance was also reflected in the expansion of women's football in Scotland during the late 1970s. This was evident in the organization of international fixtures (for example, fixtures were organized against the Republic of Ireland and Wales in 1976) and an increase in the number of teams producing players of international standard. For example, the Scotland squad for the Pony Home International Championship of May 1976 included representation from seven club teams in that country including Edinburgh Dynamo, Motherwell AEI, Westthorn United, East Fife Ladies, West End Ladies, Dundee Strikers and Lochend Thistle. Since the formation of the Scottish WFA in 1971, the organization of women's football in that country (including international fixtures) had been their responsibility, though this responsibility was subsumed by the Scottish FA in 1998 following the formal affiliation of the WFA to the Scottish FA. In 1991, the Scottish Sports Council appointed Sheila Begbie as Women's Football Coordinator with responsibility to develop girls' and women's football in conjunction with the SFA. However, some developments were occurring at a comparatively slower rate in Scotland than elsewhere in the UK. The Scottish WFA was the last of the UK women's football associations to affiliate with their respective men's association.[5] The SFA also invited Sheila Begbie and the SWFA to be housed within their office headquarters in Edinburgh (Lopez, 1997: p. 156). The SWFA has since been renamed Scottish Women's Football Ltd (SWF) and is currently housed at Hampden Park (Glasgow), the national stadium of Scotland and a seat on the SFA Council is occupied by SWF executive administrator, Maureen McGonigle (Macbeth, 2002).

The Scottish Women's Football League (SWFL) formed in November 1999 and in 2002/2003, the Premier Division broke away to become the Scottish Women's Premier League (SWPL). Maureen McGonigle explains that this change was administered in the hope that, "by highlighting the country's top 12 women's teams, those who can help the game progress may, at last, sit up and notice" (Mawhinney, 2002: p. 13). In the 2005/2006 season women's football in Scotland was organised into two main leagues — the Thompson's Solicitors Scottish Women's Premier League (a national league accommodating the top 12 teams) and the SWFL — which accommodates two national divisions and two regional divisions, comprising 38 teams in total. In 2005, the SFA Annual Review reported that 7,050 women's footballers were registered in that country and over 100,000 girls participated in either girls'-only or mixed football within the SFA's co-ordinated schools programme, at primary and secondary school levels (SFA Annual Review, 2005). Several women's teams are currently supported by, and integrated into community structures at professional men's clubs including Falkirk, East Fife, Queens Park, Hamilton Academicals, and Hibernian. Development centres are also open to females under the age of 18 and youth leagues are run throughout the country (Pearson, 2003). An official magazine named 'Miss-Kick', devoted to women's football in Scotland, was launched by the SWF Ltd in May 2001 and the women's game has begun to receive more positive press and media coverage over recent years, particularly since the national squad attained a top 20 European ranking in 2002. Indeed, in recent years the SFA have introduced several key developments in girls' and women's football at the grass roots level, including the introduction of an SFA co-ordinated schools programme, a club development package, and the funding of nine development officer posts for girls and women's football. The Scottish national squad narrowly missed out on qualification for the UEFA European Championships 2005 which were held in England, and coincided with the Women, Football and Europe Conference (from which this book is drawn). In January 2006 however, the Scottish squad had climbed to 29th place in the FIFA World Rankings.

Given the evident developmental progress since the 1970s that is necessarily outlined in brief here, one current concern is the extent to which women's football can expand further in Scotland in the continued absence of significant financial and organizational investments. The possibility (and sometimes the necessity) for talented Scottish players to pursue professional careers elsewhere is illustrative of this ongoing concern, and this concern is also shared by others.[6] Maureen McGonigle believes that the Scottish talent drain can be explained as follows:

> That is because Scotland is not offering them anything and it's about time they did. They want to keep their talent here, be proud of their talent. But they need the support and they need people to put their money where their mouth is. (Maureen McGonigle, quoted in Pearson, 2003: p. 12)

It also appears that transformations towards the professionalisation of the women's game are occurring more rapidly elsewhere than within Scotland and, increasingly (as is also the case with some Republic of Ireland players), a number of Scottish players are developing their playing potential in more professionalised structures around the world, for example, in the United States, Iceland, Germany and England. In their *Report on the Reform of Scottish Football* published in December 2005, the Scottish Parliament Enterprise and Culture Committee identified women's football as a key aspect of Scottish "Football's Future" (Scottish Parliament Enterprise and Culture Committee, 2005b: para.118) and acknowledged "the importance of integrating and encouraging the development of women's football" at national levels and within professional and semi-professional Scottish men's clubs (Scottish Parliament Enterprise and Culture Committee, 2005b: para.131). However, the extent to which such integration will be supported throughout Scotland, and the pace and level at which integration occurs has yet to be seen.

Conclusion

This chapter has attempted to redress the dearth of historical research on Scottish women's football and it has sought to demonstrate that the development of women's football in that country has been "constitutively inserted into the struggles, the forms of compliance and opposition, social reproduction and transformation, associated with changing patterns of social development" (Gruneau, 1981: p. 10). In so doing, it has identified the ways in which developments in women's football have occurred within the context of wider social developments in Scotland, particularly in the dominant sport culture. Given the dearth of research and the relative neglect of this topic area, there are clearly some issues which warrant further investigation.

One area of note includes the scope for testing the adequacy of subcultural theories in future empirical analyses of women's football in Scotland and other countries, particularly given the recent developments in subcultural research on neotribal movements, new social movements and subcultural legacies. Although international histories of women's football tend to recognise that the game has generally been marginalised in relation to dominant sports cultures, it is significant that, despite its 'subcultural' existence in many societies, none of the emerging histories have explicitly conceptualised women's football in this way. This has been done effectively in research on a range of other sport subcultures (for example Donnelly, 1993) and there is scope for subcultural theories to inform future research on the history of women's football.

In his discussion of resilience and transformation in sport subcultures, Donnelly (1993: p. 123) argues that there are continual challenges to the dominant culture that must be answered or accommodated, and these challenges often come in the form of residual and emergent sport subcultures. The dominant sport culture in Scotland is overwhelmingly male and, arguably, football-dominated despite women's involvement in folk football since the seventeenth century.

Cohen (1955, cited in Clarke, 1974: p. 436) suggests that, subcultures that have emerged as a solution to the distinctive characteristics of their locations in the social structure, are likely to continue for as long as the structural problems persist. This claim also warrants further investigation in the light of the social developments highlighted in this chapter and the more recent theoretical developments in the area of subcultural theory. In Scotland, women's football emerged as one solution to the varied structural problems associated with the First World War. Though it was then defined largely by the charitable function it served, it was supported for as long as this structural problem persisted such that women's participation in football *for football's sake* gradually became more anachronistic and came to represent a challenge to the dominant sport culture in Scotland.[7]

Pre-war disagreements and arguments (generally based on dominant medical opinion at that time) about women's participation in, and association with football emerged as one opposition to the women's game and this opinion was disseminated through the Scottish press. Yet, women's football in Scotland did not cease to exist but, rather it came to have a residual status. As Clarke (1974: p. 437) suggests, "images in terms of which the subculture is transmitted to a wider public either by word of mouth or through the mass media play an important part in the reaction process" and reactions to subcultures have consequences for their development. Although strong negative or positive reaction can lead to amplification or assimilation of the subculture, Clarke (1974: p. 437) recognises that there are various stabilising positions which are "usually achieved by the sub-culture removing itself sufficiently far from contact with non-members to avoid providing an obvious target for public complaint or exploitation". In the case of Scotland, the women who were involved in playing football had little or no control over their removal from contact with non-members.

Despite being subjected to a relatively high degree of hostility and relative subordination throughout its development, women's football in Scotland has gradually developed into a competitive, structured and institutionalised sport. Since official recognition was given by the SFA to women's football in 1974, women's football is transforming, at least at the structural level, toward being incorporated into the dominant sports culture. However, forms of hegemonic masculinities, manifest within Scottish sport and football culture, have continued to work to subordinate the women's game such that it continues to be marginalised on a number of levels (for example, in terms of media exposure and financial investment). Therefore, on the basis that it is played by women, it could be argued that women's football is not yet fully incorporated into the dominant sports culture in Scotland (Macbeth, 2004). In other words, it has not yet made the "transformation from subcultural to cultural" (Maguire *et al.*, 2002: p. 176) and this process is likely to take some time.

Finally, as I have said from the outset, this chapter represents a further contribution to the emerging body of international research on the history of women's football. By examining the development of women's football within the wider Scottish context, this chapter has not only focused on an understanding of resilience and transformation in women's football, but it has also provided an essential historical context in which to locate future analyses of women's football in contemporary Scottish society. These final remarks are also predicated on the potential for future research on the history of women's football, and the experiences of women footballers in contemporary societies, to be informed by subcultural theories.

Notes

1 Although the minute of 11th November 1970 appears to imply the formal existence of a Women's Football Association in Scotland, this was not officially established until the following year.

2 The Swedish Football Association (SFF) met UEFA's recommendations in 1972 and "decided that women's football should be organized under the leadership of SFF and that women should be incorporated into all the organizational levels" (Hjelm and Olofsson, 2003: p.190). In West Germany, 'ladies' football' was officially recognized by the German Football Federation (DFB) in 1970. The Danish Football Association (DBU) admitted women's football into its organization in February 1972 (Brus and Trangbaek, 2003: p. 106).

3 SFA minutes record the following: Women's Football (Item 319. Executive and General Purposes Committee). A letter from UEFA was noted. (SFA minutes, 9th May 1973).

4 Women's Football (Item 70. Executive and General Purposes Committee). It was agreed to give recognition to women's football. (SFA meeting, 29th August 1974).

5 The affiliation of other UK women's football associations to their national Football Associations occurred earlier in the 1990s (Williams, 2003b)

6 See Liston (2006) who shares a similar concern about the 'talent drain' in women's football in the Republic of Ireland.

7 Donnelly (1993: p. 124) explains that resilience refers to "instances of sport subcultures where the form and meanings and ways of the sport survive to become anachronistic and possibly oppositional to the dominant sport culture".

References

Bourke, A. (2003) 'Women's football in the republic of ireland: Past events and future prospects', *Soccer and Society* Vol. 4, No. 2/3: pp. 162–181.

Bairner, A. (2000) 'Football' in Jarvie, G. and Burnett, J. (eds) *Sport, Scotland and the Scots*. East Lothian: Tuckwell Press, pp. 87–104.

Brus, A. and Trangbaek, E. (2003) 'Asserting the right to play — women's football in Denmark', *Soccer and Society* Vol. 4, No. 2/3: pp. 95–111.

Carlyle, A. (Rev.) (1795) 'Inveresk', *in Old Statistical Account, Volume 16*, pp. 1–49 and 642–643.

Chambers, R. (1858) *Domestic Annals of Scotland from the Reformation to [the Rebellion of 1745]*. Edinburgh: Chambers.

Clarke, M. (1974) 'On the concept of "subculture"', *British Journal of Sociology*, Vol. 25: pp. 428–441.

Cohen, A. K. (1955) *Delinquent boys*. Glencoe, Illinois: Free Press.

Cook, E (2000) Unpublished personal scrapbook and letters. Courtesy of Jean Williams.

Cox, B. and Thompson, S. (2003) 'From heydays to struggles: Women's soccer in New Zealand', *Soccer and Society* Vol. 4, No. 2/3: pp. 205–224.

Donnelly, P. (1993) 'Subcultures in sport: Resilience and transformation', in A.G. Ingham and J.W. Loy (eds) *Sport in social development: Traditions, transitions, and transformations*. Champaign, Illinois: Human Kinetics, pp. 119–145.

——— (2000) 'Interpretive Approaches to the Sociology of Sport', in Coakley, J. and Dunning, E. (eds) *Handbook of sports studies*. London: Sage, pp. 77–91.

Dunning, E. (1999) *Sport matters*. London: Routledge.

Dunning, E. and Sheard, K. (2005) *Barbarians, gentlemen and players: A sociological study of the development of Rugby Football* (2nd Edition). Oxon: Routledge.

Elias, N. and Dunning, E. (1986) *Quest for excitement: Sport and leisure in the civilizing process*. Oxford: Basil Blackwell.

Fasting, K. (2003) 'Small country — big results: Women's football in Norway', *Soccer and Society* Vol. 4, No. 2/3: pp. 149–161.

Fittis, R. S. (1975) *Sports and pastimes of Scotland*. Edinburgh: E. P. Publishing.

Glasgow News (1881) 'Female football players', *Glasgow News*, May 9th.

Gruneau, R. (1981) 'Review of "Surfing Subcultures of Australia and New Zealand"', *ICSS Bulletin* No. 21: pp. 8–10, cited in Donnelly, P. (2000) 'Interpretive approaches to the sociology of sport', in J. Coakley and E. Dunning (eds) *Handbook of sports studies*. London: Sage, pp. 77–91.

Hall, M.A. (2003) 'The game of choice: Girls' and women's soccer in Canada', *Soccer and Society* Vol. 4, No. 2/3: pp. 30–46.

Hargreaves, J. (1994) *Sporting females: Critical issues in the history and sociology of women's sports*. London: Routledge.

Hjelm, J. and Olofsson, E. (2003) 'A breakthrough: Women's football in Sweden', *Soccer and Society* Vol. 4, No. 2/3: pp. 182–204.

Hong, F. and Mangan, J.A. (2003) 'Will the "Iron Roses" bloom forever? Women's football in China: Changes and challenges', *Soccer and Society* Vol. 4, No. 2/3: pp. 47–66.

Hope, C (Rev). (1845) 'United Parishes of Wandell and Lamingtoune — Presbytery of Biggar, Synod of Lothian and Tweeddale', *The New Statistical Account of Scotland, Volume 6, Lanark*, Edinburgh: William Blackwood, pp. 805–845.

Koh, E. (2003) 'Chains, challenges and changes: The making of women's football in Korea', *Soccer and Society* Vol. 4, No. 2/3: pp. 67–79.

Liston, K. (2006) 'Women's soccer in the Republic of Ireland: Some preliminary sociological comments', *Soccer and Society*, Vol. 7, No. 2/3: pp.364–384.

Lopez, S. (1997) *Women on the ball: A guide to women's football*. London: Scarlet Press.

Lynch, M. (1992) *Scotland: A new history*. London: Pimlico.

Macbeth, J.L. (2002) 'The Development of Women's Football in Scotland', *Sports Historian* Vol. 22, No. 2: pp. 149–163.

——— (2004) *Women's football in scotland: An interpretive analysis*, unpublished Ph.D Thesis, Scotland: University of Stirling.

——— (2005) 'The "pals", the "professionals" and the "conformers": The meaning of football in the lives of women footballers in Scotland', in J. Magee, A. Bairner and A. Tomlinson (eds) *The bountiful game? Football identities and finances*. Oxford: Meyer and Meyer Sport, pp. 79–97.

Maguire, J., Jarvie, G., Mansfield, L. and Bradley, J. (2002) *Sport worlds: A sociological perspective*. Champaign, Illinois: Human Kinetics.

Majumdar, B. (2003) 'Forwards and backwards: Women's soccer in twentieth-century India', *Soccer and Society* Vol. 4, No. 2/3: pp. 80–94.

Markovits, A.S. and Hellerman, S.L. (2003) 'Women's soccer in the United States: Yet another American "exceptionalism"', *Soccer and Society* Vol. 4, No. 2/3: pp. 14–29.

Mawhinney, L. (2002) 'The goal is to make it to the top', *The Herald (Glasgow)*, Scottish Media Newspapers Limited, August 6th, p. 13.

McCuiag, M. (1997) 'A game of two sexes', *The Herald (Glasgow)*, Caledonian Newspapers Limited, February 8th, p. 2.

——— (2000a) 'A brief history of women's football', at http://www.scottishfa.co.uk/museum/women_index.htm. Date accessed: 05/09/00.

——— (2000b) *Celtic and the people's game — the role of women in the history and development of Celtic Football Club*, unpublished.

Melling, A. (1999) '"Plucky lasses", "pea soup" and politics: The role of ladies' football during the 1921 miners' lock-out in Wigan and Leigh', *International Journal of the History of Sport* Vol. 16, No. 1: pp. 38–64.

Newsham, G. (1997) *In a league of their own!*. London: Scarlet Press.

Pearson, L. (2003) 'Net gains and goals', *The Scotsman*, The Scotsman Publications Limited, October 14th, p. 12.

Pfister, G. (2003) 'The Challenges of Women's Football in East and West Germany: A comparative study', *Soccer and Society* Vol. 4, No. 2/3: pp. 128–148.

Polley, M. (1998) *Moving the goalposts: A history of sport and society since 1945*. London: Routledge.

Saavedra, M. (2003) 'Football feminine — development of the African Game: Senegal, Nigeria and South Africa', *Soccer and Society* Vol. 4, No. 2/3: pp. 225–253.

Scottish Football Association (1924) *Meeting Minutes*, Scottish Football Museum Archive.

——— (1925) *Meeting Minutes*, Scottish Football Museum Archive.

——— (1949) *Meeting Minutes*, Scottish Football Museum Archive.

——— (1970) *Meeting Minutes*, Scottish Football Museum Archive.

——— (1973) *Meeting Minutes*, Scottish Football Museum Archive.

——— (1974) *Meeting Minutes*, Scottish Football Museum Archive.

——— (1976) *Meeting Minutes*, Scottish Football Museum Archive.

Scottish Football Association (2005) *Scottish Football Association Annual Review 2005*, Glasgow: Scottish Football Association. At: http://www.scottishfa.co.uk. Accessed: 13th March 2006.

Scottish Sport (1921) 'The football playing women: "A most unsuitable game"', *Scottish Sport*, December 6th.

Scottish Parliament Enterprise and Culture Committee (2005b). *Report on Reform of Scottish Football: Volume 1*, (13th Report, 2005 [Session 2], SP Paper 456). Edinburgh: Scottish Parliament. At: http://www.scottish.parliament.uk/business/committees/enterprise/reports-05/elr05–13–vol01.htm. Accessed: 13th March 2006.

Stirling Observer (1896) 'The female footballers in Stirling', *Stirling Observer*, July 4th.

Sugden, J. and Tomlinson, A. (1999) 'Digging the dirt and staying clean: Retrieving the investigative tradition for a critical sociology of sport', *International Review for the Sociology of Sport* Vol. 34, No. 4: pp. 385–397.

The Herald (1921) 'Measures to prevent women footballers', *The Herald*, December 6th.

Votre, S. and Mourao, L. (2003) 'Women's football in Brazil: Progress and problems', *Soccer and Society* Vol. 4, No. 2/3: pp. 254–267.

Williams, J. (2003a) *A game for rough girls? A history of women's football in Britain*. London: Routledge.

——— (2003b) 'The fastest growing sport? Women's football in England', *Soccer and Society* Vol. 4, No. 2/3: pp. 112–127.

LES FEMMES, BALLE AU PIED — A HISTORY OF FRENCH WOMEN'S FOOTBALL

Laurence Prudhomme-Poncet

Centre de Recherche et d'Innovation sur le sport (CRIS), Université Claude Bernard Lyon

Introduction

Whereas the World Cup in men's football has become an important media event, especially in France when the country hosted and then won the 1998 tournament, women's football receives little coverage in comparison and remains on the margins. Football is synonymous globally with masculinity and being a 'man's game'. In France this is no different. The governing body, the French Football Federation (FFF), has only 2% women registered and despite the recent support of Aime Jacquet, the Technical Director of Football, for the development of women's football in France, women's football there receives little encouragement.

Women's football in France has had a chaotic development and its history is characterized by a complete interruption in the middle of the 20th century. Thus, when considering the history timeline, women's football in France has two stages: from 1917 until 1937 and from 1965 to the present. For reasons that will become clear in this chapter, there was a gap in development of the game from 1937–1965. This chapter emerges out my doctoral thesis, *Ces dames du ballon rond* (Prudhomme-Poncet, 2003), which chronicled the factors surrounding the disrupted growth of women's football in comparison to the development of French men's football during the 20th century. This chapter provides an overview of the history of women's football in France with particular focus on the two stages and the reasons for the period of interruption in the mid 1900s.

Stage 1: The birth and early death of women's football in France (1917–1937)

The pioneers

In France, the first sign of women playing organized football occurred in 1917, approximately 30 years after men first played. It is recorded in the daily paper *L'Auto* (October 2, 1917) that two teams from *Femina Sport* played a match in late September 1917. *Femina Sport* was founded in 1912 in Paris as a female multi-sports association to encourage physical education for girls and women, workers and employees (*Journal Officiel*, July 27, 1912). The football match in 1917 was connected to the rise of other open air sports that were encouraged by *Femina Sport* and the match appeared a few weeks after the first interclub meeting of athletics, a few months before basketball and cross-country running competitions. At this stage it is important to recognise the overall importance of *Femina Sport*.

The early pioneers of *Femina Sport* were Therese Brule, her sister Jeanne and also Suzanne Liebrard, all employed in clerical jobs. *Femina Sport* practiced remedial gymnastics and took part in different gymnastics meetings where they obtained first place in the Ludin gymnastics Challenge at Melun in 1914. The organisation also formed a swimming team in 1913, swam in that team, practised French boxing, and took part in athletics events. *Femina Sport* photo archives from 1912–1925 contain images of women playing a variety of sports (private archives of *Femina Sport*, Stade Elisabeth, Paris). Indeed Suzanne Liebrard was a national champion in the hurdle race, the long jump and the javelin events (*L'Auto*, July 16, 1917). Whilst many of the activities organised by *Femina Sport* were individual sports, they also tried basketball and hockey before playing football (Paysse, 1918). A key point to note is that because of World War One, pedagogues and doctors had begun to support physical education programmes for women, though this did not necessarily include contact team sports such as football.

After a few football matches among themselves in 1917, women's teams from *Femina Sport* then played against boys' school teams. They first played against the third team of Lycée Buffon and lost 6–1 (*L'Auto*, October 29, 1917), then and a week later played against *Lycee Charlemagne* before competing against five Parisian well known boys' teams (Stade Français, Club Athletique de la Societe Generale, Club Français, Club Athletique du

XIVe and Union Sportive Commerciale). In sixteen matches they had one victory, two draws and 13 defeats; but the fact that girls and boys competed against each other was remarkable given that non-mixing was the rule at school and in society (Perrot, 1998). However Pierre Paysse — a gymnast who was horizontal bar world champion in 1906— helped organise the matches as he was a gymnastics teacher in two secondary boys' schools and recognised that girl's teams had no opposition. The contests ended after six months because the federation of athletics (Union des Societes Françaises des Sports Athletiques, USFSA), the first amateur multi-sports federation managing about twenty sports, prohibited its member clubs from playing football against women's teams. However by this stage two other ladies football teams, *Academia* and *En Avant*, had been formed and women took greater control of organising their own football events and meetings. In November 1918, one year after the first emergence of women's football, women's teams competed against each other with *En Avant* playing *Femina Sport* (*L'Auto*, November 11, 1918) and then *En Avant* against *Academia* (*L'Auto*, January 6, 1919).

A marginal organisation

The USFSA, with its mandate to refuse women to participate in most sports, though tennis and hockey were accepted and supported, was key in the formation of the Federation des Societes Feminines Sportives de France (FSFSF) in January 1918. Due to the success of the summer athletics games organised by *Femina Sport*, the head of *Femina Sport*, Pierre Paysse, and Albert Pelan from the women's sections of *En Avant*, spearheaded the official founding of the FSFSF as a sports organization for women. Even though women and girl footballers first began competing against men and boys there was not enough support, through FSFSF, to sustain women's football. The French Football Federation (FFF) was formed in 1919 but refused to accept women (Eyquem, 1944) though this ban did not exclude women from playing on football grounds of men's teams, something which occurred in England in 1921 (Williams, 2003: p. 33).

In 1919, Alice Milliat, a sales representative by profession and brilliant oarswoman, became Chair of the FSFSF and from then on the organisation was managed only by women. Milliat is described by Newsham (1994: p. 27) as a person with "knowledge and experience of association football [that] was probably unequalled by that of any other woman in France". Milliat was a particular advocate of women's sports and had articles published in newspapers, such as *Le Soldat de demain* and *L'Auto*, in support of women competing in sport. One particular piece, *Le football feminin* (Milliat, 1920), was a kind of answer to detractors in which Milliat promoted the development of women's football and concluded with the hope that one day women in France would play in provincial and international matches. Another article, *La progression du football feminine* (Milliat, 1923), featured a very brief history about women's football and described the sport as "one of the healthiest and the most enthralling sports" (Milliat, 1923). Milliat pleaded for support, encouragement and finance for women's sport organisations, tried to encourage women referees to participate in the popular men's sports of basketball and football, and was also particularly vocal in her support for women to be included in the Olympic Games. Even though the FSFSF was run by women for women it rejected accusations that it was a feminist movement. The *Conseil National des Femmes Françaises* (CNFF) did however create a football competition for women, *La Française*, (named after their newspaper), members of FSFSF were not formally engaged in feminist movements and, for example, the FSFSF did not campaign for the right of women to vote. Nevertheless, we can consider the practice of sports by women as a sort of 'feminism in action' and playing football, despite scathing criticism, was a way to protest about the exclusion of women from sport (*La Française*, January 21, 1922). In a sense, women's participation in the male domain of sport, and especially football, was seen as a way of offering resistance to what was going on in broader society.

The FSFSF initially organised cross country, basketball, hockey, athletics and swimming championships but established the first official football championship in 1919 (*L'Auto*, January 11, 1919). By this stage the FSFSF established specially adapted rules for women based on the men's rules (Paysse, 1918), rules which were definitively agreed after some minor teething issues in 1923 (Les Sportives, November 19, 1923). The main differences involved smaller dimensions of the playing field and a shorter match in terms of length (one hour instead of one hour and thirty minutes). The game was thus referred to as *edulcore, denicotinise* which when translated means 'sweetened, sanitized' (*L'Auto*, February 14, 1926) and *adouci, adapte, feminise* which means softened, adapted, more feminine (Pefferkorn, 1921). However the adaptations and associated descriptors reinforced the traditional view of women as naturally weak and delicate creatures who should be protected. Even though that during the 1920s signs of female emancipation, as symbolised by the short "bob" haircut, were emerging, the traditional image of the woman as a wife and mother remained predominant and adaptations to the rules partly reinforced these.

In the first championships in 1919 Only two teams competed — *Femina Sport* and *En Avant* — and the first match, which drew considerable spectator interest, ended with a victory for *Femina Sport* while the return leg ended goalless to crown *Femina Sport* as champions (*L'Auto*, March 24,1919). In 1921 six clubs took part and *En Avant* won the Championship of Paris and then beat the provincial team *Sportives*, of Reims, to become and became France Champion. *Femina Sport* then began an advertising campaign to encourage more female clubs to be formed(*L'Auto*, December 6, 1923). In 1924, 16 teams competed: as well as Parisian teams there were provincial teams from Reims, Rouen and Toulouse, a clear indication of the dissemination and popularity of women's football in France. *Femina Sport* won the 1924 tournament and went on to dominate the competition for the next ten years. As well as the National Championships, a national Cup competition, similar to the one in the men's game, was held from 1922 until 1926 but failed to be established as it had to be compressed after the championships were over so as not to encroach on the summer athletics season.

In 1920 an invitation by Dick, Kerr Ladies FC from Preston, England resulted in Alice Milliat selecting a touring team composed of players from *En Avant*, *Femina Sport* and *Sportives* to play in matches to raise money for war charities (Newsham, 1994). According to Newsham (1994: p. 24) the invitation arose to the French team materialised because:

> It seemed to the management of Dick, Kerr Ladies that the next step in the evolution of the women's game would be to invite a team from France over to England to play football, for obvious charitable reasons. The defence of French soil by British soldiers during the recent war had set up strong ties between the two nations, and what better way for France to give something back than to send a women's football team to England to play for British charities?

Four matches were played in Preston, Stockport, Manchester and London with the first one, at Preston North End's Deepdale ground, attracting 25,000 spectators. Details of the trip can be found in Newsham (1994: pp. 24–30) but a return trip was organised in the autumn of that year with Dick, Kerr Ladies playing in Paris, Roubaix, Le Havre and Rouen. This trip was particularly poignant as "some of the players had lost brothers in the war and they hoped to place wreaths on public memorials to British soldiers in the four towns where their matches where to be played" (Newsham, 1994: p. 32). The tour was the first time an English women's team had officially toured and Dick, Kerr Ladies confirmed their superiority by securing three victories and a draw. The match at Roubaix drew the largest crowd, 16,000 spectators, and women's football made it to the front page of *Miroir des Sports* by featuring as a new subject for caricaturists (Miroir des Sports, November 4, 1920). A further benefit of the French-Anglo links was the establishment of an annual fixture between the French and English ladies teams but these fixtures did not become regular features as women's football in France, as the next section will demonstrate, ran into particular problems.

The rise and rapid fall of women's football

After a euphoric period in the early 1920s, women's football in France started to stagnate. One of the difficulties was that it was Parisian dominated, and despite teams in Reims, Rouen, Toulouse and Marseille, and at no time were there more than 15 competing clubs. Also women's football became a target for criticism by doctors because of the physical toil involved with non-competitive forms of physical exercises for women receiving support. At the same time accusations of 'shamateurism' in men's football were formulated (*Miroir des Sports*, September 1, 1921) and in general football was regarded as the most controversial of women's sports (*L'Auto*, October 29,1921). In spite of the special rules for women's football the sport was considered unsuitable for women owing to the perceived levels of violence involved, the contentions that football made women players appear masculine and also the perceived fears that playing the game would make women infertile. According to Henri Bard, ex-captain of the French national football team, football was a violent game that was potentially dangerous for woman (Bard and Diffre, 1927); hygienists and doctors condemned women's football as an activity unsuitable for women (Cezembre, 1922); and wearing shorts and football boots was supposed to make women ugly and manly (Pefferkorn, 1921). An article in the newspaper *L'Auto* (February 21, 1922) featured the quote:"football is not a game for woman because it is too rough and requires sustained and hard efforts". In essence, football was culturally viewed as a male combative sport incompatible with feminine grace and beauty and the game was seen as a dangerous and pernicious show. "The spectators, simply attracted by a vague curiosity of sex, wish to see what sort of showing the women give of themselves in an exercise which is as inappropriate as possible to women" (*L'Auto*, December 8, 1921). Football, like other competitive / combative sports at the time, was not socially acceptable for women and those who played football were slandered as being a 'garçonne"– translated to English as 'tomboy'.

Alice Milliat noted the decline in the late 1920s and early 1930s and in 1931 only eight teams took part in the French championship (*L'Auto*, September 22, 1931 and November 18, 1931). Consequently the FSFSF decided to abandon football in 1933 because of the lack of arenas, a lack of money and the propaganda campaign against women's football (*L'Auto*, May 4, 1933). Such pressure had already taken its toll on women playing rugby union a few years before (*L'Auto*, September 29, 1927) and the FSFSF then focused its efforts on the development of basketball, a sport that was considered much more respectable as it was regarded as non-contact, less tiring, and gracious. Continued difficulties caused the collapse of the FSFSF in 1936 on behalf of men's institutions and the few surviving women's teams still playing created a separate federation which also collapsed for the same reasons in 1937 (*L'Auto*, September 28, 1938).

Consequently the fight to establish women's football during the inter-war years was a difficult task. Women's football suffered too much criticism by numerous players, journalists, doctors to sufficiently develop it. As Christine Bard clearly points out, "the fright of masculinization for all emancipated women as artists, intellectuals ... was a *collective obsession* during the 1920s" (1999: p. 161). Moreover, the development of men's professional football from 1932, under the auspices of the FFF, and the economic and financial crisis within the FSFSF, strengthened the influence of opponents of women's football. Traditional ideals of womanhood and the family gained new significance in this period and from 1931 articles against women's participation in the workplace increased. In 1933, several congress members in Paris insisted on women's place being in home (Bard, 2001: p. 68.) so playing football, and other competitive / combative sports duly received little support and encouragement.

Intermittent and sporadic interest

During the Second World War the Vichy government encouraged women's sports in order to help the war cause but still prohibited football as an activity for women (Eyquem, 1941). Following the Second World War, football was still considered a male domain while at the same time women were encouraged to retreat into domesticity and maintain their place in the home. Women's football was not supported but international matches against England continued in the 1930s, the last one before the outbreak of the Second World War taking place in 1937 (Newsham, 1994). In June 1947 a French team returned to England and played five matches in eight days (Newsham, 1994) and played again in 1948, 1949 and 1951 against Dick, Kerr Ladies who by this time were representing England (Newsham, 1994). In these matches the French team were composed of players from others sports — basketball, athletics and swimming — and not surprisingly lost all the matches. There are no records of any more French international matches in this era but Newsham (1994) makes references to how the post-Second World War French teams were of a much poorer standard than their pre-war counterparts, something which could have been a factor in their further decline.

Stage 2: The new age of women's football (1965–present)

The beginning: a fun 'sideshow'

Women's participation in football re-emerged in the 1960s though this was as a mere sideshow as they were present to help the male teams to raise money. At the time football was attracting more and more boys but the number of spectators of both amateur and professional competitions had stopped increasing (Wahl, 1989: p. 267) and women were seen as a way of regenerating such interest. At Humbecourt in 1965, Gerstheim in 1967 and Reims in 1968, the idea was the same: to dress up women footballers to attract a lot of interested male spectators. Football for women was thus was only tolerated in this 'humorous' or 'ridiculous' sideshow and women were given a merely traditional and conformist role as an accompaniment to men. This 'resurgence' of women's football was therefore only a parody, but at the same time it was a sign that women were interested in football and could be motivated for future competitions. Most of the women involved would already have kicked a football for fun with their brothers and friends or at least would have watched them playing and it is fair to say that there was female interest in playing the game this period.

An acknowledged but criticized practice

Appearing first as side shows to the men's game to attract spectators, the popularity of women's football began to increase with local and regional competitions being established. Contrary to the Parisian-dominance of the early twentieth century the re-birth of women's football was further-reaching, with the Reims and Alsace regions particularly prominent. In Reims in the Champagne region a championship was established in 1968–69 with thirteen teams competing, a championship won by the local Reims team (*L'Union*, February 12, 1969). The Reims club played an important function in popularizing women's football with journalist Pierre Geoffroy very active in support of women's football. In Alsace in Eastern France, the first women's club established was *FC Feminin de Schwindratzheim* in 1968 and a regional championship involving nine teams was established for 1969–1970, a championship won by *Schwindratzheim* (Alsace foot, July 3, 1970). The championship was so popular that by September 1971 25 teams entered (Alsace foot, October 1, 1971).

A key factor in the popularisation of women's football beyond Paris was that by the 1960s the men's game was popular throughout France and the sport could thus have been considered to have 'national' dimensions. This meant that more women were exposed to the game, initially as spectators of the men's game or as recreational players with male family members and male friends. By 1971, there were more than 2000 female players, such was the popularity; and in Lyon, as an example, there were more than 40 clubs. It needs recognising in this re-birth era that some women's clubs were established as female sections of male clubs rather than as independent women's clubs in their own rights.

Given this rising phenomenon and in spite of opposition some fifty years earlier, the FFF officially recognized women's football in March 1970 (*France Football Officiel*, April 15, 1970). A key reason in this could have been the FFF's anxiety about the possible creation of an autonomous organisation for women's football, as was the case in other European countries at the time. However the FFF also recognised that the popularity of women's football would bring more members to the FFF and generate interest in football amongst husbands and children of women members. The FFF established'a commission, *Commission centrale du football feminin* (CCFF), to take charge of organising women's football at the national level with assistance from regional committees (*France Football Officiel*, August 5, 1970). The first CCFF was composed of two women and eight men but became progressively more female-dominated the longer it existed and its first key action was to establish *le Statut federal feminin* in 1972 to formalise age categories, rules of the game, and to forbid teams having mixed composition (Annuaire 1972–1973, FFF). In terms of rule adaptations, women played with a slightly smaller ball, corners were taken from closer to the goal, the duration of the match was 70 minutes, a handball resulting from a person protecting her chest was at the referee's discretion, more substitutes were permitted, the goalkeeper could release the ball into play from further forward, and a chest protector was recommended for goal-keepers (*France Football Officiel*, August 5, 1970). Some of these adaptations however reinforced the traditional idea of women needing 'protecting', even if this was not the intention of the CCFF.

In 1974, the FFF organized its first national championship with sixteen teams involved. *Stade de Reims* were particularly dominant and defeated *VGA Saint-Maur* 9–0 in their first match before winning 5–0 against *Arago Sport d'Orléans*. Despite the resurgence of popularity and the official involvement as part of the FFF, traditional arguments on the roughness of the game, the poor technical level of women players and the masculinization of their bodies were voiced. The expression 'tomboy' was popularised in French language to describe women footballers and replaced 'garçonne', used in the 1920s. In 1988 a spectator wrote: "...tell me what is really feminine in a female football player? Her haircut worthy of the military? Her hairy legs or her Rambo-like build! I couldn't see hairs on their chins but that's because I am losing my sight" (*Femme Foot*, 1988: p. 12). The fear of women becoming masculinized is not specific to football players but is part of a broader argument when women enter fields / space that are traditionally regarded as masculine. Women's football in France in both phases of its popularity could not avoid become embroiled in the same argument.

However, these suspicions about the femininity of women football players are counterbalanced by opinions which idealize rather than stigmatize the female body. It is true that women players can remain highly feminine and despite their involvement in football can still be considered as 'real' ladies. Journalists in *Foot Supporter Magazine* (1977) portrayed female players as housewives and mothers but also as elegant women who wear skirts and dress after the matches. However this portrayal could also be viewed as a trivialisation of female footballers by focusing on their mothering qualities and appearance rather than their footballing ability. Contrary to criticism put forward at the beginning of the century, in this period no medical arguments were raised against women's practice of football. The medical reports made at the request of the FFF actually supported women's football. According to doctors A. Hurez and J. Merault, football is not a dangerous activity for the female body (*France Football Officiel*, November 4, 1970), a report that certainly contrasted with views from some fifty years earlier.

Throughout the 1970s, 1980s and 1990s, women's football in France continued to progress. The national French Championship has been established since in 1974 and, like other European countries, provided France with a formal structure that permitted competition on the international scene. France entered the inaugural European Women's Tournament in 1982 and despite winning their first match they failed to qualify for the latter stages of the tournament. The popularity of women's football throughout Europe resulted in UEFA establishing the Women's European Championships and France have competed in each of the six held so far — but has never gone further than the quarter-finals stage — and also at the World Cup. 1998 was a particularly special year for French football as not only did the men's national team win the World Cup on home soil but the women's Under-19 team won the European tournament. At present there are three women's national leagues and 48,000 members (2%) of the FFF are females. Like other European countries however, there is no infrastructure to support a fully professionalized system for women's football in France and television and media coverage and sponsorship revenue are a poor relation in the female's game when compared to that of the men's.

Conclusion: An "offside" game?

In France, the first recorded game of football between women took place in 1917 in Paris and the most well known and successful team of the era was *Femina Sport* of Paris. The initial success of women's football at the beginning of the 1920s was made possible by the particular context at the turn of the century. Women were encouraged to become physically fitter to assist the war cause and women discovered football (and other athletic pursuits) as a kind of emancipation. Women's football had its own specific growth pattern, independent of the football authorities even though the organisation of competitions was similar to that of men's competitions. However women's football attracted of a lot of criticism during the 1920s, particularly references to 'la garçonne' and gradually the game declined toward the end of the 1920s. The period of absence was halted at the beginning of the 1960s as women's football developed in a social context that was more favourable to women. After the 'sideshows' of the late 1960s the game became more popular and spread throughout the country but, significantly, did not attract many spectators. At the end of 1970, the most successful team — *Reims* team — could only attract an average of about 200 or 300 spectators. Despite firther progressions in the sport nowadays the top teams like as *Juvisy* (near Paris) and *Lyon* still do not attract many spectators. It seems that women's football in France will remain condemned as an 'anonymous' sport that attracts little by media interest. On television, in contrast with men's football, women players are almost completely absent and the qualifying matches for the 2003 World Cup and the 2005 European Championships were not broadcast on the main channels. In specialised press like *l'Equipe*, *France Football*, *Onze Mondial*, women's football is not given much space, a situation very different to sports such as tennis who regular feature female stars. Moreover, successive attempts to produce magazines on women's football have failed as *Le football au feminin* (at the beginning of the 1980s) and *Football feminin* (at the beginning of the 1990s) did not survive more than a few editions. The latest attempt, *foot-feminin.fr,le Magazine*, appeared in 2001 but disappeared after four issues.

Finally, women's football remains an amateur sport and the distance between the professional men's game and the amateur women's version is continually increasing. It is doubtful that the integration of female teams within major professional clubs, like *Olympique Lyonnais* did in 2005 when they incorporated a female team, will be enough to reverse the present trend of growth in the men's game and under-development of the women's. Today, football is still widely regarded as a 'man's game' in which women are still seen as marginal. The relatively poor showing of France at major international tournaments has not helped to create a 'spirit of success'. In 2000 *L'Equipe Magazine* (October 28, 2000) proclaimed that "women are the future of football" because of the popularity and growth of women's football on the back of the 1998 World Cup success of the men's team. However, six years on there is little evidence to support L'Equipe's claim and unless significant investment in the women's game occurs it will continue to be on the margins of French football, despite boasting a history that stretches back almost 100 years.

References

Alsace foot, 3 July, 1970 and 1 October, 1971.
Annuaire 1972–1973, French Football Federation.
Bard, C. (1999) *Un siècle d'antiféminisme*. Paris: Fayard.
——— (2001) *Les femmes dans la société française au XXe siècle*. Paris: Armand Colin.
Bard, H. and Diffre, H. (1927) *Le Football-association*, Paris: Doin et Cie.
Cezembre, J. (1922) 'Quelques sports qui ne semblent pas réservés aux femmes', *Miroir des Sports*, 9 November.
'Comment devenir une "femme-foot"' (1977) *Foot Supporter Magazine*, No. 4
Eyquem, M. T. (1941) 'L'organisation du sport féminin', *Tous les Sports*, No. 5.
——— (1944) *La femme et le sport*. Paris: Editions Susse.
Milliat, A. (1920), 'Le football féminin', *Le football Association*, 17 April 1920.
——— (1923), 'Le football féminin', *L'Auto*, 6 December 1923.
Newsham Gail, J. (1994) *In a league of their own! The Dick, Kerr Ladies Football Team Lancashire*. Pride of Place Publishing.
Onze Mondial (June 1997).
Paysse, P. (April 1918), 'Le football et la femme', *Les sports feminins*, No. 28.
Pefferkorn, M. (1921) *Le Football-association. Theorie et pratique du jeu de football*. Paris: Flammarion.
Perrot, M. (1998) *Les femmes ou les silences de l'histoire*. Paris: Flammarion.
Prudhomme-Poncet, L. (2003) *Histoire du football feminin au XXe siècle*. Paris: L'Harmattan.
Wahl, A. (1989) *Les archives du football. Sport et société en France (1880–1980)*. Paris: Gallimard/Julliard.
Williams, J. (2003) *A Game for rough girls? A history of women's football in Britain*. London and New York: Routledge.

THE HISTORICAL DEVELOPMENT OF WOMEN'S FOOTBALL IN NORWAY: FROM 'SHOW GAMES' TO INTERNATIONAL SUCCESSES[1]

Bente Ovèdie Skogvang

Hedmark University College

Introduction

Various forms of football were played by indigenous people in countries such as the United States, Chile, Ireland and Britain with *calcio* in Italy and *soule* in France proving particularly popular (Bromberger, 1995; Folds & Harris, 1979; Giulianotti, 1999; Guttmann, 1991; Oliver, 1992). Upper class Japanese women and Native American women played folk football (Williams, 2004) and there is evidence that women in Ireland and the British islands (Lopez, 1997; Newsham, 1994, 2005; Williams, 2004; Williamson, 1991) and France (Prudhomme-Poncet, 2005) played football at the beginning of the 1900s. However, it is well documented that women's football, both in individual countries and globally, has been significantly under-developed during the twentieth century, especially in comparison to the men's game.

Even so, it is possible to see that Italy, Denmark and Sweden have pioneered the major developments that have occurred in women's football. Norway, the country of interest to this paper, has also contributed to the development of women's football and can be considered one of the world's leading nations in women's football at present. However, as in other countries, the journey for women's football in Norway involves 'show matches', a ban by the game's authorities and a subsequent struggle for acceptance and integration into the Norwegian Football Association (NFA) before widespread popularity and acceptance was achieved. This chapter assesses the development of women's football in Norway by dividing its history into three stages:

1. 'Show matches' and curiosity — the 1920s to 1960s;
2. Struggle for acceptance and inclusion in the NFA — the 1970s until 1988;
3. Popularity increases and further international success: 1988 until present.

Stage One: 'Show matches' and curiosity — the 1920s to 1960s

In 1922 the NFA Executive Board member, Per Christian Andersen, described "football as a game for strong men and powerful boys and men" with any notion of women as players being regarded as something strange and monstrous (Goksøyr & Olstad, 2002: p. 79). Even though it was accepted in the 1920s and 1930s that Norwegian women should have a more active role, football was regarded simply as a man's game. However, there was initial interest in women playing organised football and one of the earliest recorded matches featured *Moss Ladies Team* who played against a men's team in 1921 and also against a fellow female team from Askim later that year. Further recordings of matches involving women are quite sketchy but nonetheless in 1928 Crown Prince Olav attended a match between Sonia Henie's team — Henie was a famous ice-dancer of the time — and a men's team. 4000 spectators attended and following a draw Henie's team was awarded the match because of the style in which they performed (Goksøyr and Olstad, 2002).

In 1930 the sports magazine Idrettsliv featured a photograph of *Fjeldstrands Idrettsforenings Ladies*, a team consisting of nine players, and commented that "there is played some football by ladies around the country" (Goksøyr & Olstad, 2002: pp. 80–81). Another recording includes a match in Brumunddal in 1931 when a 'show match' between a women's team and a men's team featured as part of the St. Heinz Day celebrations. The match was not viewed seriously as can be seen in the emphasis on novelty but, nevertheless, it inspired the formation of *Hamar Idrettslags Ladies Team* (Goksøyr & Olstad, 2002) who played against a touring team from Bolton Wanderers in July 1931. There is little other evidence of matches in this era though Fretland (1996) states that a match between men and women in Aurland, Sogn occurred in 1937 with the women's team consisting of only nine players. According to the same source, a match between *Aurland* and *Kapp Idrettsforening* women's teams also took place that year and this match is regarded as a 'real match' as it was formally officiated by a referee. In general, however, it can be concluded from the limited accounts of this era that women playing football did so in 'show matches' against men's teams with the purpose of providing extra spectators interested mainly by the entertainment and novelty factors.

Even though the initial involvement of women in football was not taken particularly seriously, two clubs — *Kvik* in Trondheim and *Brandbu* in Hadeland — did establish women's football sections, but this was a rare occurrence at the time. As was experienced in other countries at the same time, women playing football was not particularly welcomed. The situation is summed up by the following example regarding the women's team from the Fløya club in Tromsø, northern Norway, in 1931. The newly formed women's team decided to organise a match to raise funds for a banner and Harald Rønne, an instrumental figure in football in the region, wrote to the NFA seeking permission as it was generally not seen as appropriate for women to take part in football or any other physically demanding activities. Owing to the slow mail system at the time the reply from the NFA in Oslo arrived after the game had taken place. According to Hansen:

> It took a long time before the NFA answered the letter. Because the match was announced, the Fløya Ladies played without the permission from the NFA. It was a great match between two teams of players from Fløya's Ladies department. As expected a lot of curious people came. The girls played in 'ski boots' and long 'stretch pants', and the spectators got a historical and adventurous football experience. Not all the movements were gracious and controlled. It was a tough game, and the girls left the pitch with blue marks both here and there after kicks which were both controlled and uncontrolled. But it had been fun, and it brought money to the banner and the wish for a repeat match was big. (1994: p. 28)

Another game was arranged but a few days after the first game took place a letter was received form the NFA with the following instruction: "Ladies should not play football. That was not only because it was unsuitable for women, the ladies could also get injuries that destroyed their reproductive organs. Fløya should therefore not allow or let ladies enter the football field. Fløya has to follow that because football was for boys and men!" (Hansen, 1994: p. 29). Owing to the late arrival of this letter, one game had already taken place but the clear view of the governing body prevented another one from being organised.

This view of 'football as a man's game' was common at the time and not just in Norway. Playing football was considered an activity that made women masculine and also exposed them to damaging their reproductive organs (Fasting, Scraton, Pfister, & Bunuel, 1999; Lippe, 1982, 1997; Pettersen, 1985). Fretland (1998: p. 98) comments that "many people spoke against women's sports. It was not medically defensible for a woman to take part in competitive sport. She could not stand the same pain as the man and must be saved from health injuries. All together it was against the healthy ideal for women to do hard sports. Neither was it aesthetic to see sweaty female bodies!". Football was thus considered too tough and physical for women to partake in, with gymnastics and handball more preferred for women.

As evidenced in the letter from the NFA to Harald Rønne regarding Fløya Ladies, the governing body took a dim view of women playing football and banned it from occurring (Lippe, 1997). Even though this historical stage has shown that there was some organised football for women, especially in 'show matches', it was intermittent and sporadic and did not receive support from the NFA. Consequently women's football remained under-developed and poorly supported until the late 1960s and early 1970s, as the next stage demonstrates.

Stage Two: The struggle for acceptance and inclusion in the NFA — the 1970s until 1988

The subsequent development of women's football has to be viewed in relation to the development of Norwegian society in general and the progress of the women's movement toward the end of the 1960s and early 1970s. The Gender Equality Council was established in 1972 and in 1979 the Gender Equality Act came into force to strive to achieve gender equality in Norway. The Nordic philosophy of equality stresses that equal opportunity is not enough and that active efforts are required to promote the status of women (The Gender Equality Ombuds Person, Council T.G.E., 1994).

In 1981 a gender quota was enacted under the Gender Equality Act which required that any committee of at least four people had to have at least two members of each sex as members. This was changed in 1988 to a 40% representation of both sexes on all boards, councils and committees, a feature that was later incorporated into the local Government Act in 1992. In 1990 the Norwegian Sport Association took into the by-laws that: "All national congresses, executive committees, councils and boards shall have representation proportional to the percentage of men and women in the organisation. However, every board must have at least two members of each sex. If a committee has three or fewer members it is not bound to this rule" (The Norwegian Confederation of Sports Laws, 2–4, 1994)

Given that the context was of gender equality in the early 1970s it is no surprise to learn that Norwegian women began playing football again, though it was viewed as part of the anti-authoritarian wave that was popular in Norwegian society at this time. Women did not want to stay behind or be suppressed and that sporting interest was to be more than merely supporters of men's sport. Pettersen (1985: p. 126) states that women of this era "wanted to take part, move borders, and break barriers" and playing football was part of this mandate. In the early 1970s the goal of the NFA was to 'spread and lead the sport of football' (Fotballforbund, 1974) though there was resistance within the NFA to include women's football as part of the development plans. Even though references at the time were made by some NFA (male) members to the positive aspects of women's football, the reality was somewhat different. Arguments preventing women from being formally accepted by the NFA included how playing football made women more masculine, it affected their reproductive organs and it encouraged lesbianism (Pettersen, 1985; Lippe, 2001). Also there was the view that if the NFA formally accepted women it would make football a "frøkensport" — a sport for wimps (Goksøyr & Olstad, 2002). Even though there was clear desire by women to play football, the view of the NFA remained the same between the 1920s and 1960s: women should not play football.

Despite such resistance and a lack of support from the governing body, men and women played together in unofficial leagues and tournaments just as they had done in Stage one. In June 1970 a match between two Bergen women's teams — one from Brann and the other from Sandviken — took place and a month later the Amazons from Grimstad played BUL-Oslo. This match attracted much interest and was popularly considered the 'first' ever women's match but the previous section demonstrates this not to be the case as matches between women's team's had taken place some 40 years earlier. Nonetheless, the Amazons–BUL-Oslo game is viewed as having much significance in forwarding the cause for women's football.

The newspaper *Dagbladet* was an important supporter of women's football in this stage and it featured articles in support of women's football. Together with Ellen Wille and Torgeir Røyert from the Frigg club, *Dagbladet* initiated the Norway Cup in 1971, a tournament which men and women's teams were able to enter but not play against each other. Mixed teams were also not permitted but different categories and age ranges were featured. Initially 16 teams entered the women's competition with the handball team, *Vestar*, winning the first two tournaments but BUL-Oslo gradually became the dominant team. The tournament increased the number of categories for girls and women throughout the late 1970s as it became more popular — the 1977 tournament attracted 57 women's teams while the numbers of girls and women's teams had risen to 249 by 1982 (Torkildsen 1993). Progress has been steadily maintained since and 450 girls and women's teams (out of 1435 teams in total) entered in eight category ranges in 2004 (www.NorwayCup.no). As well as the Norway Cup, the Norwegian Championship was also established in 1978: it provided a league competition for women and not surprisingly BUL-Oslo won the first championship.

It is also important to consider other forms of organised women's football in the 1970s as well as the Norway Cup and championship. Leagues for girls and women were formed throughout Norway during the 1970s as the game steadily diffused. In eastern Norway 'The Runar League', organised by the Runar Sport Club, established a local league for women which later became known as 'The Easter League' ('Østlandsserien'). In the west of the country, the regional football association (Rogaland Football Association) was the first one to organise a league on a regional basis in 1973 and six teams entered. *Haugar* won the league in its first year, one point ahead of *Mulier*, a team that became infamous in Norwegian football when they were 'accepted' into the NFA in 1974. The NFA did not know that *Mulier* was a woman's team — despite the fact that 'mulier' means 'woman' in latin — but when they did *Mulier's* application was rejected! Glåmdal FA established a regional league for women in 1975 and regional leagues were also formed in central Norway (1981), western Norway (1983) and northern Norway (1985) — which meant that by 1985 women's leagues were established in all parts of Norway (Hansen 1994, Goksøyr & Olstad, 2002).

As well as regional leagues, local leagues were established by Øvrevoll Ball Club in Oslo and Torp Club in Østfold. So it would seem that women's football was relatively well accepted and became increasingly popular in the 1970s and early 1980s.

Unfortunately, this is too romantic a tale as those at the centre of developing women's football from the 1970s encountered significant problems with the NFA despite successfully establishing clubs, leagues and tournaments. The ethos of the NFA to 'spread and lead the sport of football' (Fotballforbund, 1974) did not, however, include girls and women as the NFA still refused to accept women's football. As well as the barriers outlined previously (physical issues, reproductive factors, and lesbianism) the lack of playing grounds, dressing room facilities, organisers and referees were factors that prevented women's football from being accepted and subsequently developed. Indeed some men's football clubs openly discriminated against women's clubs. One example was the *Ullensaker/Kisa's* Ladies team who were not allowed to play at the men's ground but rather had to rent a playing ground even though they were part of the men's club (Goksøyr & Olstad, 2002).

What was required was firm leadership and commitment from those dedicated to women's football in the face of such resistance. One of the pioneers was Målfrid Kuvås who is popularly regarded as the 'Mother of Women's Football in Norway'. Kuvås started her football career in 1952 as a 10 year old girl playing for *Børsa Boy's Team* in Sør-Trøndelag in the middle of Norway but, like many of her colleagues, she stopped playing in her puberty as there were no girl's teams, and playing in boy's teams was too difficult. Aged 18, Kuvås moved to Oslo and continued her sporting career by competing in athletics, skating and handball before returning to football in 1969. With football becoming popular again for women at this time, Kuvås was the captain of the *BUL-Oslo* team and helped organise the women's match between *Amazons* of Grimstad and *BUL-Oslo* in 1970. From then on she was a very important figure in the development of women's football. Kuvås then served *BUL-Oslo* for 25 years and her service to football was rewarded when she became the first woman to receive the NFA's Order of Merit Gold at the NFA's anniversary congress in 2002.

Per Ravn Omdal, who is currently a Vice-President of FIFA the world's governing body, was a particular supporter of women's football in his time at the Norwegian FA and had the view that "men and women can use the same dressing rooms and the same shower but at different times". Unni

Hole, from Herd in western Norway, attended the NFA's annual meeting in 1973 and presented the case that as girls and women played football all over the country they should be accepted into the NFA. Later in the same year, the NFA did not formally accept women and girls as members but did decide that women should follow the same rules as men's football with a few exceptions: women played shorter halves (2 x 30 minutes) and they used a size 4 ball which was smaller and lighter (Goksøyr & Olstad, 2002).

Having seen the popularity of women's football rise in neighbouring countries such as Denmark and Sweden the NFA's Executive Board announced in 1974 that: "the stead[il]y increasing interest for women's football in other countries has not yet propagated to Norway, even if women's football is increasing in some regions. Until further notice, the Norwegian FA do not want to be active in that area of our sport." (Fotballforbund, 1974: p. 11). The NFA were not yet going to accept women's football, but under severe pressure established a Women's Committee in 1975 that consisted of Ellen Wille from Frigg, Grete Einarsrud from Ullensaker/Kisa and the General Secretary of the NFA at the time, Nikolai Johansen. Johansen had been a particular opponent of women's football but gradually changed his mind and became a supporter of it. The Women's Committee that he chaired acted as a 'watchdog' body to oversee the establishment of leagues and cups for girls and women. As well, women were encouraged to take courses as leaders, coaches and referees and seek election to NFA committees.

In 1975, 91 girls and women's teams in 17 regional FAs were registered, an impressive figure for the inaugural year. With such numbers it was hard for the NFA to refuse women anymore and at their Annual General meeting of 1976 women were accepted into the NFA, with acknowledgement that "Women's football was established and had reached Norway forever." (Torkildsen, 1993). However Per Pettersen, the manager of the women's national team from 1978–1982 wanted full acceptance for women's football (Goksøyr & Olstad, 2002) — in other words Frigg wanted the same development processes and policies as existed in the men's game. This was met with some resistance but in 1982 the NFA did sign a sponsor deal for women's football in the first step to the commercialisation of the game for women. In 1984 it was agreed that girls and women should have the same opportunities as boys and men in Norway and follow the same 'skills development model', often in mixed sessions. In 1985 the Executive Board of the NFA decided that there should be at least one woman in every committee of the NFA, which was seen at the time as a significant step forward. The numbers of women's teams and players registered with the NFA continued to increase and by 1988 nearly 2500 teams were registered.

The development of women's football in other European countries in the 1970s and 1980s cannot be ignored as an influential factor in the NFA accepting women into the organisation and seeking to promote the women's game. Italy in particular had been a key proponent of women's football and had hosted an 'unofficial' World Cup in 1970, a tournament organised by Federation of Independent European Female Football (FIEFF). A further World Cup was held in 1971 — this time in Mexico — and the success of these tournaments struck a chord at UEFA who passed a motion in favour of member countries taking control of women's football, a motion that was formally adopted by UEFA in 1971. UEFA established a Women's Committee in 1971 that bizarrely was all-male, but the committee was wound up in 1978 having failed to organise any international competitions. A new committee was set up in 1981 and this time it included two women members — Pat Gregory from England and Hannelore Ratzeburg from Germany. The first UEFA-organised Women's European Championships took place between 1982–84 and Pat Gregory had this to say of UEFA's eventual involvement in women's football: "UEFA woke up and realised that if they didn't do something, the whole thing [women's football] would be out of their control" (cited in Lopez, 1997: p. 59). A further positive result of UEFA's involvement with the development of women's football was that women's football was to come under the control of individual governing bodies within Europe, as had already occurred in Norway (in 1976) and later in other countries such as Italy (1986) and England (1993). This gave women's football across Europe formal recognition within national (for example, NFA) and the international governing (UEFA) bodies.

Norway entered the inaugural UEFA European Championships, held between 1982–84, and narrowly failed to make the semi-finals but in the next championships (1984–1987) as not only did Norway host the tournament but they won it. This success was evidence of the development of Norwegian women's football and marked the beginning of a glory period for women's football in Norway. In terms of administrative progress Ellen Wille became the first female to be elected member to the NFA's Executive Board in 1985 and she was also the first woman to address in the FIFA's Annual Congress in 1986. Wille suggested that FIFA should establish a Women's World Cup and that women's football should be included in the Olympic Programme, two proposals that eventually bore fruit in the next stage.

Stage Three: Popularity increases and further international success — 1988 until present

The European success of 1987 was built upon the strong membership of women's football clubs and by 1988 the number of women's teams registered to the NFA had increased to 2496. Goksøyr & Olstad (2002) argue that the popularity of women's football increased because of the success of the national team and positive media coverage. The 1987–89 and 1989–91 European Championships saw Norway lose both finals to Germany but Norway triumphed again in the 1991–93 tournament and, again, as hosts. In the first five UEFA European Championships, Norway had appeared in four finals and triumphed twice, a very impressive return. On the world stage, FIFA organised an invitational tournament in Guangzhou, China in 1988 and followed this with the first Women's World Cup in China in 1991. The United States of America won the inaugural tournament but the next tournament, staged in Sweden, was won by Norway with the team collating a 23–1 goal difference throughout the tournament. This was not only a victory for the team itself but also reward for those in Norway who had demonstrated commitment to their belief that women should play football. After all it was a Norwegian woman, Ellen Wille, who had raised the matter of a Women's World Cup at the 1986 FIFA Congress. In a visit to Norway in 1999, current FIFA President, Joseph S. Blatter, described how female pioneers like Wille had influenced the world's football agenda, and commented:

> I do remember Mexico City in 1986 very well. There was a young woman from Norway, Ellen Wille was her name. She was small, and the table for speakers was tall, when she entered it on the FIFA Congress in Mexico City. Wille criticised us because we had not written anything about women's football in FIFA's Annual Report. I was the General Secretary at that time. President João Havelange criticised me because of that. Havelange told me: 'From now, you must remember the women's football!'. That was the first time in FIFA's history that a women talked at the congress.

The successes of Norway at European and world level had greatly promoted the virtues of the 'Norwegian model' of football development which had boys and girls developing their skills in programmes that at times mixed the sexes. This model had been adopted by the NFA in 1984 and within 11 years Norway had become world and European champions. In the early 1990s the NFA sought to have women contributing to all levels of Norwegian football as they worked on developing football as a family pastime (Goksøyr & Olstad, 2002)

In 1996 the NFA permitted boys, men, girls and women to play in the same teams at all levels and programmes were launched to recruit more women as players, coaches and referees. Several recruitment projects were initiated and elite clubs for women were developed throughout the country. Mette Hammersland, the current Vice President of the NFA, initiated recruitment projects for girls and women such as *Lillejenteprosjektet* (Little girls project) and *Fotballjenter mot år 2000* (Football for girls in the year 2000) as the popularity of the game increased. Football has been the most popular sport for women in Norway since 1995 and has continued its upward journey. 3064 teams were registered in 2002 and 5932 in 2005, popularity no doubt assisted by the national team's continuing success — they lost in the final (again to Germany) of the 1995 European Championships but won the Olympic Gold in Sydney 2000 in front of 90,000 spectators. This was a phenomenal achievement and reward for investment in the development of girls and women's football in Norway. There was also administrative progress in this era. Karen Espelund, who had been a member of the NFA's Executive Board since 1988, was elected as Vice President of NFA in 1996 with responsibility for developing men's and women's elite football. Espelund was the first women ever elected to this position, is the General Secretary of the NFA today, and is also Chair of UEFA Women's Football Committee. In 2006, the NFA provided funding for elite women's clubs to employ administrative leaders responsible for managing the development programmes at their clubs.

Conclusions

There is little doubt that women's football has developed significantly in the last 30 years and Norway is one of the leading nations both in terms of international success and the 'Norway Model' of development programmes. However, like women's football in other countries, support for women's and girl's football, especially from national and international governing bodies is relatively recent. Even though there are accounts of women playing football in Norway from 1921 it was not until 1976 — 55 years later — that they were accepted by the NFA. There has been considerable progress for women's football in Norway since then as the game has rapidly increased in the popularity stakes. As well as 5932 registered women's and girls clubs in 2005, it is estimated that women make up 30% of the spectators at men's matches in Norway. However, even though much progress has been made and stage three provides a very positive picture, more could be done. Elite women's clubs usually rely on a small number of key personnel who volunteer their time to conduct the necessary roles and duties and despite the recent NFA appointments support for women's and girls football is far outweighed by that provided to boy's and men's football. Particular problems that face the women's game — globally as well as locally — concern the difficulties of attracting sponsors, spectators and media interest. The successes of the national team on the European and world stages did attract media interest, particularly from television, but television coverage was restricted. Progress was eventually made in 2005 when a deal was struck to show live matches from all the 2005 European Women's Championships matches in England whilst the NFA and the Norwegian Broadcasting Company (NRK) agreed that the football programme '4-4-2' would show 15 minute highlights from the women's Premier League. A further deal between another channel, TV2 and Canal Digital, with the NFA has been negotiated for 2006–9 and will see increased coverage of women's football both at league and national levels. This chapter has provided a history of women's football in Norway and its journey from 'show matches' to international success but there is still much more to be done to further develop the game in Norway for its girls and women of the future.

Note

1 This chapter reflects my personal exgagement with Norwegian football as a player, coach, referee and NFA committee member. I consider myself part of the history of women's football in Norway, having been one of the pioneers who started a women's team in my home village of Manndalen in northern Norway in the early 1970s, before playing at Level Two in the Norwegian league system and also in the 'Regional federation team' in Northern Norway. After a period of coaching at junior level I qualified as a referee and have been on the FIFA list of international women's referees since its inception in 1995. I have refereed matches at the 1995 World Cup in Sweden, the 2001 European Championships in Germany, and I also had the privilege of refereeing the first ever Olympic Games final between the United States and China in 1996. As well as this, I was a member of the Executive Board of the NFA from 1996 until 2002 and was also on the Board which selected candidates for the Executive Board from 2002–2004. Presently I am involved in the process which selects candidates for the NFA elections and I also sit on the NFA Regional Football

Association's Referees Committee. This varied involvement with women's football in Norway (and beyond) has provided me with many experiences including the stimulus to conduct academic research on Norwegian women's football. This chapter is the first to come from my recently completed doctorate (Skogvang, 2006) which studied the history, development and current state of men's and women's football at elite level in Norway.

References

Bromberger, C. (1995) 'Football as world-view and as ritual', *French Cultural Studies, Vol. 41*: pp. 293–311.

Council, T. G. E. (1994) *The Norwegian Act on Gender Equality.*

Fasting, K., Scraton, S., Pfister, G., & Bunuel, A. (1999) *The experience and meaning of sport and exercise in the lives of women in some European countries*. Oslo: International Olympic Committee and Norwegian university of Sport and Physical Education.

Folds, S., & Harris, P. (1979) *America's soccer heritage: A history of the game.* Manhattan Beach: CA: Soccer for Americans.

Fotballforbund, N. (1974) *Norsk Fotball i 70-årene. Mål og midler. Handlingsprogram.* Oslo: Norges fotballforbund (NFA).

——— (1974b) *Arbok 1974.* Oslo: Norges Fotballforbund.

Fretland, F. (1996) *Sogn og Fjordane Fotballkrets 75 år 1922–1997.* Sogndal: Sogn og Fjordane Fotballkrets.

Giulianotti, R. (1999) *Football: a sociology of the global game*. Oxford: Polity Press; Blackwell Publishers.

Goksøyr, M., & Olstad, F. (2002) *Fotball! Norges Fotballforbund 100 år.* Oslo: Norges Fotbalforbund.

Guttmann, A. (1991) *Women's sports: A history.* New York: Colombia University Press.

Hansen, J. R. (1994) *I "futtbollens" tjeneste. 75 år med Troms Fotballkrets.* Tromsø: Troms Fotballkrets.

Lippe, G. v. d. (1982) *Kvinner og idrett. Fra myte til realitet.* Oslo: Gyldendal Norsk Forlag.

——— (1997) *Endring og motstand mot endring av femininiteter og maskuliniteter i idrett og kroppskultur i Norge: 1890–1950 — med sideblikk på Tyskland, Sverige og Danmark. En feministisk analyse av empirisk materiale.* Oslo: Norges idrettshøgskole.

——— (2001) *Idrett som kulturelle drama. Møteplasser i idrettssosiologi og idrettshistorie.* Oslo: Cappelen Akademisk Forlag.

Lopez, S. (1997) *Women on the ball. A guide to women's football.* London: Scarlet Press.

Newsham, G. J. (1994) *In a league of their own! Dick Kerr Ladies Football Team.* London: Scarlet Press.

——— (2005) *'Focus: Dick, Kerr Ladies'*, Paper presented at Women, Football and Europe, Preston, June 14th.

Oliver, G. (1992) *The Guinness Record of World Soccer*. Enfield: Guinness Publishing.

Pettersen, P. (1985) 'Damefotball. Idrettshistorie og viktig skanse i likestillingskampen', "Drillo" Olsen, E. (ed) *Fotball–mer enn et spill.* Oslo: Cappelen Forlag A/S.

Prudhomme-Poncet, L. (2005) *'Women of the ball — A history of French women's football'.* Paper presented at the Women, Football and Europe Conference, Preston, England, June 14th 2005.

Skogvang, B. O. (1999) *The culture in Norwegian elite football — Consequences for female and male players.* Paper presented at Women's Worlds 1999, Tromsø, Norway, June 22.

——— (2000) *The Path to Women's World Cup in Football.* Paper presented at Gender and Sexuality in Sport Settings, Norges idrettshøgskole, Oslo.

——— (2006) *Toppfotball — et felt i forandring. Doktoravhandling* Oslo: Norges idrettshøgskole.

The Norwegian Confederation of Sports Laws, 2–4, 1994.

Torkildsen, R.-K. (1993) *Norsk kvinnefotball — en historisk undersøkelse om norks kvinnefotballs utvikling. Hovedfagsoppgave.* Oslo: Norges idrettshøgskole.

Williams, J. (2004) 'The fastest growing sport? Women's football in England', in F. Hong and J. A. Mangan (eds) *Soccer, women, sexual liberation. Kicking off a new era.* London, Portland, Oregon: Frank Cass.

Williamson, D. J. (1991) *Belles of the Ball.* Devon: R & D Associates.

www.FIFA.com (2006) The International Football Association's (FIFA) web site.

www.fotball.no (2006) Norges fotballforbunds internettside, the Norwegian Football Association's web-site: Norges Fotballforbund.

www.NorwayCup.no (2006) Internet page for Norway Cup: Norway Cup Football Tournament.

SECTION TWO: EQUITY

FOOTBALL IN ENGLAND AND THE GENDERED WHITE MASK

Colin King

Introduction

In 2007 the celebration of the abolition of slavery will commence, however, this chapter argues that the political and economic legacies of slavery continue to resonate in the experiences of black women in the modern game of football. It explores the echo of post-colonialism inside the exclusive male cultures of management and coaching. In particular, how white men control access to power in the game and how black women face racism and sexism. Firstly, the chapter examines how men, maleness and whiteness influence black women's experiences. Secondly, it explores, through a focus on a prominent black female manager, the ways race, gender, and national identity impact on black women's experiences. I make the argument that the institution of football is built upon the ideology of the slave trade and black people as commercial products. The discussions highlight how black women negotiate such a context through the masks of race and gender. Finally, I argue that male writers have failed to represent the experiences of black women in English football and consequently have not appreciated the manner in which maleness influences racism and sexism in, this case, coaching. In short, the central argument is how the 'gendered white mask', used by black women, reveals the fantasies of the women's game, and the powerful influences of white men.

Games of whiteness and gender inside football

Previously, I have used the metaphor 'play the white man' as a way to explore how institutionalised racialised cultures operate in football coaching and management (King, 2004). Such an analysis is influenced by the work of Franz Fanon (1967) and his critical commentary of post colonial Algeria. For me, a critical engagement with the notion: 'play the white man' enables an examination of the narratives, pressures and performances, enforced by white men on racial 'others' to comply. I suggest that these practices, which also force black women's compliance, are often neglected. As Dyer (1998) argues maleness, similar to whiteness, is made natural, absent and invisible. I argue that this is the case in football and explore how this impacts on black women's experiences of management and coaching.

When maleness is made visible, it is often polarised in white feminist thought (O'Donnell and Sharpe, 2000), as omnipotent and a distinct masculine paradigm that is oppressive. In the context of football white male writers have focused on maleness (cf Williams, 1991; Back, Crabbe and Solomos, 2002) as a way to understand class relations, in particular, the operation of masculinity in hooligan cultures. It is worth making the point that maleness becomes more complex when considered in relation to whiteness. Whiteness and maleness are evident throughout the culture of the game, from the board room to the field of play. Frakenberg (1993) suggests that rarely are the links made between how maleness operates on a subconscious level and how it shapes the experiences of black women. For me, reflexivity helps reveal the silences and complexities of black maleness.

I was born in an era when masculine heterosexual roles are strongly defined and demarcated. Race and maleness, in this context, means that black men have the power to give orders. It is assumed that black women comply. Heterosexuality is viewed as compulsory and homosexuality is pathologized as a disease. In addition, sport is understood as something black men are good at and participation is encouraged. In short, racial stereotypes help construct black boys' and men's masculine identity as athletic (Carrington, 1986), educationally 'subnormal' (Coard, 1967) and defiant (Sewell, 1997).

In relation to normative notions of the family, black families are often viewed as not conforming to the archetypical nuclear family. The nuclear family in Britain is socially, culturally and politically sanctioned. Black families that display different relations are often devalued and viewed as dysfunctional. Black mothers are often held accountable for the different patterns in family relations and are therefore understood as incompetent (Davidson, 1997). Within sports studies these stereotypes are often perpetuated. For example, Cashmore (1982) colludes with these views through his description of the single parent black family, and his argument that white teachers become replacement father figures.

The configuration of black families in Britain is further complicated by legacies of colonialism and slavery. The implications, as Wallace (1990) suggests, for black men as fathers and sons in black families, is collusion with the ideologies constructed in the slave period by white men. Roideger (1991) reveals how black women have been sexualised through the practices of slavery. As a result they are understood in sexual terms as available, easy, and worthless. In addition to these processes of sexualisation, hooks (1991) argues that as a result of black men's feelings of exclusion from white society, black women are forced to experience the anger and resentment of black men. Clearly, black women face layers of oppression, which inevitably influence their participation in sport. Davidson (1997) argues that black women constantly face complex denials of their identity. Many are denied the opportunity to self-actualise in British society and the institution of sport. Mac an Ghaill (1988) is one of few writers who reveals the complex mechanisms black women use to survive power relations in the black community and succeed in the British educational system. To date, black women's negotiation of sporting practices has not been considered in detail, this is especially the case in relation to the institution of football. I argue that not only do post colonial processes related to slavery have important implications for black women's employment in sport, but also, discourses of gender equity that have favoured the inclusion of white women in positions of power in sports organisations.

Practices in sport help produce the illusion of a level playing field. However, it is evident that social relations in football reflect white privilege, for example, white men occupy almost all positions of power with white women in administrative positions, black men as coaches and black women as cleaners. It is possible to apply Roideger's (1991) analysis of social relations of slavery to the institution of football. More specifically, how 'others' become involved in processes of competition that surround the privileged position of white men. In this competition, as Wallace (1990) discusses, black men collude to protect their own positions without speaking out for black women. So in the current debate about the barriers facing black players in the transition into management and coaching, few mention the double forms of oppression black women face. I argue that black men are myopic to the plight of black women. This might be explained by current relations between black men and white women. As the 2001 Censor data shows 70% of black men are now in relationship with white women. I suggest that this might affect their ability to understand discrimination faced by black or mixed race women and that this might be relevant to an understanding of black women's experiences of football.

It is important to analyse the experiences of black women inside the English game to reveal the impact of maleness and racism. The emergence and evolution of the women's game reflects processes of exclusion, which have denied opportunities for women. In a very rudimentary way this is reflected in the ruling, issued by a male institution, banning girls from playing with boys after the age of eleven. Research by Scraton et al. (2005) provides some evidence to suggest that black women experience inclusion/ exclusion differently to white women and findings highlight the ways clubs are set up and controlled by white men. Generally, both national and local governance of the game reflects a white hegemony. There are few black women in positions of power. That said it is possible to explore some of the experiences of a black female manager to consider the struggles faced by black women and analyse how race and gender operate together.

Managing the 'gendered white mask' in football management

I argue that the ideology and legacy of slavery has affected the experiences of black women in sport. To make the point, I provide an analogy between Rosa Parks, the American Civil Rights Leader in the 1960s and a black woman currently coaching and managing. Both women can be understood in the context of neo-colonial western society. Welsing (1991) refers to post-colonial symbols in the lives of black people and this enables a reading of how black women are treated. Rosa Parks' refusal to give up her seat on a bus can be read as a post-colonial symbol. She challenges the assumption that black people must give up their seats for white people. We can liken the bus to the institute of football, more specifically managing and coaching, and the privileging of whiteness. Rosa Parks' presence on the bus and the presence of a black woman manager in the game contests white hegemony, but both women battle, in different ways, to maintain their presence.

During an interview with a black female manager it became apparent that her life in the game represented a series of negotiating the power of white men. As I have suggested previously these negotiations often involve processes that Fanon (1967) refers to as the 'white mask'. Fanon successfully identifies the ways black men in post-colonial Algerian society adopt the white man's language and culture in order to be valued:

> The black man has two dimensions, one with his fellows, and the other with the white man. A Negro behaviour differs with a white man and with another Negro. The self division is a direct result of colonial subjugation. (1967: p. 40)

I extend Fanon's arguments to include a gender dimension to the white mask and suggest this is relevant to black women in sport. The type of racism that operates in the social relations between men does not adequately explain the conditions that black women are forced to endure in society and in sport. Therefore the 'gendered white mask', applied to football contexts, reflects the pressures black women encounter. I suggest this 'gendered white mask' is a complex psychological tool, which is used to survive gender and racial hierarchies and simultaneously runs the risk of rendering blackness and femaleness invisible. It is through this new gender dimension that we can now begin to analyse a black women's experiences of managing:

> I think somebody needs to break through and probably act as a voice or a spokesperson, it can be done and you should not be intimated by the whole set up. Cause I believe it is scary, it's scary to put yourself out there unknown in a white world, in an all white situation, it's scary because colour always becomes an issue. (Black female manager, interview 1997)

This black manager reveals the psychological fear that confronts black women when whiteness is invisible but present. For her, whiteness creates anxiety. During the interview, I could see the link between her consciousness and the performances needed to survive in a world in which she is being judged as a black person, and, judged in relation to stereotypes concerning lack of motivation:

> Because we are black and I think we think we go so far, it's hard. It's very difficult unless black people see somebody else doing it. I don't think we are [seen as] driven, we are not [seen as] driven as a race, we are [seen as] easy, we are [seen as] more kind of laid back, but fear, fear stops you going into the unknown, it's frightening. It is the fear of failure or being laughed at. (Black female manager, interview 1997)

Her comment reveals the impact whiteness has on black women and how this can lead to potential self-exclusion from the management structures of English football. It illuminates the damage to the psyche, and reminds me of what Fanon (1967) refers to as 'negrophobia'. Practices surrounding 'negrophobia' conceal the ways white men act to create inferiority in the lives of black women, as evident, so vividly, in the experiences of Rosa Parks. What materialises is a system in which white men unconsciously lead black women to internalise stereotyping. Such a system is based on assumptions about black women's limitations and incompetence. The closer black women get to see and experience the perceptions and actions of white men, the more gendered the 'white mask' becomes:

> I play the game [white mask], "oh yeah, nice to meet you", I think they think they are really clever, and if they say jump, you say how high. It's the 'old boys' network, I believe it is tokenism they are not really interested in women's football. I think it is because of Equal Opportunities Policies and all that stuff and there were so many issues around colour. I think they needed to put somebody in there sooner or later to make it look good and if that's the case and I am the guinea pig I don't mind I can get in there and change things (Black female manager, interview 1997).

For this woman, the power of white men is not visibilised but appears more in the form of Goffman's (1956) notion of secret codes. The covert nature of racial and gendered power, I argue, encourages black women to move from a 'white mask' to adopt a 'gendered white mask' that operates on both a political and emotional level.

I argue that the presence of black women, in the institution of football, represents an illusion of multi-culturalism and gender equality. Similar to Rosa Parks fifty years ago, black women have become more sophisticated in translating white men's rationale to make black women 'honorary white' and 'honorary male'. In the quote above, the black women is aware of the cosmetics of equality as is evidenced by her reference to 'tokenism'. Black women in sport, therefore, represent the fallacy of open access, especially inside the coaching structures of English Football. More research is needed on the ways white men, and black men, respond to black women in sport in order to reveal the intricate ways racism and sexism operate together at both the social and psychological level within sporting organisations:

> In terms of institutional racism nobody tells you they are discriminating against you, the culture of the organisation makes you know where your place is. As a black person you have got to know that part of British culture means that you are trying to co-exist with a group of norms that you are grappling with. The people within that world will manipulate processes to suit themselves, they appoint people in their own image. White people are still at the top, white people still have the power. (Sir Herman Ousely, Chair of the Commission for Race Equality, interview 1997)

To date, application of the concept institutional racism has not explored how black women are affected by institutional practices. We know very little of the experiences of black women inside the cultures of sports management and coaching. When we talk about racism in the aftermath of the murder of Steven Lawrence, and the Amendment to the Race Relation Act 2000, there is still an unspoken connection to how black men have been discriminated against. In the context of football, evidence of challenge to institutional racism tends to express black men's concerns, for example, the Professional Footballers Association's setting up of the Black Players Forum and focus on barriers facing black professional male players. The presence of black players at top level football has meant that some black men represent an elitist group within football culture. Such developments occlude the gender dimension of racism. It might be that in football, black women now see maleness as institutional on both sides of the colour line. In other words, the different ways both black and white men control their progress. I suggest, using the work of Goffman (1956) on performance and the preservation of self, that black women in the context of English football exist inside the codes and rules of the men's game in which they are controlled by other people's scripts. The above reference to 'tokenism' supports this claim.

For me, the presence of a black woman manager in regionally recognised football stadium for the European 2005 Championships warrants critical analysis. The stadium hosts men's fixtures during the season and the field of play, technical area and spectating areas are usually dominated by men. Again we can liken this public space to the public transport spaces facing Rosa Park. In this context and given that the football business has been the domain of white men, I observe the presence of a black woman in the technical area. She has long locks, wears an England 'Umbro' tracksuit, she is a manager; breaking national barriers black men have not. The apparent success of this black manager could be understood as a celebration of the end of post colonial racism. This black manager's presence contests the traditional signature of football management; white middle-aged male. This juxtaposition of images, white male coach, black female coach, reflects the contradictions of the women's game. The appearance of a black woman manager reveals the illusions of a new multi-culturalism. I argue it is more complicated than simple processes of liberation and emancipation. Her presence disguises the ways black women have to perform inside the masculine world of management and coaching. For a deeper understanding of these negotiations it is important to remain mindful of the histories of both football and colonisation, for example, the banning of women by the FA, in the early 1900s, from 'male pitches' and the ways slavery confined black women to specific spaces on the plantation. Previously, I have likened the racial relations evident on the plantation to the spatiality of football. I have argued that black men are now allowed access to the field of play but not the board rooms. In this case a black woman manager is visible in the space between the field of play *per se*, and the board room.

When we analyse the challenges facing black women having to integrate into exclusively [white] male spaces a new perspective of women's football emerges. It is a perspective that focuses on black women's experiences of gender *and* race. My advocacy is that a gendered white mask is adopted. Such a strategy is similar to Goffman's (1956) notion of 'front stage' and 'back stage'. I suggest that black women have to act in certain ways in the 'front stage', in this case the public spaces of management and coaching to 'achieve' within the rules of white male culture. To further illustrate this point I discuss how black women face forms of discrimination whilst being mentored to obtain a FA Level 1 coaching qualification.

Coaching race and gender assimilation in football coaching

In my role as project manager for the Martin Shaw King Trust in Lambeth, London, I have been involved with various aspects of football. Despite the illusion that football is a level playing field governed by a system of meritocracy it is evident that most administrative, coaching and management structures lack significant representation of women, in particular, black women. For example, in 2005, there were only 7 women who held the UEFA A Licence coaching badge. The dominance of men inside the coaching structure influences the design and delivery of coaching qualifications, and concomitantly invitation to coach and recruitment of coaches. Despite the recruitment of women development officers and a separate women's committee inside the Football Association, the inequalities that exist for 'other' women have not been addressed. Given this premise, the Martin Shaw King Trust sought to address the issues surrounding black women gaining coaching qualifications through a mentoring coaching scheme. The scheme was set up to provide opportunity for local black working-class women participating at grassroots level.

The FA qualification system entails a certain amount of indoctrination into practices that have historically been used to symbolise white male culture. For example, how instructions are delivered, how skills and practices are set up and how coaches are expected to appear. These practices produce a certain style of coaching, one which men recognise.

In setting up the course I was interested in how both black men and black women would respond to this white English male mode of coaching. More specifically I was determined to redress the omissions of the scheme in relation to the needs of 16 black women from inner-city Lambeth. I wanted to avoid what hooks (1991) describes as the 'terror of whiteness', in other words forcing the women to talk, walk and perform to the same norms of a white male order. This proved difficult given that the course is overviewed by a white male county structure. Referring back to some of the points I make earlier I was aware that as a black man I became part of these gendered and racialised practices, where white men and black men regulate black women's experiences of coaching. For the women involved, gender relations operate beyond male dominance in football culture and implicate their relationship with black men from their own community. For example during the course there was some evidence that local black men challenged the women's active involvement. For the women it was difficult to perform in front of watching men. The black male gaze in one instance concluded with the comment — 'what the hell are they doing here?' On another occasion five men walked on to the playing area, making comments about the shape of the women, suggesting they 'couldn't play'. One woman left the pitch because she felt harassed. When the men were challenged about their behaviour they denied the arrogance of their actions, stating 'I didn't do anything wrong'. More research is needed to further explore the conflicts and tensions between black maleness and black women's experiences of coaching. For example, what are the implications for the black community if black women surpass black men in the coaching structures of English football?

To make the experience as comfortable as possible for the black women candidates on the free Level 1 McDonald course, we seriously considered the discriminatory constraints they often face. For example, a lack of finance, the traumatic experiences of being indoctrinated by negative male images, being excluded and undermined by partners and being told 'football was not their place'. It appears that participation in football repeats the types of oppression that resonate in the private lives of black women. Many were constrained by child care, and in other ways denied self-expression and their own individuality. Black women also faced a male ideology that the women's game is dominated by a lesbian culture. Such an ideology can be used by men to test black women's status and belonging to the black community.

The course was run by two white women, in a local community centre, during weekends and at times convenient to the group. The course was free and for women only. Despite being free of male officials' presence, I argue, maleness and male traditions continued to influence the women's experiences in the ways they were asked to appear for the assessment; with socks pulled up, shirts tucked in and wearing shorts. The structure and design of the course and assessment, including log book, child protection and first aid courses, I argue, reflects codes of whiteness. For the women to succeed, their behaviour, 'front stage' (Goffman, 1956), represents assimilation into codes and practices, and this is when the gendered white mask reappears.

Concluding comments

For maleness and gender equality to operate inside the development of the women's game, white and black men have to give up gender privileges, especially in relation to the needs of black women. Making an analogy with the MacPherson Report (1999), I argue that 'institutional maleness' in football must start with individual men and reflection on their attitudes, practices and exercise of power over black women. It is evident that the codes, rituals and practices surrounding maleness, and whiteness, escape critical reflection. In this chapter I have discussed how both maleness and whiteness impact on the experiences of women manager/coaches who identify as black. I have argued that in order to be actively involved these women adopt a 'gendered white mask'. The gendered white mask represents the ways women negotiate white male power, and, used in this way, as identified by Fanon, reminds us of the racialised and gendered culture of colonisation. Previously, I have argued that power within the men's game is not dissimilar to processes of racialisation evident during slavery, plantation culture, colonisation, and post-colonialism. Like Fanon, I focus on black men's experiences however such an approach occludes the complex experiences of black women. To date, critical commentary on sport, moreover football, has not discussed in detail the ways black women experience whiteness and maleness. This chapter provides a starting place.

References

Back, L. Crabbe, T., Solomos, J. (2002) *The changing face of football. Racism, identity and multiculture in the English game*. London: Berg.

Carrington, B. (1986) 'Social mobility, ethnicity and sport', *British Journal of Sociology of Education* Vol. 7, No. 1: pp. 3–18.

Cashmore, E. (1982) *Black sportsmen*. London: Routledge and Kegan.

Coard, B. (1967) *How the West Indian child is made educationally subnormal*. London: Penguin.

Davidson, S. (1997) 'What has been the contribution of social policy to the assessment process of black children. A study of one Local Authority: Department of Government'. Brunel University. Unpublished papers.

Du Bois, W.D. (1903) *Souls of a black folk*. New York: Dover Publications.

Dyer, R. (1988) 'White', *Screen* Vol. 29, No. 4: pp. 44–56.

Fanon, F. (1967) *Black skin, white mask*. London: Pluto Press.

Frakenberg, R. (1993) *White women, race matters: The social construction of whiteness*. London: Routledge.

Goffman, E. (1956) *The presentation of self*. London: Penguin Books.
hooks, b. (1991) *Black looks*. Boston MA: South End Press.
James, C.L.R. (1963) *Beyond a boundary*. London: Serpent's Tail.
King, C. (2004) *Offside racism*. Playing the white man. London: Berg.
Mac an Ghail, M. (1988) *Young gifted and black: Student-teachers relations in the schooling of black youth*. Buckingham: Open University Press.
MacPherson, W. (1999) *The Stephen Lawrence Enquiry. The Report of an Inquiry by Sir William Macpherson of Cluny*. London.
O'Donnell, M. Sharpe, S. (2000) Uncertain masculinities. *Youth, ethnicity and class in contemporary Britain*. London: Routledge.
Rodney, W. (1980) *How Europe underdeveloped Africa*. London: Routledge.
Roediger, D. (1991) *The wage of whiteness*. London: Verso.
Scraton, S., Caudwell, J. and Holland, S. (2005) '"Bend it like Patel": Centring 'race', ethnicity and gender in feminist analysis of women's football in England', *International Review for the Sociology of Sport*. Vol. 40, No. 1: pp. 71–88.
Sewell, T. (1997) *Black masculinity and schooling: How black children survive modern schooling*. England: Treham Books.
Wallace, M. (1990) *Black macho and the myths of the superwomen*. London and New York: Verso.
Welsing, C. (1991) *The Isis papers*. Chicago: Third World Press.
Williams, J. (1991) *Lick my boot — Racism in English Soccer*. Leicester: Department of Sociology, University of Leicester.

A 'FAIR GAME'? BRITISH-ASIAN FEMALES' EXPERIENCES OF RACISM IN WOMEN'S FOOTBALL

Aarti Ratna

University of Brighton

Introduction

Racism in sport is said to be waning. It is implied that with the right political elbow grease, residual 'misunderstandings' can be eliminated for good (Gilroy, 1997). The English Football Association's (FA) policy on the issue firmly states that incidents of racism will not be tolerated. This policy is summed up by the FA's slogan: '(R)acist and anti-social behaviour has no place in football' (FA, 2005). Without de-valuing the FA's anti-racist initiatives, Burdsey (2004) suggests, in his research about British Asian[1] male football players, that the idea that racism is declining is problematic because it fails to acknowledge racism at the grass-root levels of the game. In contrast, Johal (1998) argues in his article about British-Asian female players that, "(U)nlike in the men's amateur and non-league game, in women's football there are very few incidents of racism, or racist antagonism, both on the pitch and in the organisational set-up" (p. 203). However, with no empirical evidence to support his claim, Johal's argument is merely speculative. In my current doctoral research about British-Asian females who play at elite levels of women's football, I found that many 'white' development officers, coaches and players whom I interviewed suggested that "there is no racism in their game". They claim that, like the title of the official FA's women's football magazine, women's football is a 'fair game'. Yet many of the British-Asian female players themselves felt that racism was present in their experiences. Other empirical research also indicates that women's football is not a virtuous space void of racism altogether (Hargreaves, 1994: p. 254; Scraton, Caudwell and Holland, 2005: p. 78). There is clearly a need to investigate the discrepancy between the dogma that racism does not exist in women's football and the reality of the situation.

Whilst there is a burgeoning of studies regarding race and racism in men's sports such as football, cricket and rugby (Bains and Patel, 1994; Burdsey, 2004; Carrington and McDonald, 2001b; Long, Hylton, Welch and Dart, 2000; Long, Carrington and Spracklen, 1997; McDonald and Ugra, 1998), with a few exceptions — e.g. Hargreaves (1994) and Scraton *et al.* (2005) — little research has examined the phenomenon of race and racism in women's sport. I address this particular void by examining how British-Asian females' experience of playing women's football is mediated by issues relating to 'race' and racism. In this chapter I suggest that the use of 'coping mechanisms' by the research participants indicates the presence of racism in the women's game. Such coping strategies ranged from the outright denial of racism, the admission of racism but preferring to focus on sexism, down-playing racism and vocally opposing racism. To begin with, I introduce ideas about 'race' and racism in sport and then explain the research methodology, methods adopted and my own position as the researcher.

British Asian sporting females: ideas about 'race' and racism

For some time now it has been acknowledged that 'race' does not exist in any scientific sense (Banton, 1998). Nevertheless, the concept of 'race' still has currency as many people in society continue to act as if 'race' is a fixed and objective category demarcating inherent biological and cultural differences (Solomos, 2003; Solomos and Back, 1996). Such ideas about 'race' are based on differences including those of skin colour, country of origin, religion, nationality and language. In the context of sport, the consequences of this type of thinking are illustrated by the reproduction of *common-sense* ideas (St. Louis, 2004). These ideas become deeply ingrained in people's hearts and minds to the point that they are assumed to be 'natural', and hence do not warrant remark. In the case of British-Asian females, common-sense thinking tends to regard them physically weak and incapable of playing tough competitive sports like football (Lewis, 1979: p. 5). In the place of biological arguments, it is assumed that females of British-Asian heritage are restricted from participating by religious/

cultural prohibitions as well as by over-protective parents who do not allow them to play, preferring them to cook, clean and pursue their academic studies (Dixey, 1982: p. 108; Lewis, 1979: p. 5; Lyons,1990: p. 3).

In this type of interpretation, the heterogeneity of the British-Asian community living in England is ignored (Raval, 1989: p. 237). The assumed lack of British-Asians at elite levels of sport, male and/or female, is arguably reflective of the process of 'othering' (Parmar, 1990: p. 101). That is, an explanation which reduces their sports participation to the 'backwardness' of *the* British-Asian religion/culture rather than as symptomatic of wider socio-cultural constraints and inequalities. The diversity of South Asian religious and cultural affiliations in this type of argument is also neglected. By shifting attention to biological and cultural explanations, racism in the sporting lives of female British-Asians is denied (Raval, 1989: p. 239). Carrington and McDonald (2001a: p. 59) suggest that in order to avoid such ethnocentric and stereotypical thinking we must begin to problematise the wider society in which racial discourses operate to include some groups of people by excluding others. And Susan Birrell (1989: p. 186) argued, that the analysis of 'race' needs to move away from descriptive studies about crude biological and cultural differences to an understanding of how racial relations of power are produced, re-produced and contested in and through sport.

Bulmer and Solomos (1999: p. 124) claim that when an institution conveys the message that it does not advocate racism, this may only partially guarantee the absence of racism. It may be seen that various practices and policies are used by the institution in various ways "to protect the advantages of a dominant group and/or maintain or widen the unequal position of a subordinate group" (Bulmer and Solomos, 1999: p. 351). In this way, institutionalised forms of racism are interwoven with individual racist actions, intentional or not, in and through particular settings, in complex ways (Bulmer and Solomos, 1999: p. 124). Back *et al.* (2001: p. 6) suggest that in football, overtly racist gestures and chants interplay with less obvious forms of racialised codings to demarcate 'insider' and 'outsider' groups. Hence racism can be defined as the personal and/or institutional "practices, procedures, and actions that have the effect of excluding, providing unequal access, or in some way disadvantaging racialised groups of people" (Knowles and Mercer, 1992: p. 109, emphasis added). In this way we can see how actions, procedures and practices that are invisible and thus not considered by their perpetrators to be racist, may nonetheless have an excluding and/or disadvantaging effect (Bulmer and Solomos, 1999: p. 351).

Through changing historical points of reference, racism may manifest in plural and complex forms with residual forms of racism being replaced by changing and 'new' forms of racism (Brah, 1996: p. 154; Bulmer and Solomos, 1999; and Carrington and McDonald, 2001b). In order to make sense of these changing forms of racism they must be linked to wider political, cultural, social and economic circumstances that give rise to and alter these racist formations (Solomos and Back, 1996: p. 26–7). Racism though, like nationalism, ethnicity and class, is also gendered. Rattansi (1993: p. 37) argues that racism is based upon several axes of differentiation, including gender specifically, as well as age, class, religious belonging, and other social positioning(s). Hence, racism is not a parallel dynamic of power but articulates with other forms of oppression, for example sexism and homophobia. Parmar (1988: p. 197) succinctly justifies this conceptualisation in the case of 'Black' women — the political identity which refers to both Afro-Caribbean and British Asian women — that:

> It would not be useful to dissect these different power systems and attempt to strip them away as if they formed separate layers of oppression, because the daily subjective and objective experiences which form the matrix of young Black women's lives are fashioned by their fusion.

Researching the lives of British-Asian females

In most of the academic literature about British Asian females, their stories about racism and other forms of oppression are invisible. These experiences are hidden amid the over-generalisation of 'white' women's experiences (Brah, 1996; Bhopal, 1998; Mirza, 1997). Cassidy (1995: p. 32–3) refers to the marginalisation of knowledge about ethnic minority groups of women as evident of 'white solipsism'; a racist process in itself as dominant groups of 'white' women have the power to speak as if their experience is wholly representative of all women's experiences. Black and British-Asian feminists are as a result utilising identity politics to uncover the diversities that may exist in and between women as a whole (Amos and Parmar, 2005; Brah, 1996; hooks, 1984, 1989; and Mirza, 1997).

The point of this feminist work is to acknowledge that social identities are never static but dynamic and inter-connected across time and space (Sarup, 1997: p. 47; Jacobson, 1997; Hall, 1996). Rutherford (1990: p. 19) refers to the intersecting of our various social relations and identities as the process of articulation. Butler (1999: p. xvi) suggests that sometimes social relations find their 'most powerful articulations through one another'. The sexualisation of racial gender norms, for example, cannot be viewed simply through a 'gender' lens but calls to be read through multiple lenses at once (Scraton, 2001: p. 183). Therefore, it would be useful to focus on the politics of articulation (Crenshaw, 2003: p. 176; Rutherford, 1990: p. 19–20) to help explain the diverse and fluctuating dimensions of British Asian females' experiences of racism in football. Avtar Brah's conceptualisation of 'difference' is especially useful for this analysis. She argues that the subjective experiences of British Asian girls and women should be viewed across the *multiple* positions that these females identify. That is:

> At the most general level 'difference' may be construed as a social relation constructed within systems of power underlying structures of class, racism, gender and sexuality. At this level of abstraction we are concerned with the ways in which our social position is circumscribed by the broad parameters set by the social structures of a given society ... Difference may also be conceptualized as experiential diversity. Here the focus is on the many and different manifestations of ideological and institutional practices in our everyday life. (Brah, 1991: p. 171)

Brah (1994) alludes to the construction of difference at many levels: the level of the subject (agency) and at the levels of the political, institutional and ideological (structural). Scraton *et al.* (2005: p. 76–77) use this analytical framework to understand how British-Asian (and Black) female football players' experiences of racism, for instance, are structured by wider parameters related to power and the unequal distribution of football resources/ knowledge, in conjunction with experiential levels concerning team interactions and sub-cultural values and norms.

Methodology and method

In order to understand how British Asian females' identities articulate and to give voice to their experiences of racism in football, I adopted a qualitative research approach. I specifically used semi-structured interviews to examine the 'life histories' of these football players. Tierney (2000: p. 540) suggests that 'life histories' are useful when the research participants are from minority/disadvantaged groups e.g. disabled people, women, racialised groups etc., because they are given the opportunity to 'speak' about their lives in a way that makes sense to them as members of a 'minority' group. In addition to the interviews, I trained as a football player with a predominantly British-Asian female football team. I also attended training sessions with other British-Asian girls and women that were included in this research. This participant observation enabled me to observe and analyse the subtle interactions between the players, coaches, and managers that elucidated aspects of their racialised and gendered experience.

The sample

This research is based on the views and experiences of 19 British Asian female football players. Fourteen of the British-Asian girls and women had played or were playing for teams that competed at various levels of the Women's Football Pyramid, the elite organisation of women's football in England. I also interviewed five British-Muslim girls and women that represented the UK team at the 2005 Muslim Women's World Games in Iran. Hence, the British Asian females that I interviewed played at elite levels but differed in terms of the length of their playing careers, standard of play and their own playing aspirations. Furthermore they held different religious beliefs and were of varying ages and class backgrounds. I also interviewed the coach of a predominantly British-Asian female football team and a County women's football development officer. These interviews allowed me to develop background details about the history of women's football, knowledge about particular teams, opinions regarding the participation of British-Asian females in the game, and of course, views about racism. I do not suggest that the nature of racism portrayed in this chapter is typical of the experiences of *all* British Asian girls and women that may be playing the game throughout the country. The oral testimonies of the players interviewed for this study are used to explore the subtle and nuanced operation of racism in and through the spaces of women's football.

In this chapter I have chosen not to use 'ethnic' pseudonyms to personalise the research participants. This is because the complexity and meanings associated with the naming of children of South Asian descent could cause offence if randomly applied and/or used incorrectly. Arguably, appropriating 'ethnic' pseudonyms does not reflect the changing modern times that many of the research participants included in this study have grown up with. As the research participants are living in a British context, many second/third generation parents themselves are also choosing to give their sons and daughters 'English'-sounding names. Additionally — though there is not enough space here to expand upon this point — the adoption of 'English'-sounding names may be used to negotiate access and entry into spaces of work, education, sport and other socio-cultural arenas from which British Asians have historically been excluded. With regard to this research, many of the research participants explicitly mentioned that they do not want to be 'named' solely in terms of their ethnicity, but rather as *players* of women's football. Therefore, the research participants included in this paper will be referred to as Player 1, Player 2, Player 3 and so on. In order to also protect the anonymity of these British-Asian females, pseudonyms are given to the women's football clubs for which they play or have played.

Myself as researcher

As a female postgraduate student of British Asian background interested in the sociology of sport I am empatheticwith the feelings of Marshall (1994) who, in relation to academia, expressed the following:

> I was angry that white lecturers perpetuated a racist account of social life and that white students failed to recognise this. Instead of articulating my despair I internalised it. Often I remained silent in seminars. I felt alienated by discussions that excluded my reality. The creative energy to use the pen as a weapon against such racist and sexist misinformation was frequently suppressed by the fear that I needed to conform in order to survive and ultimately to pass my degree. (p. 107)

Similar experiences and my own growing confidence within academia have led me to believe that I must join those who speak out against racism (and sexism) in sport. In this task I adopt the 'passionate objectivity' stance of Hargreaves (2002: p. 10–11) who chooses to engage with issues of inequality and discrimination in sport from her own position within the political and social context of the period and of the research, rather than to separate them.

Research findings

The denial of racism

It became apparent that the research participants who played at elite levels of women's football selected various coping mechanisms in order to construct responses to forms of inequality and discrimination evident in the game. Many of the females who have been playing football for several years, mostly for well-known teams, are reluctant to acknowledge that racism even exists in women's football. These British-Asian players re-iterate the viewpoint of many women's football development officers, coaches, and players. In addition, these players perceive their racialised differences to be unimportant in this arena. For example, a Catholic player of Indian origin who has unsuccessfully trialled for one of the top clubs in the country, now playing for a Division One team commented:

> I don't really have time to think about it (racism). Y'know when you're playing the opposition you sort of just, it doesn't, your colour doesn't really come into it, if you see what I mean? You sort of just get on with the game. I mean you notice it but you don't dwell on it, you see what I mean? (Player 3)

The basis of this argument is grounded in Player 3's belief system that if 'colour' does not matter in women's football, then there cannot be incidents of racism. It is assumed in this thinking that, as football is 'colour-blind', anyone with the right talent and determination will automatically rise to the highest levels of the game. In other words, Player 3 articulates the notion that women's football is a 'fair game'. Even though she does 'notice' racialised differences between the players, she chooses not to focus upon the significance of these differences. Another participant, of Sikh-Indian heritage, alluded to the subtle effect of being racially different to the other players. She had joined a Premiership club from her local (predominantly British-Asian) community club at the time of the interview, and felt that even though there is no obvious racism in the women's game, she did feel a sense of 'racialised' outsider-ness that she had not felt before:

> I haven't actually come across any racism in women's football but playing for 'City''football club, them (other players, coaches, and

> staff) being all white having a few black people, *I did feel a bit out of it.* (Player 1)

Sexism and not racism

From a starting point of outright denial, the participants who have played football for some length of time begin to account for their beliefs by highlighting the continued importance of sexism, over racism, in women's football. I would suggest that this is because they know about the discrimination women have had to endure in order to play football in the first place (Pettus, 1998; Polley, 1998; and Williams, 2003). Many of the participants felt that this represented their experience of playing, when women's football was not as popular in this country as it is at present. Alongside their 'white' (and a few 'black') team-mates they have regularly had to deflect stereotypes about women's rightful place being at home (Birrell and Cole, 1994; Hargreaves, 1994). In addition, as pointed out by a women's football development officer I interviewed for this project, many female squads have had little support from the chairmen of the men's teams to which their teams are adjoined. Therefore, in relation to the prevalence of gender stereotypes about body size and shape in women's football (Caudwell, 1999; Cox and Thompson, 2000; Mennesson and Clement, 2003), many of these girls believe that sexism is still a major problem. For example, Player 4, a girl of Sikh-Indian heritage who has played for mainly 'white' teams, explains:

> That's what I mean about 'race' not being a problem kind of thing, as we're still proving we're girls. I mean that there's a lot of stereotypes like female footballers have to be butch or a lesbian to play women's football (laughs), and stuff like that. So 'race' doesn't really come into it.

Without under-valuing the relevance of sexism, it would be wrong to assume that this is the only form of discrimination that occurs in the game. A common belief amongst the participants of this study is that as women *they know* what it feels like to be discriminated against, and therefore they would not dream of discriminating against any other group of women. It follows, then, that women's football is depicted as a 'fair game' that includes various social groups. Yet this assertion neglects evidence of racism and other forms of oppression, like homophobia, classism, ageism, and religious hatred, for example, in addition to the underpinning power (im)balances and divisions that privilege some groups of women over others. With further probing, the idea that racism does not exist in the women's game begins to be questioned.

De-prioritising issues related to racialised difference

The process of denying racism and focusing on sexism for the older players may be seen as a coping mechanism. When pushed to explain her opinion, one of the oldest players in this study, of Sikh-Indian heritage, who has played for many top women's football teams throughout her career, explosively remarked that even though she is aware of racism in women's football, and at times incidents are really bad, she cannot (or will not) recite any examples. She dismisses them and prefers to use other excuses as she hates to play the 'race' card:

> ... I am one of these people that I don't want to accept that 'race' is an issue because it shouldn't be that way. As soon as you start sayin' 'race' is an issue, if you don't get into the team on the weekend you're sayin' it's because 'race' is an issue. I think that there might be a point where it absolutely is and you're just not getting in the team because you're 'Asian'. But I don't think it does you any good. I think you just have to think I wasn't good enough and use every other excuse under the sun until it's just obvious that 'race' is the issue...When it actually comes to the stage that it's really becoming difficult it's much easier to give up if you've got that excuse: 'Yeah it's out of my control, I'm good enough but I'll never get there. It's because I'm 'Asian''...I think at the moment we just expect it to be there so if something doesn't go your way it's very easy to call the 'race' card. I hate, I mean there is lots of racism as well, but I just think that sometimes we need to start from the other side ... (Player 5)

Player 5 argues that it is more beneficial for her 'to start from the other side' and focus on positive rather than negative things. Negative things only de-motivate her, and other British-Asian players like her, from making it at higher levels. The players who do not make it or who use the 'race' card have, in her belief, not worked hard enough. Like the arguments utilised in previous ethnocentric research, she also perpetuates the racial meritocratic ('fair game') nature of football by choosing to blame British-Asians as individuals rather than the detrimental impacts of racism (Lovell, 1991). More realistically, though, I would suggest that Player 5 has not only made it due to her talent, self-determination and sheer hard-work, but also as a result of her ability to tolerate racism and 'get on with it' (see quote below). For someone with her playing credentials she knows quite clearly what it takes to play the game at elite level:

> I mean look, as a British-Asian player you have your own problems whether they be one of racism or something else, but you just got to get on with it for the sake of your own sanity... (Player 5)

Individual acts of racism

When incidents of racism were acknowledged by the females who had played for many years and also by some of the new younger British-Asian players, they were reduced to something minor and insignificant. For example, Players 3 and 5 see racism as if it is the act of ignorant individuals rather than reflective of women's football in general. Nevertheless, when Player 5 talks about 'joking' around with her team-mates, it can be argued that it is far from minor and insignificant. As noted by Les Back, although many people realise that racism is wrong, young whites repeatedly use racist discourse to characterise racialised groups (1996: p. 179). Player 5 may disregard the situation as trivial and reflective of the immaturity of her team-mates, but it reflects the whiteness of women's football and the racial assets that make a player a 'normal' and accepted member of the team, and non-whites the racist butts of exclusionary jokes. The incident related below highlights how 'joking around' normalises racist interactions between player 5 and other 'white' players. Interestingly in this quotation, the unusual choice of kabbaddi — a tag style of game played in the Indian sub-continent — as a training ground practice perhaps only serves to heighten player 5's feeling that she is 'made to stand out':

> I mean ... 'United' and 'Albion' were fantastic clubs and I've got loads of wonderful friends from also 'Palace' football club. But 'Palace' was really a little bit backward...things like you were made to play kabbaddi and you know that it's just all a bit cheesy...and that you're just made to stand out. It's also people saying 'oh look,

> there's your sister' when any old 'Asian' woman walks past the training ground. I just never felt that I fitted in but then I had some really good friends. I think it just depends on the dominant cliques...So you just felt a bit stood out that you were the only 'Asian' when I was there. But I'm not sure what it was, whether it was racism, I hate using the word 'racism'. But it was just some ignorant individuals.

Player 3, who had grown up in a predominantly Sikh area of England, suggested that when she was joking around with her team-mates her racialised difference was implicitly referred to, even though she herself does not strongly identify as a British-Asian but prefers to align her identity with her Catholic beliefs. These jokes were based around the South Asian cuisine of curry, even though Player 3 claims that at home they tend to eat a mix of 'English' dishes and traditional South Asian cuisines. Furthermore, British-Asians do not *all* eat 'curries' which resemble the food that is served at an Indian restaurant. People from the Indian sub-continent have a diverse range of diets according to various regional and religious traditions. Yet, 'curries' are used to 'other' and make fun of British Asians, as Player 3 related:

> I just found it funny, they always say things though like "we're coming round to your house on Sunday for a 'curry'" and I'm going "yeah if you want""... I mean they used to do that sometimes but ... I don't take anything offensively, they haven't said anything to me to make me feel overly-conscious about the colour of my skin or anything ... everything that they say you take it as a joke.

It may be argued that the deeply ingrained racist practice of joking around is not simply the act of an ignorant individual or a one-off incident, but that such jokes form a regular banter between team members. As racism is perceived to be nonexistent, complaints about such banter would probably be treated as trivial and construed as the player not being able to take a joke, or, the player having 'a chip on her shoulder' (see Fanon, 2003: p. 62). With this kind of reaction likely, British-Asian players probably choose not to complain or retaliate.

Speaking out against racism

The younger British-Asian girls I interviewed for this study, who have been playing for only a few years and who play for predominantly British-Asian squads, perceive and experience racism differently from the older group of British-Asian females. Their experience of racism is not from within their own teams but in relation to other teams. This distinction gives them the sense of confidence to collectively oppose racism whereas those females who play for predominantly white teams do not have the same 'back-up' (Interviewee 1) to take a stand against their own team-mates. At all opportunities, the girls who play in predominantly British-Asian clubs are not afraid of taking a defiant stand. For them, women's football is not such a 'fair game'. British Asian female players tell anyone who will listen about their racist tormentors. To them, verbal abuse about their South Asian heritage is something that they have learned to cope with, by either telling the referee or their coach, who will report it to the Disciplinary Committee of the local FA if the referee does not. They are especially keen to take a non-violent approach in order to avoid giving the club and perhaps British-Asian youths in general a bad name (see Alexander, 2002). This coping strategy is summed up by Player 10, a young girl of Gujerati-Indian heritage who lives in a pre-dominantly Gujerati-Indian district of England:

> A lot of the teams we play against are all-'white' and there can be a lot of racism. When we play they stare and make jokes about us ... For example, 'Hope you ate enough chapattis'. Sometimes you can hear them calling you a 'Paki' under their breath. But we don't care about name calling; we just have to beat them. Sometimes when they see we can challenge them they get angry and do fouls and bad tackles. To be fair the ref has always told them off and told 'em it's not on, but it still happens. I think it comes down to racism ... if you look at sport now, there aren't many 'Asians' in sport and all the football girls are 'white'-British, you don't see any 'Asians', you don't see many 'blacks', they're all 'white'. The newer girls play a lot of basketball and they tell us 'bout the racism in that. I don't like it. But they help us handle it so we do the same as them. But I can never get used to it. When we first joined 'Kingsley' we were told to expect the worst. Football can be really racist and the best thing is to ignore it. Not to lower yourself to their level. Report it to the ref or tell Coach. Y'know there will be racism but it makes us

> stronger in a way that we're all together and no one can knock us like that. (Player 10)

So, the British-Asian players who compete for this team choose to take the higher moral ground and fight back where it counts: by winning matches on the football pitch. Their ability to retaliate in this way is aided by the guidance of some of their British-Asian team-mates who have also been prey to racism in other women's sports. The long-term damaging effect of handling racism has repelled many of them from furthering their football careers. They choose instead to study hard and work for a non-sporting career.

Discussion: "One of the 'white' girls"?

The adoption of coping mechanisms reveals that racism does feature in women's football in subtle and nuanced ways whether the British-Asian players included in this study explicitly and/or implicitly refer to the subject or not. Changing and emerging forms of racism are not always easy to decipher, which partly contributes to some people's opinion that they are fading. Furthermore, the intersection of sexism and racism makes examples of racial discrimination even more intangible than when focusing on racism in itself. Forms of racism have become so complex that even the people who are affected by them at times find it hard to label them as such (Long and Hylton, 2002: p. 92). For this reason "the denial of racial discrimination is common because quite simply it can be denied due to its invisibility" (Solomos, 2003: p. 77). Indeed, although many of the participants of this study genuinely believed racism did not exist in the women's game, other aspects of their oral testimonies indicated the opposite.

The older British-Asian players included in this study are a case in point as they chose to ignore racist incidents, and/or to go along with the idea that racism is evident outside but not inside women's football. In Philomena Essed's study of racism in the Netherlands and the United States, she found that the 'black' females she spoke to also avoided discussing racism and comprehension of racism seemed to be absent. Essed explains this lack of knowledge by suggesting that, "(T)he women do not define themselves as 'black' or are ambivalent about defining themselves as members of a racially or ethnically dominated group" (1991: p. 77–78). This also may be why the British-Asian players in this study are keen to de-prioritise their 'race'. But no matter how much they attempt to be seen as 'just another football player', as noted by Mukherjee (1988: p. 212) about British-Asian teachers, their visible skin colour will always demarcate them as belonging to a racialised minority: "(F)or those of us who have *made it* we can never escape the reality of colour, however hard we try to pretend we are other".

At the time when the older participants began to play football they were among the few ethnic minority players, therefore to speak out against racism might perhaps have jeopardised their football careers. Nirmal Puwar (2004) argues, in reference to racialised groups of female politicians in the UK, that as they cannot change their visible skin colour difference, they instead choose to perform other social identities in a way that positions them closer to the dominant and valued identities of that arena. Puwar uses Judith Butler's concept of 'performativity' to explain this process of identity management. That is, as we do not have a gendered/racial inner self, our identities are constituted through a stylised repetition of acts that conform to (and subvert from) the social norms and values of various institutions (Butler, 1997: p. 406). Puwar (2004: p. 150) explains, for racialised minorities in the elite spaces of Parliament and Whitehall, that:

> Whilst they have to accept that skin colour is a permanent feature of their bodily appearance, they can change or slowly 'whitewash' bodily gestures, social interests, value systems and speech patterns'... Adherence to the norms and values of this hegemonic culture is almost a condition of entry.

In the case of the British-Asian players in this study, it may be suggested that they have spent many years repetitively de-prioritising their skin colour differences and British-Asian heritage in order to appear as "one of the 'white' girls". To affirm their status, their beliefs and thoughts have to match the ones of the dominant group. Therefore British-Asian players align their views to the dominant 'white' ideology that racism does not exist within women's football. As a result of under-playing their racialised differences they can fit more comfortably with their 'white' peers. Under the surface of imagining women's football as inclusive, it may be that players are afraid and lack the power as individuals to speak out against the norm.

The younger British-Asian girls who have been playing for only a few years and those females who play for predominantly British-Asian squadsare more likely to speak out in opposition to racism. Far from the dogma that British-Asian females are too meek and mild to rebel, these girls have the attitude that they can look after themselves and struggle with racism "on their own terms and in their own culturally specific ways" (Parmar, 1988: p. 200). With the rise of 'black' and 'feminist' coalitions in association with growing youth politics, many British-Asian females are defining their own ways of being young, female, and Asian living in England. They refuse to accept their stigmatised position in 'white' society. Instead, from their own marginal positions, they choose to challenge racism and expose the false racial meritocratic ideology (Carrington and McDonald, 2001a: p. 56) operating in the supposedly 'fair game' of women's football. Although it is difficult to determine the success of their voices, this type of cultural resistance helps them to feel a part of a unit instead of feeling 'out of place' in the context of women's football.

Conclusion

Feagin and Vera (1995) propose the term 'sincere fictions' to describe the ability of 'white' people, through their day-to-day practices and/or through institutional policies, to claim their anti-racism whilst simultaneously — intentionally and/or unintentionally — continuing to act in racist ways. The victims of racism, on the other hand, have very little power to overturn such discrimination. The process of 'sincere fiction' is evident in women's football as, despite the belief of many 'white' coaches and development officers that their sport is a 'fair game', the findings presented in this chapter suggest the contrary. The football achievements of the participants in this research are a testament to their tolerance thresholds in dealing with hidden and unacknowledged forms of abuse. As indicated by this chapter, all the interviewees use coping mechanisms in order to enable them to enter and stay involved in the women's game. The coping strategies ranged from outright denial of racism, emphasising sexism over racism, de-prioritising the significance of 'race' and racist jokes, to reducing racism to the acts of ignorant individuals, and finally learning to rise above racist abuse. The idea that racism does not exist may be genuinely felt by some participants of this study, but it is a position that is potentially damaging as it masks and perpetuates subtle, but 'real' forms of racism. The sad conclusion to this paper is that the British-Asian football female players interviewed for this study are forced to 'sink or swim': if they do not learn to cope with racism their participation is hindered, and if they continue to participate their enjoyment is dampened by on-going discrimination.

Note

1 The term British-Asian is adopted to refer to British citizens of South Asian descent. I do not suggest that British-Asians are a homogenous group but acknowledge the diversities and differences that exist between them.

References

Amos, V. and Parmar, P. (2005) 'Challenging imperial feminism', *Feminist Review*, 17: pp. 44–63.

Back, L. (1996) *New ethnicities and urban culture: Racisms and multiculture in young peoples lives*. London: Routledge.

Back, L., Crabbe, T. and Solomos, J. (2001) *The changing face of football: Racism, identity and multiculture in the English game*. Oxford: Berg.

Bains, J. and Patel, R. (1994) *Asians can't play football*. Solihull: Asian Social Development Agency.

Banton, M. (1998) *Racial theories*. Cambridge University Press.

Bhopal, K. (1997) *Gender, 'race' and patriarchy: A study of South Asian women*. Aldershot, Hants, England: Ashgate.

Birrell, S. (2001) 'Women of color, critical autobiography, and sport', in M.A. Messner and D. F. Sabo (eds) *Sport, men and the gender order: Critical feminist perspectives*. Champaign Illinois: Human Kinetic Books.

——— (2002) 'Feminist theories for sport', in J. Coakley and E. Dunning (eds) *Handbook of sport studies*. London; Thousand Oaks; New Delhi: Sage, pp. 61–76.

Birrell, S and C. Cole (eds) (1994) *Women, sport and culture*. Leeds: Human Kinetics.

Brah, A. (1996) *Cartographies of diaspora: Contesting identities*. London and New York: Routledge.

——— (1991) 'Questions of difference and international feminism', in J. Aaron and S. Walby (eds) *Out of the margins*. London: Sage, pp.168–76.

Burdsey, D. (2004) 'Obstacle race? "Race", racism and the recruitment of British Asian professional footballers', *Patterns of Prejudice* Vol. 38, No. 3: pp. 279–299.

Bulmer, M. and Solomos, J. (eds) (1999) *Racism*. Oxford and New York: Oxford University Press.

Butler, J. (1999) *Gender trouble: Feminism and the subversion of identity* (10th anniversary edition). New York; London: Routledge.

——— (1997) *Excitable speech: A politics of the performative*. London: Routledge.

Carrington, B. (1998) '"Football's coming home" but whose home? And do we want it?: Nation, football and the politics of exclusion'. In A. Brown (ed) *Fanatics! Power, identity, and fandom in football*. London and New York: Routledge: 101–123.

Carrington, B. and McDonald, I. (2001a) 'Whose game is it anyway? Racism in local league cricket' in B. Carrington and I. McDonald (eds) *Race, sport and British society*. London and New York: Routledge: pp. 49–69.

Carrington, B. and McDonald, I. (eds) (2001b) *Race, sport, and British society*. London and New York, Routledge.

Cassidy, B., Lord, R., and Mandell, N. (1995) 'Silences and forgotten women: Race, poverty and disability' in N. Mandell (ed) *Feminist issues*. Ontario: Prentice Hall, pp. 32–60.

Caudwell, J. (1999) 'Women's football in the United Kingdom: Theorising gender and unpacking the butch lesbian image', *Journal of Sport and Social Issues* Vol. 23: pp. 371–86.

Crenshaw, K. (2003), 'Mapping the margins: Intersectionality, identity politics and the violence against women of colour' in L.M. Alcoff and E. Mendieta (ed) *Identities: Race, class, gender and nationality*. Malden; Oxford; Victoria; Berlin: Blackwell Publishing Ltd., pp. 175–200.

Cox, B. and Thompson, S. (2000) 'Multiple bodies: Sportswomen, soccer, and sexuality', *International Review for the Sociology of Sport* Vol. 35, No. 1: pp. 5–20.

Dixey, R. (1982) 'Asian women and sport — the Bradford experience' in the British Journal of Physical Education, 13 (4), pp. 108–14.

Essed, P. (1991) Understanding everyday racisms, An interdisciplinary theory. Newbury Park; London; and New Delhi: Sage Publications.

Fanon, F. (2003) 'The fact of blackness' in L.M. Alcoff and E. Mendieta (ed) *Identities: Race, class, gender and nationality*. Malden; Oxford; Victoria; and Berlin: Blackwell Publishing Ltd., pp. 62–74.

Feagin, J.R. and Vera, H. (1995) *White racism: The basics*. New York and London: Routledge.

Fielding, N. (2001) 'Ethnography' in N. Gilbert (ed) *Researching social life* (2nd Edition). London; Thousand Oaks; New Delhi: Sage Publications, pp. 145–163.

Gilroy, P. (1997) 'Diaspora and the detours of identity' in K. Woodward (ed) *Identity and difference*. London, Thousand Oaks and New Delhi: Sage Publications, pp. 301–346.

Hall, S. (1996), 'Introduction' in S. Hall and P. du Gay (ed) *Questions of cultural identity*. London: Sage.

Hammersley, M. and Atkinson, P. (1995) *Ethnography: Principles in practice*. London: Routledge.

Hargreaves, J. (1994) *Sporting females: Critical issues in the history and sociology of women's sport*. London: Routledge.

——— (2002) *Heroines of sport: The politics of difference and identity*. London: Routledge.

hooks, b. (1989) *Talking back: Thinking feminist, thinking black*. Boston, Mass: South End Press.

——— (1984) *Feminist theory: From the margins to the centre*. Boston, Mass: South End Press.

Jacobson, J. (1997) 'Religion and ethnicity: Dual and alternative sources of identity among British-Pakistanis', *Ethnic and Racial Studies* Vol. 20, No. 2: pp. 238–256.

Johal, S. (2001) 'Playing their own game: A South Asian football experience' in B. Carrington and I. McDonald (eds) *'Race', sport and British society*. London; New York: Routledge, pp. 153–169.

——— (1998) 'Forgotten sisters' in J. Bains and S. Johal *Corner flags and corner shops: The asian football experience*. London: Victor Gollancz.

King, C. (2004) 'Race and cultural identity: Playing the race game inside football', *Leisure Studies* Vol. 23, No. 1: pp. 19–30.

Knowles, C. and Mercer, S. (1992) 'Feminism and anti-racism' in J. Donald and A. Rattansi (eds) *'Race', culture, and difference*. London; California; and New Delhi: Sage Publications Ltd., pp. 104–125.

Lewis, T. (1979) 'Ethnic influences on girls P.E.' *British Journal of Physical Education* Vol. 10: p. 5.

Long, J. and Hylton, K. (2002) 'Shades of white: An examination of whiteness in sport', *Leisure Studies* Vol. 21, No. 1: pp. 87–103.

Long, J., Carrington, B. and Spracklen, K. (1997) "Asians cannot wear turbans in the scrum": Explorations of racist discourse within professional rugby league', *Leisure Studies* Vol. 16, No. 4: pp. 249–59.

Long, J., Hylton, K., Welch, M. and Dart, J. (2000) *Part of the game? An examination of racism in grassroots football*. London: Kick It Out.

Lovell, T. (1991) 'Sport, racism, and young women' in G. Jarvie (ed) *Sport, racism and ethnicity*. London; NY; and Philadelphia: The Falmer Press.

Lyons, A. (1990) *Asian women and sport*. London: Sports Council.

Marshall, A. (1994) 'Sensuous sapphires: A study of the social construction of black female sexuality' in M. Maynard and J. Purvis (eds) *Researching women's lives from a feminist perspective*. London and New York: Taylor and Francis, pp. 106–124.

Mennesson, C. and Clement, J.-P. (2003) 'Homosociability and homosexuality: The case of soccer played by women', *International Review for the Sociology of Sport* 38(3): pp. 311–30.

McDonald, I. and Ugra, S. (1998) *Anyone for cricket? Equal opportunities and changing cricket cultures in Essex and East London*. London: University of East London.

Mirza, H.S. (1997) *Black British feminism*. London: Routledge.

Mukherjee. T. (1988) 'The journey back' in P. Cohen and H.S. Bains (eds) *Multi-racist Britain*. London: Macmillan Education, pp. 211–225.

Parmar, P. (1990) 'Black feminism: The politics of articulation' in D. Rutherford (ed) *Identity: Community, culture, difference*. London: Lawrence and Wishart, pp. 88–100.

——— (1988) 'Gender, race, and power: The challenge of youth work practice' in P. Cohen and H.S. Bains (eds) *Multi-racist Britain*. London: Macmillan Education, pp. 197–210.

Pearson, G. (1993), 'Talking a good fight: Authenticity and distance in the ethnographer's craft' in D. Hobbs and T. May (eds) *Interpreting the field: Accounts of ethnography*. Oxford: Clarendon Press, pp. vii-xx.

Pettus, E. (1998) 'Soccer: From the suburbs to the sports arenas' in L. Smith (ed), *Nike is a Goddess, the history of women in sports*. New York: Atlantic Monthly Press, pp. 245–266.

Phoenix, A. (1994) 'Practising feminist research: The intersection of gender and 'race' in the research process' in M. Maynard and J. Purvis (eds) *Researching women's lives from a feminist perspective*. London and New York: Taylor and Francis, pp. 49–71.

Polley, M.(1998) *Moving the goalpost: A history of sport and society since 1945*. London and New York: Routledge.

Puwar, N. (2004) *Space invaders: Race, gender and bodies out of place*. Oxford and New York: Berg.

Rattansi, A. (1993) 'Changing the subject? Racism, culture, and education' in J. Donald and A. Rattansi (eds) *'Race', culture, and difference*. London; California; and New Delhi: Sage Publications Ltd, 11–48.

Raval, S. (1989) 'Gender, leisure, and sport: A case study of young people of South Asian descent — a response', *Leisure Studies*, 8: pp. 237–240.

Rutherford, J. (ed) Identity: *Community, culture, difference*. London: Lawrence and Wishart.

Sarup, M. (1996) *Identity, culture and the postmodern world*. Edinburgh: Edinburgh University Press.

Scraton, S. (2001) 'Reconceptualizing race, gender and sport: The contribution of black feminism' in B. Carrington and I. McDonald (eds) *'Race', sport and British society*. London and New York: Routledge, pp. 170–187.

Scraton, S., Caudwell, J., and Holland, S. (2005) '"Bend it Like Patel': Centring 'race', ethnicity and gender in feminist analysis of women's football in England', *International Review for the Sociology of Sport* Vol. 40, No. 1: pp. 71–88.

Solomos, J. (2003) *Race and racism in Britain* (3rd Edition). Basingstoke; Hampshire; and New York: Palgrave Macmillan.

Solomos, J. and Back, L. (1996) *Racism and society*. Basingstoke: Macmillan.

Stanley, L. and Wise, S. (1990) 'Method, methodology and epistemology in the feminist research process', in L. Stanley and S. Wise (eds) *Feminist praxis, research, theory and epistemology in feminist sociology*. London: Routledge, pp. 20–60.

St. Louis, B. (2004) 'Sport and common-sense racial science', *Leisure Studies* Vol. 23, No. 1: pp. 31–46.

Sudbury, J. (1998) *Other kinds of dreams: Black women's organisations and the politics of transformation*. London and New York: Routledge.

The Football Association (FA) (2005) 'Football for all'. Http://www.thefa.com/TheFA/EthicsAndSportsEquity/RacialEquality/Postings/2005/10/KickItOut_WeekofAction.htm, 13th October 2005.

Tierney, W.G. (2000), 'Undaunted courage, life history and the postmodern challenge', in N.K. Denzin and Y.S. Lincoln (eds) *Handbook of qualitative research* (2nd Edition). Thousand Oaks; London; New Delhi: Sage Publications, Inc., pp. 537–553.

Williams, J. (2003) *A game for rough girls? A history of women's football in Britain*. London: Routledge.

HACKNEY WOMEN'S FOOTBALL CLUB: LESBIAN UNITED?

Jayne Caudwell

University of Brighton

Introduction

This chapter[1] offers an account of a women's football club based in North London, England. As advertised on the club's website Hackney Women's Football Club (HWFC) was founded in 1986 and "was the first totally women run team and the first predominantly lesbian team in London, possibly even the UK" (http://hackneywfc.intheteam.com/modules/page/page.aspx?pc=home). In women's football generally, the club is unusual because it has been, and continues to be, run by women, and because it dares to be publicly 'out'. Given these two fundamental principles it is worth documenting the club's history with particular reference to players' experiences of football and sexual/gender politics. This chapter, therefore, provides detail on the challenges faced by players at the club. In particular, it explores the shifting nature of homophobia and, the unrelated, drift from an overtly lesbian feminist agenda. Players at the club have, in the past, received direct homophobic abuse, both verbal and physical, during play and training. With the introduction of policy by the governing body and other agencies, such as local authorities, this abuse has declined. Interestingly, the most recent form of homophobia appeared on the club's web site, posted by an anonymous perpetrator. The move from a strident lesbian feminist politics is reflected in meeting agendas and minutes from meetings. Membership is no longer exclusively lesbian although all of the club's business and social events take place in lesbian bars/pubs in North London.

A brief note on methodology

Discussion and analysis presented here are informed by qualitative research that includes analysis of archival material and club documents, and semi structured interviews. The findings support current work[2], as well as informing this chapter. The semi-structured interviews occurred in two phases. Firstly, three club members, who had been at the club for over ten years, were interviewed. Next, a further three members, who have also been at the club for over ten years, were approached for interview. Prior to interview these players were given a draft of this chapter and then asked for comment. The draft chapter was used to stimulate discussion on HWFC and their experiences of playing. The research aims to capture the past and present of the club. The semi structured interviews, with long standing members, involved discussions on previous experiences at the club. Clearly, the interview findings are specific to the group of women who participated in the research. Their experiences provide a particular account, which offers valuable insights into HWFC.

HWFCUK[3]

The club was set up by a group of women who had met through a *Football for Women* class organised by the Local Authority (London Borough of Hackney). One of the women interviewed for the research joined the club in 1992. In 1997 she completed her MA dissertation in Women's Studies and Education, entitled *'We can't even shoot straight — issues of power and safety in a feminist lesbian football team'* (Huggett, 1997). As her account demonstrates, the setting up of the club emphasises a lesbian feminist political agenda:

> These lesbian women felt it was important that a safe space existed for lesbian women to play football in... The team was set up to be run in line with feminist principles of collective responsibility in decision making and also for a non-competitive squad selection policy to operate. (p. 3)

Over the course of the club's history, members have engaged with lesbian feminist principles in a variety of ways. The extent of the engagement has varied and currently the lesbian feminist agenda is not as apparent as it has been in the past. That said, the club remains publicly 'out' and the focus on providing a safe space for women, predominantly lesbians, to play football still exists as one of the main aims of the club. For example, the *Shoreditch Sport and Leisure Directory* (March, 2004) advertises HWFC as a predominantly lesbian team and provides information on training and playing venues. This public service information for the communities of East London further reinforces the club's advocacy that "all women are welcome" and that members of the club want "to enjoy our game and play as a team". At the time the club was founded, members accepted an equal opportunities policy which continues to have currency, and includes the following statements:

> 3.2 In the spirit of the club, all members will uphold the rights of all women to be free from oppressive, prejudicial and discriminatory treatment on the grounds of their gender and we challenge all sexism.
> 3.3 [...] We reject all forms of anti-lesbian and anti-gay behaviour. We challenge all forms of heterosexism and homophobia.
>
> 3.4 We uphold the rights of Black women, women of colour and women of all nationalities and cultures to be free from abuse and discrimination on the grounds of their colour, race, culture and/ or nationality. We challenge all racism.

Similar statements are included for disabled women, older women and working-class women. In the early years members were encouraged to look at "who is empowered and who is silenced in the group" (Huggett, 1997: p. 25). Agenda items for meetings illustrate that the club was discussing racism. On March 6th 1994, the anti-racism working party reported that the anti-racism policies should be implemented and that commitment to these should be matched with action. The minutes from a meeting on 11th December 1994 document the club manager's dissatisfaction with the "lack of commitment by the majority of the club" to address and challenge racism in the game. A concerted approach by the club has meant that over time members have endorsed the anti-racist policy. Most incidences documented illustrate how some players are faced with taunts or comments from opposition players and spectators. In particular, during seasons 2003/4 and 2004/5 one team and their spectators directed racist (and homophobic, which I return to later) comments towards certain players at Hackney. Abuse involved reference to skin colour and the letters of complaint sent to the league quote taunts prefixed by "black" and "yellow". During an interview a player recollects her experience of being identified through discourses of white hegemony.

> I was going up for a corner, and I was going up in the box and this girl from the team pointed at me and said 'I've got the coloured one'. I thought 'have I got a number on my shirt?' you know what I mean, why point out my colour, which made me really aware. Our manager went up to their manager after the match and said exactly what had happened, and he kind of — not dismissed it — he said 'right we understand', but I don't think he did anything about it.

Practice at the club indicates that members are active in challenging racism and upholding section 3.4 of the Club's equal opportunities statement devised in 1986. The move to address racist behaviour has probably been aided by the wider campaign to 'Kick Racism Out of Football' introduced initially in 1993 (Kick it Out, 1993). Despite the national campaign's focus on men's elite football and lack of representation of women's experience in promotional materials, it is evident that Hackney and the league take steps to reprimand racist behaviours: for example, according to letters sent in seasons 2003/4 and 2004/5, the league issued the team involved in the incident noted above a severe warning and the incident was recorded at league meetings.

The ebbs and flows of the influence of lesbian feminist politics at the club can be plotted via events, incidents and committee meeting minutes. For example, events such as Gay Pride and the Gay Games have been a large part of the club's collective identity. Participation in the Gay Games has been regular but it seems that attendance during the late 1980s and 1990s demonstrates an approach whereby members went *en-masse*. For example, for the Sydney Gay Games 2002 the club struggled to send one team and numbers were made up by players who played for other clubs. In comparison, two teams, *The Wildcats* and *The Amazons,* attended the New York Gay Games, 1994. One player commented on New York during an interview:

> JC What's your most vivid memory of the 90s?
>
> J I suppose it was the Gay Games, going to New York for the Gay Games. You know the dyke march there and Stonewall however many years it was.
>
> JC 25 years.

The links between football, sexuality and politics came together at this major event. Stonewall represents a significant incident in the history of sexual politics when lesbians, gays, drag queens, to name a few of the groups, fought back against police brutality and public discrimination, prejudice and harassment. On 27th June 1969, riots took place outside Stonewall Inn in New York's Greenwich Village. This public display of defiance reflected the beginning of the modern Gay Rights Movement. In order to attend New York Gay Games the club embarked on a huge fundraising project to ensure all players who wanted to take part could do so financially. In fact, the club continues to raise funds and monies are made available for players who might not otherwise be able to make financial commitments to big annual events. In more recent times the ethos of concessions and club funding has been protected at committee meetings and this has ensured good attendance at local events such as Clacton 11-a-side and 7-a-side tournaments. Clacton 11-a-side weekend tournament has been running for over twenty five years and HWFC have a history of attendance, and a good relationship with the long standing organisers of the event (mostly men). Usually two teams enter the 11-a-side tournament and in 2004 four teams entered the 7-a-side. Players are visibly 'out' at these events. Women often hold hands, kiss and stand or lie in each others arms. At Clacton, HWFC is understood as a lesbian club by organisers, officials, participants and spectators. In this way, the club demonstrates a display of lesbianism despite the lack of sexual politics inherent in the actual event.

Returning to events such as the Gay Games and Gay Pride, in the late 80s and 90s members of the club not only spent time raising funds, they also worked together to create the paraphernalia that may accompany attendance. For example, individual members have team artefacts such as playing kit, t-shirts, flags, banners, pendants and song books. The song books are collections of lyrics compiled by players to be sung to familiar tunes — a familiar practice within football culture. These player-devised lyrics help illuminate the lesbian feminist agenda. Here are some examples from the *Hackney Women's Songbook, Pride 1993:*

1. A woman needs a man like a fish needs a bike,
   I'm proud to be a woman and I'm proud to be a DYKE.
   So if you want to join us, you can join us if you like.
   Cos' that's what we are marching for.

2. Here I stand with a knife in hand,
Free castrations on demand.
The WOMEN'S ARMY is marching,
Oh sister don't you weep.

3. I am LESBIAN, a big butch LESBIAN,
That's why I'm marching here today.
Nobody tells me who can love me,
So you can take all your CLAUSES away.

I am a DYKE, Mum, a (hairy/happy) Dyke, Mum,
I want the world to know I'm GAY.
So please don't blank me, you should thank me.
Cos' I'm marching for all Women today.

Reference to 'clauses' signals UK legislation (Section 28, 1986) introduced by a Conservative government and right wing attempts to regulate (lesbian) sexuality. A long-standing member articulated her understanding of why HWFC was established, linking its foundation with the wider political and social context of the 1980s and 1990s.

> I think it was more focused on lesbian politics when I was first there (joined 1992). The Pride marches were political statements then.... The major aim for Hackney was to provide a safe space for lesbians to play football in. I think that's why Hackney was tight it was about protection, about lesbians against the rest of the world sort of thing. You know... being a lesbian wasn't easy then. ... We were under siege, under siege because of our sexuality. (Emma)

The mention of the 'clauses' in their songs demonstrates Hackney's engagement with the broader politics of gender and sexuality. Emma's comment makes clear how important the club was for its lesbian members. A consideration of one final song sang at Gay Pride contributes to understanding the particular challenges the club faced within the context of football and the relationship the team had, as an out lesbian team, with those officials who oversee the game.

Our politics the league don't suit
They want to give Hackney the boot
They bring the game into disrepute

> Not like mighty Hackney
> We are lesbians and we're proud
> Why should we not shout it loud
> We'll stand out in any crowd
> We love Hackney women

In 1991, an article appeared in the *Guardian* newspaper entitled *Innings and Outings.* The journalist Maggie Davis exposed HWFC as an out lesbian team in the national press. Some members seemed satisfied with being 'out' in the context of football but not in the national media. The 'outing' was supported and premeditated by some members of the club, but not all. The exposé caused discussion within the club and led to a more sensitive approach to appearing nationally as a lesbian team. Not only was it some of the players who preferred not be 'outed' in the national press, the Women's Football Association (WFA) also took issue with Hackney coming out *en masse*. In a similar incident, the WFA challenged HWFC on the grounds that the club's 'out and proud' stance effected the reputation of women's football. An interview with a past club secretary (1992–1996) provides evidence:

> ...and the WFA had this thing about us [HWFC] appearing on *Out* [Channel 4 TV programme], without their permission. The WFA charged Hackney of ... probably bringing the game into disrepute. And Hackney asked what and when we'd get a hearing and really challenged the WFA. You know, and you talk about articulate women who were up for a fight... So I've always liked that about Hackney. If you have problems [related to anti-lesbian practices] in the workplace there will be someone who can tell you where to go [for information and help] and back you up.

The former club secretary went on to talk about how the club had also dealt with the official representative of the Greater London Regional Women's Football League (GLRWFL), the league secretary. The league secretary serves as part of an organisation that governs the competitive fixtures in which HWFC participate. It was during a fixture with another team that players at Hackney experienced homophobic comments and practices.

> ...being a lesbian wasn't easy. You know, in the early 90s, the attitude you got from other teams, you know, we got kicked to pieces on a five a-side game, by a team that was good at football

> but were just kicking us. We reported the things they did to us and things they said to us but the league was powerless to deal with it effectively. The league secretary phoned me up about it. She received my letter and wanted to know what I wanted to do about it. She phoned me up [laughs] I was at school [her workplace] and we had this conversation without saying the word "lesbian" and we were trying to have this conversation about the issues without mentioning that we [Hackney] were lesbian... [laughs] very funny. We never got them to do anything about it. I think the league has felt intimidated by Hackney, more intimidated by the ideas of what they think we are.

It is worth making the point here that the ability to challenge the institutional control of the game suggests that some members are familiar with official discourses of equal opportunity. This familiarity is further evidenced in club policy and the language used to articulate the political concerns of the club.

During the season 2004/5 one of the teams, at Hackney, was the target of homophobic and anti-lesbian comments from the opposing players during an 11-a-side league fixture. The team managers and club secretary discussed the issue and it was decided that a letter be sent to the league complaining about the opposition's behaviour towards players at Hackney. The club secretary, who self-identifies as heterosexual, wrote and sent the letter. The two players who received the most direct homophobic comments also identify as heterosexual. This rather peculiar situation points up to two key aspects of the club. Firstly, the club remains predominantly lesbian although more heterosexual women now play at the club compared with previous years. The three heterosexual women in this incident were keen to make the point of addressing homophobic behaviour on the field of play. This contrasts with the early 1990s incident mentioned above when both women struggled to utter the word 'lesbian'. Clearly, there are changes in how homophobia is understood as unacceptable and changes in methods to challenge homophobia. Second, the league took the complaint very seriously and issued an official policy on anti-homophobic and anti-racist behaviour (GLRWFL committee meeting, November, 2004). All clubs competing in the GLRWFL must now sign this document before they are permitted to take part in fixtures for season 2005/6. Again this contrasts with the incident in the early 1990s.

An unusual incident of homophobia occurred at the end of the season 2004/5. The club website received severe homophobic comments that were extremely personal. The website contains information related to the club's history, philosophy, training, fixtures, tournaments, match reports and elected members. It is also used by members in a 'fun' way to post comments and photographs. The web site has developed as an integral part of the club and the intrusion was understood as a violation of HWFC and its members. At the AGM, members voted in support of reporting the homophobia to the local police. The discussion that surrounded the vote evidenced familiarity with hate crime, homophobic crime, computer crime and the confidence that the incident warranted serious attention by the authorities.

The most brutal homophobia experienced by players at Hackney occurred over 10 years ago, in 1995. Minutes from an Emergency General Meeting (EGM, 28.01.95) documents events that took place during a training session at a Local Authority leisure facility in North-East London. The club used the outdoor pitches on Wednesday evenings and shared these facilities with men. Despite the indoor facilities being given over to a 'women only' night, it was not considered financially viable to do the same with the outdoor facilities. In an all too familiar scenario, HWFC had to challenge a group of men who were playing on their pre-booked pitch. The coach of Hackney, Gill, asked the men to get off the pitch. The records, which are lengthy and written in note form, show that one of the men pushed and then punched Gill:

> ...she (Gill) fell over he started kicking her, Ali tried to intervene, Gill tried to defend herself, [the man] threw punches at Ali... eventually backed off. ..."come on Mick its only a bunch of women" ... "it's not a woman it's a lesbian", backed off shouting abuse, threatened to come back and get us, "fucking bunch of lesbians."

After this very distressing experience, the EGM was called to discuss the 'physical assault of two of our players'. In a letter sent to the leisure facility, local council, local police, and Sports Council the club requested that fences surrounding the pitch be repaired, that the area be patrolled and a member of security be present at change-over, surveillance cameras installed and better lighting in the area. Remarks made in the letter highlight the fierce challenge made by the club:

> What price do we have to put upon women's safety? Surely any commitment to equal opportunities must mean commitment to

> providing women with a safe opportunity to play football. Men do not face verbal or physical assault just for 'daring' to ask for a pitch they have pre-booked. We are in no position to intimidate men off of the pitch...

The discussions, liaisons and resolutions which resulted from the assault are detailed at length, requests are forceful and the issue of women's safety is the central concern throughout.

From talking with women who have played at the club since the late 1980s and early 1990s and reviewing the documentary evidence, it is apparent that the club associated strongly with lesbian feminism. This political agenda framed the footballing experiences of the women who were members during the first ten years or so of the club's existence. A large majority of the members identified as lesbian and very few women joined the club who identified as heterosexual. A more recent analysis of the club's politics indicates a shift away from an explicit lesbian feminist political agenda. A longstanding member (joined in 1989) explains this change in the following way:

> I don't think you need to hide your sexuality if you join a mainstream football team now... a straight team. I don't think you have to hide but I think you would have had to then, and if you would have come out it would have been very unpleasant but it's not such an issue now. (Deb)

It is evident that the club continues to focus on issues surrounding women and football: for example, all coaching, managing and administrative posts are held by women. This is rare within women's football in England. Some of the women are qualified coaches and the club has funded these qualifications and other courses. The club continues to run a system of committee/club meetings and all officer positions are elected. Most members are aware of club politics on an everyday level and this means that there is a familiarity with key aspects such as the concessions policy, which is a sliding scale of training/playing payment according to earnings status (£2 unemployed, £3 earning under £15,000 pa, and £4 over £15,000 pa). There are some high earners at the club and it was suggested another band of payment be introduced. After some discussion it was made apparent that those women on high salaries have contributed sums of money ranging from £400 to £1000 in the form of sponsorship of kit and one-off payments to club funds when the club has been in financial difficulty.

The club's constitution continues to stipulate that sexist, racist and homophobic practices will not be tolerated and members are aware of the everyday politics that underpin the club's philosophy. For example, players are discouraged from using the phrase "man on" when warning team-mates of an imminent tackle and most players will use "woman on", although there has been some slippage with newer and younger members. Despite this awareness of wider political issues, members no longer rally and demonstrate *en masse* and minutes of meetings demonstrate less engagement with politics *per se*.

Interestingly, the political shifts emerging at the club are accompanied by a more relaxed approach to women who identify as heterosexual and women who identify as bisexual. The teams and club are no longer exclusively lesbian. Towards the end of 2004, the annual fund raising event was being discussed at a committee meeting and a member of the committee asked if men would be welcome. After a very relaxed discussion it was agreed that male partners or male friends of players could attend. After the formal meeting there was a comment from a long-standing member that the discussion would not have happened in 'days gone by', indicating that the social events at the club used to be exclusively women only.

For season 2003/4, heterosexual and bisexual players were elected as club secretary, club treasurer and summer tournament fixture secretary. At one point the women responsible for getting promotional material to magazines such as *Pink Paper* and the football magazine *Fair Game* (formerly *On the Ball* then *She Kicks*), identified as heterosexual. There has been some debate, both in official committee meetings and informally, as to whether heterosexual players have the acumen to help run and promote a lesbian football club/team. The more sceptical members of the club have been challenged with some of the slogans that have currency within both club policy; "we are women positive, we say 'no' to negative". The tensions have not been entirely resolved but it seems that a shared belief in providing a safe space for women to play football overrides any aims for the club to be exclusively for lesbian players.

Promoting the team via team photographs is an interesting issue and on the occasions when team photographs are taken to capture the team's collective identity it is often stated that players can leave the frame if they prefer not be 'seen'. This is something lesbians who are concerned about being 'outed' opt for rather than heterosexual or bisexual players ashamed of being seen as lesbian. The point here is that the heterosexual and bisexual members of the club feel comfortable in a known lesbian footballing context. However, it still remains that lesbians in heavily defined lesbian sports' spaces are not always entirely safe. Despite having carved social and sporting enclaves for themselves as lesbians, they must return to their wider social relationships within family and employment where prejudice and discrimination exist against their sexual identity ... explaining the need for some lesbians not to be seen in a [lesbian] team photograph.

Concluding remarks

Very little is known about football clubs that have socio-political associations. There is work on 'out' lesbian and gay teams. For example, Elling, De Knop and Knoppers (2003) present findings from research on lesbian and gay sports organisations in the Netherlands; and Birrell and Richter (1994) provide a specific account of the experiences of women playing softball for a lesbian feminist team in USA. In terms of gay men, Van Ingen (2003) writes about a running club in Canada; Price and Parker (2003) offer discussion on a rugby club in London; and Wellard (2002) explores the practices within a tennis club in South England. Importantly, these contributions help develop our understanding of the relationships between sport cultures and sexuality.

Predominantly, the focus for the study of football considers the game as a global phenomenon. In these representations the "people's game" is often understood as male. Less is written concerning the local, everyday experiences of [male] players. That said there are important ethnographic accounts that reveal men's experiences of 'hooliganism' (Armstrong, 1998), and valuable insights that explore how the men's game is racialised (Burdsey, 2004; King, 2004). Macbeth's ethnography of a women's team in Scotland is the first to give an account of subcultural complexities. The account of HWFC, through a focus on the local, reveals how socio-political associations impact on some women players. Such an approach contests easily-made assumptions that football is wholly 'male', institutionalised and commercialised.

At the club the relationship between football and a political agenda is apparent in the ways the women train, play, and socialise. The political agenda is evidenced foremost in the club's constitution. Interestingly, this has meant that since inception HWFC has become more inclusive, for example the increasing number of non-lesbian members reflects the constitution's feminist agenda. Clearly HWFC has forged a collective political identity, however the extent to which playing has a political inflection varies and individual members embrace political beliefs differently. The initial drive to establish a relationship between football and lesbian feminism has left a legacy, which heterosexual and bisexual members continue to uphold in their roles within the club. Despite departure from traditional lesbian feminism, the club continues to be founded on a political agenda. Currently, the political inflection promotes equity and challenges forms of discrimination based on gender, sexuality, race and class.

Notes

1 A version of this chapter appears as Caudwell, J. (2006) 'Women playing football at clubs, in England, with socio-political associations', in *Soccer and Society* Vol. 7, No. 4: pp. 423–438.

2 Caudwell, J. (2006) *Sport, sexualities and queer theory.* London: Routledge; Caudwell, J. (in press) 'Queering the field? The complexities of sexuality within a lesbian-identified football team in England', *Gender, Place and Culture.*

3 HWFCUK: this script appears across club t-shirts worn by players at summer tournaments.

References

Armstrong, G. (1998) *Football hooligans: Knowing the score*. Oxford: Berg.

Birrell, S. and Richter, M. (1994) 'Is a diamond forever? Feminist transformations of sport', in S. Birrell and C. Cole (eds) *Women, sport and culture.* Leeds: Human Kinetics, pp. 221–247.

Burdsey, D. (2004) 'Obstacle race? 'Race', racism and the recruitment of British Asian professional footballers', *Patterns of Prejudice* Vol 38: pp. 279–299.

Elling, A., De Knop, P. and Knoppers, A. (2003) 'Gay/lesbian sport clubs and events: Places of homo-social bonding and cultural resistance?', *International Review for the Sociology of Sport* Vol. 38, No. 4: pp. 441–456.

Huggett, J. (1997) 'We can't even shoot straight — issues of power and safety in a feminist lesbian football team', Unpublished MA Dissertation, Institute of Education, London.

King, C. (2004) 'Race and cultural identity: Playing the race game inside football', *Leisure Studies* Vol. 23, No. 1: pp. 19–30.

Macbeth, J. (2005) The 'pals', the 'professionals' and the 'conformers': The meaning of football in the lives of women footballers in Scotland', in J. Magee, A. Bainer and A. Tomlinson (eds) *The bountiful game? Football identities and finances.* Oxford: Meyer and Meyer, pp. 79–97.

Price, M. and Parker, A. (2003) 'Sport, sexuality, and the gender order: Amateur Rugby Union, gay men, and social exclusion', *Sociology of Sport Journal* Vol. 20: pp. 108–126.

Stanley, L. and Wise, S. (1993) *Breaking out again.* London: Routledge.

Van Ingen, C. (2003) 'Geographies of gender, sexuality and race. Reframing the focus on space in sport sociology', *International Review for the Sociology of Sport,* Vol. 38: pp. 201–216.

Wellard, I. (2002) 'Men, sport, body performance and the maintenance of "exclusive masculinity"', *Leisure Studies*. Vol. 21, No. 3/4: pp. 235–247.

Wheaton, B. (2002) 'Babes on the beach, women in the surf: Researching gender, power and difference in the windsurfing culture', in J. Sugden and A. Tomlinson (eds) *Power games. A critical sociology of sport.* London: Routledge, pp. 240–266.

SECTION THREE: EXPERIENCES

CAN FOOTBALL BE A FEMALE GAME? AN EXAMINATION OF GIRLS' PERCEPTIONS OF FOOTBALL AND GENDER IDENTITY

Ruth Jeanes and Tess Kay

Institute of Youth Sport, Loughborough University

Introduction

Whannel (1992) commented that football in Britain is viewed as virtually exclusively masculine, and it is widely observed that within the sport a culture of 'extreme' masculinity exists in which toughness and aggressive behaviour are prioritised. In Britain the sport is a source of national pride and a very visible celebration of male culture. Despite the recent [2005] televising of the women's European Championship, the men's game continues to dominate the mass media and is presented as an essential component of hegemonic masculinity. As a result of this image, men have gone to great lengths to resist and exclude women's participation in the game. However, women and girls' football continues to be the fastest growing and most popular participation sport for women (FA 2001). It is unclear what influence this shift is having on the perception of football as an exclusively male sport and, at more personal levels, how participating in football may provide a mechanism for females to challenge the numerous restrictions that surround stereotypical femininity. As Smith suggests, femininity is "continually undergoing elaboration, contradiction, reworking at the local level" (1988: p. 55) and female footballers could be viewed as being a significant part of this remodelling of repressive gender norms. The rapid growth of female football suggests that a large number of girls want and are happy to play, demonstrating they are capable of challenging 'traditional' feminine values, but little is known about this process other than the blanket assumption that participation is automatically challenging these ideals.

This chapter examines the perception girls hold about football in the context of the massive expansion of the female game and explores their participation experiences. It investigates whether playing can contribute to constructing an 'alternative' female gender identity. A group of 13 girls aged 10 and 11 have contributed their knowledge of what football means to them and discussed the potential of football to challenge or reinforce oppressive gender beliefs within their own gender identities.

Deconstructing girls' experiences of football: theoretical issues

The theoretical framework for this research uses a number of approaches drawn together by a feminist underpinning to ensure that the analysis of how gender affects the girls' values and reasoning is central to the process. In some respects, theorising the research adequately is problematic, for while the research utilises an over-arching feminist framework, it also draws on areas of cultural studies and post modernism. Both of these theoretical underpinnings have however been developed more widely to examine adult social relations. In contrast, childhood reflects a period where there is a great deal more experimentation occurring within individual identities as young people seek to find out 'who they are' (Bloustien, 2003). What this chapter seeks to demonstrate is how feminist cultural studies and post modernism can offer a number of resources that will be useful for exploring childhood and gender identity.

The postmodern epistemological positioning is grounded in the assumption that social life is fluid and continually being redefined. At a generic level, this is a particularly appropriate perspective from which to attempt to understand the dynamic worlds of children, where experimentation is encouraged and expected. However, this research more specifically uses James, Jenks and Prout's (1998) assumption that children have their own social realities which are not necessarily the same as those of adults. The 'adult' theories used may not adequately capture children's realities and the fluidity of their interactions with various discourses. These additional dynamics need to be considered when applying both theoretical positions to the current research.

When examining whether the concept of football as Britain's national sport and a representation of maleness can be contested, it has been useful to draw on elements of feminist cultural studies. In particular the reworking by feminist writers of Althusser's notion of ideology (1971) and Gramsci's (1971) concept of 'hegemony' to demonstrate how naturalised assumptions and common sense beliefs have been responsible for teaching males that sport is a significant part of manliness and the subsequent exclusion and distancing of women from this domain (Birrell and Theberge, 1994; Cole, 1994; Connell, 1995; Hall, 1996). These contributions have drawn on the traditions of cultural studies, which is founded on the assumption that cultural practices, such as sport, are areas where values, meaning and ideologies are reproduced (Cahn, 1994; Donnelly, 1988). Feminist cultural studies analyses of sport have demonstrated the power of male hegemony in the sporting arena, but also the possibilities for women to contest this space in ways that enhance their own enjoyment of leisure and possibly alter sporting structures in their favour (Wearing, 1998). A cultural studies framework can be applied to football to demonstrate that as a sport it does not simply mirror male hegemony, but actively develops and maintains dominant societal forces that create numerous sites of oppression and restriction and keep women on the margins of the game. However, Gramsci theorises that no hegemony is total or without question, and feminists have drawn on this to explain how sport can reinforce repressive gender ideologies while simultaneously providing a site of freedom from and an opportunity to challenge them (Hargreaves 1990). As we are seeing with the rapid increases in female participation, football could act as a site where this challenge occurs.

Cultural theorising maintains that resistance and transformation must occur at a structural and ideological level, but transformation also has to be achieved at a level of 'material practice' (Birrell and Therberge, 1994: p. 363). Current female participation in football can be viewed as the process of transformation at the level of 'material practice'. Feminist cultural studies recognises the potential impact such transformations could have on challenging broader cultural power relations once dominant and naturalised notions of gender relations have been broken down, but also the difficulty of doing so. There is always the potential that the dominant ideology will resist attempts at transformation and continue to maintain superiority through the cultural hegemony women are trying to break away from (Birrell and Theberge, 1994: p. 372). This theory has been used in this chapter to examine why football remains such a strong signifier of maleness, and for scrutinising the difficulties of challenging this belief due to the structural and ideological systems that surround it.

When examining, at the micro level, the impact football participation can have on girls' gender identities it has been useful to draw on elements of feminist postmodernism, particularly theorisations explaining identity construction. Post modernism focuses on deconstructing the concept of the 'subject' and moving away from a fixed and static notion of identity. Rather than a humanist perspective, which conceptualises identity as a stable and relatively fixed entity, postmodernist thinking views identity as being achieved through interactions with multiple discourses (Davies, 1993). It has provided feminist theory with a range of critical tools including discourse, deconstruction and difference (Weedon, 1987) all of which have been relevant for the current research. This research particularly draws on Bulter's (1990) understanding of identity as performative and individuals as lacking an essence or inner core of who they are — possessing, instead, multiple identities. Butler draws on the work of Foucault and Derrida amongst others to develop an understanding of identity as multiple, free floating and constructed through "regulatory practices of gender formation" (p. 17) or discourses. Gender identity is viewed as an effect of these practices and it is through enacting gender discourses that individuals construct their sense of subjectivity. Butler views gender and identity as being inseparable as "persons only become intelligible through becoming gendered", a concept which is adopted in the current research. Viewing gender identity construction in this way enables a breakdown of restrictive binaries such as male/female, masculine/feminine (Derrida, 1982). It also allows the possibility of individual agency when constructing a gender identity and the opportunity to resist as well as engage in certain discourses as suggested by Foucault (1972) and reworked from a feminist positioning by Butler. This has provided a theory of identity construction as a dynamic and multi-faceted process (Lowe, 1998). This theoretical positioning has been used to examine the gender identity construction of the girls in the current research to explore how they have developed extremely complex, very individual and multiple gender identities.

The use of a multiple and layered theoretical perspective in this study reflects the inadequacy of single theories in explaining the complexities of social life. Drawing on both cultural studies and postmodernism within an over-arching feminist perspective allows this dilemma to be confronted. First and foremost, it is important for understanding the dynamics behind gender identity construction that a feminist perspective is used to make the experiences of the girls central to the research and to ensure the research retains a political as well as a philosophical standpoint. The research aims to explore and highlight how the girls can be restricted by gender norms and values, as well as illustrate how they form their identity through these. Hegemony theory is an effective tool for understanding the status of football as a male sport and the potential influence playing can have on disrupting gender systems. However, simply using one 'truth' narrative is too simplistic and does not capture the complexity of the girls' lived experiences, the multiple roles they perform and the numerous discourses they integrate with or reject to achieve their identities. This is where postmodernist approaches to identity construction have value, in highlighting the fluidity of these processes.

Even in combination, there are limits to the potential of these theories to adequately explain children's realities. Drawing on a multiple theoretical approach does however enable examination of the the girls' interactions with social life as multi faceted, complex, and fragmented but existing within numerous hegemonic power frameworks.

Girls, football and gender identity

Research examining football, girls and gender identity demonstrates the real difficulties girls and women have had to face to access this male domain. Renold (1997), Skelton (2000), and Swain (2000) have all theorised how playing football, both formally and informally in the primary school setting contributes to the development of boys' masculine identities. Football is shown in these studies to be an essential part of a boy's development, in that it plays a significant role in defining what it is to be a real man or a boy. It is also shown to be a space that girls have not been allowed to enter. Girls, instead, define their femininity by not playing football. Swain's (2000) case study analysis in an English primary school indicated that gender ideology continues to restrict girls' participation in schools, ensuring girls have unfavourable football experiences both in lessons and informal situations. Femininity in this situation continues to be constructed as subordinated, stigmatised and marginalized— something the girls recognise but are unable to change. The research offers compelling evidence of the power of football to retain its masculine status and the ability of boys and men to restrict girls' access to it.

Numerous women and girls are nonetheless breaking into this arena and participation for them does not automatically equate to a negative experience but instead can provide a great deal of pleasure and enjoyment. The female footballers interviewed in Scraton, Fasting, Pfister and Bunuel (1999) all described their enthusiasm and willingness to play from an early age and created reasons for their involvement in the sport whilst actively reconstructing female-appropriate behaviour. This was often achieved by adopting many types of femininities to enable them to play a sport they enjoyed, but not alienate themselves from feminine practices. Scraton *et al.* (1999) argued, though, that this may not be a major challenge to the gender order. Instead, it can be simply interpreted as women crossing gender boundaries to access a sport that is associated with masculine traits.

Methodology

The research was conducted using methodological principles from feminist and childhood studies. The use of a feminist approach indicates a commitment to ensuring that female voices are heard. Adopting an approach reflecting theories developed in childhood studies has ensured a commitment to using methods which enable young people to communicate and their voices to be heard (James, Jenks and Prout 1998). This approach complements the overarching feminist theoretical framework. Girls, when examined through both a feminist and childhood sociological lens, are subordinated by both male/female and adult/child binaries. They lack power both as females and as children. The research looks to ensure the girls' voices are heard where previously they have been silenced and marginalised within the research process by both dominant gender and adult discourses.

An ethnographic approach was used, working in a single school. It was agreed with the school that we would gain access through running an after—school girls football club. The girls who attended the club were invited to take part in the research but it was not compulsory for them to do so. In total 13 girls attended: three Asian girls, one black African-Caribbean girl, and nine girls were "white". The case study was conducted in a fee-paying primary school so the majority of girls were from a fairly wealthy upper -middle-class background.

Working with the girls as coach as well as researcher allowed us to develop trust and rapport with the girls and approximate the interested 'adult friend' role advocated by Fine and Sandstrom (1988). The girls did see us as a authority figures at timesthey were far more relaxed and informal around us than with their teachers or other visitors to the school.

Data was initially gathered during the football coaching session but once we got to know the girls they agreed to meet at lunchtimes in small friendship groups. There was a rough outline for each meeting, but each was very responsive to what the girls wanted in terms of how the session was structured and what methods were used. Keeping the research child-centred and allowing the girls to feel in control at all times in the research process was therefore of paramount importance. Primarily, interviews and focus groups were used with pairs or 4 or 5 girls. In conjunction with this a number of participatory techniques were introduced, using photographs, newspapers, images and stories to help the girls with communication and to make the research process more interesting. Thomas and O' Kane (2000) maintain that drawing pictures and writing stories is often more appealing to children because they are concrete and tactile ways to express themselves rather than being verbal and abstract. Here, the participatory methods acted as prompts to improve and focus our conversations and to help the girls to describe the complex issues they were discussing.

'There is never anything about women': Girls' understanding of football

Prior to the research the girls had had very little opportunity to participate in formal football coaching. The research notes and session logs suggested that the girls never integrated football as an important part of their lives. It remained very much on the periphery of their daily routines.

The girls were initially encouraged to talk about their perceptions of football. They all considered it was England's national sport and a male game. This topic was discussed using the sports pages of a series of national newspapers as prompts on the premise that newspaper images convey cultural meanings (e.g. Humberstone, 2002). Ursula [this and all following attributions are pseudonyms] quickly commented that these pages were dominated by male sport, predominantly football, and the other girls agreed..

RJ: "So what do you notice about these newspapers?"
Ellie: "Football."
Ursula: "There is never anything about women, that is exactly what I said, women have all the pain."
Sarah: "More football. Everything in this one is like football and for boys."

The girls understood that sport was dominated by males and that football in particular took precedence in sports coverage. They also demonstrated a sophisticated understanding as to why they felt men's football dominated media attention and the potential impact this had on the profile of the women's game. They used their perceptions of the national game being exclusively male and the determination of men within football's structure to retain control to explain why women's football was excluded:

Alison: "Men don't want to show women's football because they don't want people to know that girls are good at football. They want to keep it just as a man's sport."

Helen: "Yes it is the pigs at the BBC because they are mostly men anyhow."

The girls were aware of the way men dominated and controlled the game. They realised that the women's game was often discredited by men as a 'lesser version' but perceived this was due to men being desperate to retain control of 'their' sport.

The girls' conversations illustrated that whilst participation is developing in the sport, there is a limit to how much this can alter the global perception of football and what it signifies. They still feel football is a male sport and the media continue to display it as such, keeping women on the margins of the game. Feminist critiques of the mass media maintain that it does not simply reflect reality but actively assists in producing what we view as a 'true' reality (Pollock, 1977). Whilst the media continue to ignore the female game it is unlikely that the girls' perceptions of the sport can alter. The media simply continue to generate a reality where football is constructed as male.

The girls' discussions indicate that much of men's hegemonic control over football is generated by discourses played out in the media. Helen was very disdainful of this control, referring to those who controlled televising sport as 'pigs'. The girls felt that technically there were no differences between men's and women's football, but the women's game was dismissed as inferior and kept hidden from public view. The girls also recognised the impact the lack of media attention had in ensuring that women and the public generally were disinterested in the sport because it had no profile or importance in the public eye. There was however, some division over whether female football could ever gain the popularity and status of the male game. Susan firmly stated her belief:

> "I think by 2031 the girls FA cup will be on the tele and all the women will watch it and all the men will be doing the ironing.".

Kathy was less positive:

> "Because they know if they did [televise more women's football] people wouldn't like it and then it wouldn't be a man's game anymore. By not showing much women's football that won't happen. People will just think it is only for men and that women don't even play even though lots of them do."

They understood how power was constructed within the sport and felt men intended to retain this to the detriment of the women's game: however many women were participating, they still felt it was a man's sport. Men own and control this cultural production and, as Helen indicates, the distribution mechanisms — the mass media — for the product. The girls felt women were relatively powerless to alter these perceptions whilst men had control of both football and the popular media.

Encouragingly — and possibly because the girls have grown up during the expansion of female participation— they are very aware that women's football is silenced. It is not that women don't play: they are aware that they do, but are kept outside of mainstream media attention. The girls' recognising the female game exists is a positive step towards transformation. Postmodernist and cultural studies theories stress the importance of agency and individual choice in deciding which discourses and hegemonic beliefs to take up (McNay, 1992; Barker, 2000). The girls did exercise some agency by discussing how unhappy they were about dominant discourses surrounding football: they did not simply accept them, and did feel they were unjust. However, despite this, they could not see football's national image changing significantly to benefit women. They felt men have too much invested within the sport to risk this happening and football would therefore remain a man's game.

'They don't like girls being able to do it:' Attitudes to girls' participation in the school environment

After the girls had identified the low profile of the female game at national level, they were encouraged to discuss how they felt this might affect the attitudes of their peers towards girls playing and their own participation experiences within the macro level of their school. Their conversations suggested that boys at their school considered football to be exclusively theirs. The girls were very aware and able to articulate their understanding of the importance of football to boys and their need to retain it as a male sport due to its strong links to masculinity.

RJ: "Why do you think football is so important to boys?"

Susan: "It is just that they want to prove themselves, it is a showy off thing for boys."

Alison: "Boys think it is their sport don't they, they think girls shouldn't be playing. They don't like girls being able to do it because they might be better than them and they like football because it helps their masculinity."

Alison's comments indicates that the perception, constructed by the media, that girls should not be playing football is transmitted to a local level and impacts negatively on the girls' participation. The boys within the school also viewed football as 'their' sport. They accepted the global ideology that football is not a sport for girls and actively enforced this belief within their school, demonstrating the impact global assumptions can have within local structures. The girls understood that football was a sport that allowed boys to assert their maleness and reinforce wider masculine hegemony. The girls also understood the consequences for boys of not conforming to the gender norms:

Ursula: "If you are like a boy and you don't play football then they all pick on you and bully you. If you are a girl then basically sometimes it is the other way round although girls can do it a lot more than boys".

Our discussions highlighted how much antagonism and negativity the girls faced from boys who attempted to discredit them as footballers. Inevitably the boys had opinions on the girls entering their environment and playing football, and generally these were very unsupportive. They ridiculed and undermined the girls' sessions and excluded Helen and Sally when they attempted to play with the boys. They continually suggested the girls' skills were inferior and used this as a means to make fun of them. The girls felt the boys considered their football participation was a joke and unworthy of serious attention. In doing this they devalued the girls' sessions amongst the pupils in the school. The girls were continually fighting to prove they were as good as the boys but they also recognised it would be difficult to demonstrate this due to the superior skill levels the boys had been able to develop from playing over a long period of time:

Sarah: "The boys are only better because they start playing from year 3 onwards and they just get better and better we

> haven't been playing very long, but if we had been playing as long as them then we would be as good as them."

Sally and Helen had participated in the boys' formal football sessions for a period of time and the antagonism towards girls playing was even stronger within the space the boys perceived as 'theirs'. The boys had not been able to prevent the girls entering this environment but Helen and Sally's narrative suggested they did everything possible to ensure the girls did not enjoy being in this space:

RJ:	"And did you stop going?"
Helen:	"Yes I did in the end, because they were not letting me play and I did try to play with them but they wouldn't pass me the ball. They would just pass it to the other boys."
RJ:	"Why do you think they are like that?"
Helen:	"Because they think it is their game. It is not a girls' game."
Sonia:	"They think they are better. They are always saying if you tackle someone 'you got tackled by a girl'."

Both Helen and Sally eventually stopped playing in the boys' sessions because of the constant abuse and lack of genuine opportunity. Both of them were very able players but it was easy for the boys to exclude them by not passing to them and keeping them out of the game. Even when they played well and demonstrated similar skill levels to the boys, this was used by the latter to tease the other boys rather than recognising the girls' performances. They would infer that a boy must be a weak player to be tackled by a girl. There was no acknowledgement that Helen and Sally might be accomplished players and that was why they were successful at taking the ball from the boys.

The boys' attitudes towards the girls participating were extremely negative. It was encouraging that the girls did not accept the boys' beliefs and stereotypical assumptions that boys were naturally stronger and better at football than them. They did not agree or consent to hegemonic practices but lacked any status to contest them. It is evident how powerful these discourses continue to be and how embedded they are within society. The girls also understood that there were other structural factors which limited their participation and also fuelled the boys' beliefs that they were better. However, their understanding does little to challenge or change the boys' attitudes that girls were simply inferior. The boys were extremely adept at defending their space and keeping the girls outside of this. The only way Helen and Sally could really 'play' football was to access it through the girls-only sessions. Once the two girls were removed from the masculine domain of the boys' football sessions it was even easier for the boys to disregard their abilities and the girls to be completely silenced. The football they played in our coaching was girl's football and therefore not 'real' football and therefore of little threat to the boys' masculinity. It happened outside the main school day and represented no challenge to the boys' prowess and skills within the sport.

'I enjoy it and because it is a sport that I can do': Girls' reasons for playing football

It is difficult to believe that the girls would be interested in playing football given the messages delivered to them at a global and personal level that they should not be playing. However, these were ignored and the girls gained a great deal of pleasure from participation. When asked why they enjoyed playing, the common theme for all the girls was that they found football 'fun'.

> Beth: "It is fun and like in tennis it has taken me a long time to work up to my standard but football is much more natural and I can go out and play football."

The girls saw football as different to curriculum activities they took part in and this contributed to their enjoyment. As well as being a different sport, the girls also enjoyed the football coaching because it was not dominated by what they defined as 'sporty girls'— i.e. female pupils with high skill levels in all curriculum sports. Girls within the school who excelled at traditional sports also obtained a great deal of status and power over the girls who were unable to buy into these discourses because of their lower level of physical competence. The research girls again found themselves in a position of subordination in relation to the sporty group of girls. These power dynamics were however removed in the football setting as it was a new sport in which no one was particularly skilful and in which very few of the labelled 'sporty girls' took part. This seemed to be of particular importance to the girls' enjoyment

> Karen: "Well I think it is fun and I enjoy it and because it is a sport that I can do and because apart from rounders I don't do any other sports but I actually do a sport now."

Karen: "And that Alison and Robin don't go makes it much better."

Alison: "That is part of it, that they are not showing off. They are Miss Nevill's favourites. They are good at rounders and at netball and hockey and all the sports besides football they are there."

The girls' discussion illustrated the enjoyment they gained from participating in a different sport which did not require them to be very skilful. This was particularly important to the girls because they felt they were often ridiculed by the sporty girls for not being competent or not allowed to participate because of their lack of skill. Ironically, when considering the global hegemony that surrounds football, and how the girls were excluded from the male setting, football has become in this context an arena for experiencing a sense of freedom. It is reshaped and re-identified in these sessions as something that is accessible and obtainable for them. Football was their chance to 'have a go' and play sport in a non-pressurised environment.

The girls had very personal reasons for wanting to participate in football and very personal views about what they found appealing about the sport. It was evident from their conversations that they did not necessarily see the football they participated in as being the same as football as a national sport or even the football played by the boys at school. It was seen as an alternative activity to them and the benefits they derived from it could probably have been gained from participating in any non-mainstream or feminine-appropriate sport. In a wider context, discourses constructing football as exclusively male remain dominant. Their participation does not alter this but helps them challenge more personal discourses which have constructed them as 'non sporty' girls. Football provided an environment where they could discredit this understanding of themselves and reshape their own identity accordingly.

'I am a girlie girl but I do like playing football': Football and female gender identity

As a result of football moving into a redefined context for them, participating had minimal influence on challenging and reshaping their restrictive feminine identities. The girls viewed their identities as consisting of two main components: firstly their visual image which included their physical appearance and body shape and, secondly, their behaviour. Within both of these constructs the girls felt it was possible to enact a myriad of ways of being between the polar opposites of 'tomboy' and 'girlie girl' and these could alter depending on context. They felt however, that girls tended to ground themselves closer to one particular identity and then experiment with other ways of being away from this. The girls talked about being mostly 'girlie girl' or 'tomboy' but considered it was currently possible to experiment with a range of behaviours, even if these did not reflect the core identity they wished to construct.

However, there was little evidence of a similar shifting, fragmented and multiple visual identity construction. Although there are multiple ways of developing individual appearances the girls did not experiment with any of these. This therefore, suggests that postmodern theorising is inadequate as a tool to explain the ways they develop this aspect of their identity. Their visual identity construction was much less flexible than their behaviour identity and the girls felt it was vital to reflect feminine expectations in their appearance even if their behaviour identity rejected feminine ideals. Stereotypical visual discourses are extremely limiting and insist girls have to be striving to achieve a particular ideal body shape [slender and toned, not overly muscular or fat] and had to look a certain way [long hair, clear skin and natural]. These images of females were actively consumed and maintained by the girls. Girls are playing football but no alteration in the discourses surrounding image and the female body are occurring, revealing how powerful and active these discourses are. In order to access alternative spaces the girls feel these body image ideals have to be adhered to in order that their 'post modern' and shifting take-up of behaviour discourses can be viewed as acceptable.

Football fitted into the girls' gender identities in different ways. For the girls who viewed themselves as predominantly tomboys, playing football sat easily with the identity they wanted to construct.

> Helen: "I am less girlie and other girls are more girlie and they don't like doing rough things or getting dirty which I like doing which is why football fits in well with me"

Playing football reflected the behaviour ideal associated with this particular way of 'doing girl'. For the girls who sat closer to the 'girlie girls' persona this process was more complex. They were aware that playing football was in opposition to their chosen gender identity construction, but it formed one of their multiple alternative behaviour identities which were often in opposition to their core identity and helped affirm to them that they were not 'complete' girlie girls.

Heather: "I am a girlie girl but I do like playing football and I play it because it is fun. I don't play it to be different or because I am a tomboy but I just enjoy it. But I am definitely a girlie girl. Football is just something that I do, it doesn't stop me from being a girlie girl"

The contradiction was not an issue because the girls felt that their behaviour identities were fragmented and this was something positive, to be actively sought. For Heather there was no conflict. Although she recognised that tomboys might find football appealing and it was perceived as a male sport this did not affect her decision to play. Despite identifying as a girlie girl she enjoyed football and wanted to play so ignored what cultural connotations were associated with it. To her, being a girlie girl should not prevent her playing football, although participating did not assist her with constructing the main aspect of her identity in the way it did for the tomboys. Instead it sat alongside but in contrast to her 'core' identity.

Football was not an important part of who the girls were, but playing for some was something that helped them reaffirm the non-feminine identities that they were already developing in other aspects of their lives. For other girls it helped them to be more than a rigid girlie girl, and added a further dimension to their identities which was generally viewed as positive. The girls were aware that playing football did not sit within a conventional girlie girl identity and that by playing they were stepping outside and distancing themselves to some extent from this identity, but this process was not problematic or something they wanted to avoid:

RJ: "So why is football not as important to girls then?"
Ursula: "Three words: High heels, boyfriends and make up. That is what society expects girls to be into. I'm not, I'm into football."
Heather: "I'm into high heels and make up."
Ellie: "Yes like I am into that but I still love football and playing on the Xbox."

The girls did not see the behaviour aspect of their gender identity as a singular concept but more something they could play around with. Football was part of this experimentation at times. For the tomboys, football helped enforce their main identity but for the girlie girls it provided a contrast, a change from their 'regular' identity. For all the girls, playing football did not automatically cause problems because experimentation with their behaviour was an acceptable part of their pre-adolescent identities.

Playing football alone could not be viewed as constituting a challenge to restrictive feminine stereotypes, but the girls may not necessarily attach the same meaning to their involvement in the game as it has at a national level. Playing football was redefined by the girls and moved away from being the football played as our male national sport, and instead became an activity that the girls can access because is fun and free from the established sporty girls. They did feel that their participation might be challenging the belief that girls could not play football and this held some appeal, but in reality there was actually little opportunity to have this acknowledged even within the school environment. To engage in football the girls had to be marginalised and moved out of the arena of 'real football' as defined by males. They were, to a certain extent, also removed from the 'real' sports arena because none of the sporty girls participated either. It was therefore very easy to discredit and ridicule the sessions. Whilst this created a very positive space for them, it did little to challenge the global assumptions surrounding football and instead became simply an activity in which they took part. Wearing (1998) uses post structural theory to describe how women use leisure for rewriting the script of what it is to be female beyond definitions provided by powerful males and dominant gender 'truth' discourses. To an extent this has occurred here: the girls have reshaped and redefined their own football space, but this actually neutralised football so that their version caused little conflict within their identities and ceased to be an active site where contestation of stereotypical gender identities could occur. That is not to say that football was not used at times to construct an alternative identity, but this was viewed as little more than an experimentation of the behaviour aspect of their identity.

Discussion

Scraton *et al.* (1999) argued that for women to enter the powerfully male defined and controlled world of football they have had to challenge dominant notions of 'appropriate' female sport. In this study a range of theoretical perspectives were adopted to deconstruct the extent to which young girls undertook this 'challenge'. The overall findings of the study suggested that while the football which the girls played provided valued opportunities for them to participate in an activity they otherwise could not access and allowed them to nurture important elements of their gender identities, it did not provide a site for resistance and challenge of gender norms. This discussion focuses on the two central processes that underpinned this: the process through which girls assimilated football within their gender identities, and the process through which the local context of their participation failed to challenge the global hegemonic masculinity of football.

The relationship between playing football and the construction of gender identity was a central theme in the study. The girls in the study gained considerable enjoyment from playing football, suggesting that participation might provide a site where constructing an alternative identity was possible. It became evident however that this occurred within the aspects of their identity that the girls felt are relatively flexible. On the one hand, by participating in football the girls challenged Cockburn and Clarke's (2002) assertion that constructing an appropriate gender identity is more than just appearance and girls need to behave in a certain way to be socially acceptable. The girls in the research felt it was acceptable and sometimes desirable to behave in a non typical way but it was not necessarily just through football participation that this occurred.

The fluidity and, at times, apparent contradictions in girls' performance of identity are captured by Butler's theorising surrounding the performance of multiple identities. The girls were unable to define themselves in terms of a single one type of identity: they instead discussed how they drew on a variety of discourses to create an identity that shifted between a number of gender norms. At the same time, these identities were not wholly fluid or without boundaries. Salih (2002), when examining the work of Butler, discusses how gender choices are constrained by a lack of choice. This has been evident in the current research. Although not anchored in a singular relatively fixed identity, the girls were clearly contained in their development of a gendered identity by existing discourses. If, as Butler suggests, there is not a "doer behind the deed, but that the doer is variably constructed in and through the deed" (1990: p. 142), then the girls will invariably be limited in their identity construction by the multiple but ultimately limited discourses available to them: the girls can construct their identity only within a range of established norms. There is the freedom to take up or reject traditional feminine or masculine discourses, but little scope for moving beyond this and reshaping gender norms. The girls demonstrated that they are able to move away from traditional feminine expectations and contest these using alternative discourses, but this only occurs within the limited range of options available to them. As Butler's work discusses, gender is a set of acts which occurs within a highly rigid framework and the girls have shown that this is a useful way to understand their own gender identity construction

The girls however, did talk about having a 'core' identity, something that they perceived defined who they were and was central to their identity construction. Howevermuch various aspects of their identity fluctuated, the girls viewed this core as the thing which stabilised them, a constant in an otherwise shifting understanding of themselves. They talked about defining themselves as 'mostly girlie girl' or more 'tomboy' and this they considered defined who they were. This moves away from Butler's assumption that such an 'essence' does not exist and all aspects of identity are socially constructed. It does however mirror Hall's (1992) concept of individuals as 'sociological subjects' (p. 275) which sees individual identities as shaped by culture and the subject as being socially formed, but also considers that individuals have a core self and are able to co-ordinate themselves into some sort of unity. Foucault has also struggled to theorise these contradictions in identity construction. McNay (1992) suggests that Foucault (1984) in his later theorisations viewed individuals as breaking down established subject positions through multiple identities, but this did not constitute an "abandonment of the self to flux, dissipation and fragmentation" (p.134) as is suggested by Butler (1990). Instead, McNay interprets Foucault as recognising the potential for multiple identities but perceives experimentation of these as a coherent exploration of the self within the bounds of available discourses rather than as random fluctuation.

When continuing to use Butler's framework, the girls can be interpreted as believing their identity fluctuates around this 'central core', but this core can also be viewed as being socially constructed. Identity is such an important part of an individual it is inevitable the girls want to feel they have something which is unique to them that they control and create, hence the belief in some inner self that is their own invention. However, their 'inner self' can be viewed as comprising of discourses that the girls adopt more rigidly and frequently than other aspects of their gender identity. If, as Butler suggests, gender is a consequence of "repeated acts that harden into the appearance of something we have all been doing all along" (Salin, 2002: p. 85), then the girls' core can be interpreted as their repeatedly engaging in certain discourse whilst fluctuating with others, but with the repetition providing some sort of centre and grounding. The girlie girls continued to adopt stereotypical feminine appearance and (to a lesser extent) behaviours which they felt made them 'mostly girlie girls'. However the tomboys repeatedly adopted non feminine behaviour values which they felt assisted with defining them as mainly tomboys, even if they adopted typically feminine value in different areas of their identity. The interpretation of the data using this theoretical stance would suggest that the girls' central 'core' is also culturally constructed and therefore potentially open to fluctuation or alteration depending on the context. However, currently they continue to interact at some level with relatively consistent discourses whilst in other aspects of their lives experimenting fairly freely with other gender norms available.

It is too simplistic to state that playing football redefined restrictive feminine stereotypes. The postmodern underpinning of the study recognises that the girls' identities were complex and by constructing multiple identities the girls were continually able to challenge feminine expectations in different contexts.

Butler (1993) argues that multiple narratives of the self expressed in postmodern theory are an inevitable consequence of the proliferation and diversification of social relationships, contexts and sites of interactions. Utilising this understanding, it can be recognised that the girls were likely to generate alternative identities from playing football as this provided a different context from their established lives, and they were choosing to use a different discourse which — according to normalised gender beliefs — shouldn't have been available to them. However, this need not necessarily have any wider impact on global gender beliefs and values. Equally, football is not the sole mechanism they could achieve this through: rather, it was the available vehicle during this particular time. To some extent, the effects of playing football were muted precisely because the girls felt the behaviour aspect of their identity had never been particularly restricted. Butler's theorising suggests it is possible to experiment with multiple identities and participating in football supports this argument. That said, participation does very little to break down the rigid discourses surrounding the game, nor does it have any lasting impact on the discourses surrounding the way girls and women should behave, or encourage the girls to take up alternative discourses in wider aspects of their lives. Playing football had little impact on these discourses and possibly made them more even restrictive and important for the girls to adhere to.

Football, therefore, became a space for girls to experiment with alternative identities, but it was not the only setting they had available to do this. Playing football was an example of the girls experimenting, rather than the catalyst to this process. Nonetheless, although the girls played-out multiple behaviour identities, the strength of dominant feminine discourses was very apparent. The girls adhered fairly rigidly to discourses surrounding their visual appearance. Playing had little impact on changing how they considered they should construct their visual identity: all of the girls felt it was essential to 'look like a girl' even when they were playing football. Krane, Choi, Baird, Aimar and Kauer (2004) describe this process as performing femininity to gain social acceptance elsewhere in their identity. It was this conformity — visually they remained feminine — that allowed them to adopt a more fluid shifting identity in relation to their behaviour.

Butler (1990) maintains that females recognise that society still expects them to appear feminine whatever activity they are engaging in. Discourses surrounding visual appearance are extremely restrictive, with limited choices available for females if they wish to be considered normal. Although the girls are still relatively young they are very aware of these cultural expectations and the consequences of not adhering to them. As a result the girls were adamant that participating in football was acceptable for any girl so long as she looked female, retained long hair and did not get too muscular. Alternative discourses are available but the girls did not feel it was acceptable to experiment with these in the same way they could when choosing the behaviour they wished to adopt. Krane (2001) considers women become empowered through sport to transgress the margins of hegemonic femininity and create alternative images for women. This research suggests this holistic transformative process did not automatically occur for the girls involved.

The second substantial theme in the study was the relationship between the girls' experiences of football and its hegemonic nature. The elements of the research that addressed this explored both the immediate implications of the girls' participation through the after-school football club, and the girls' broader perceptions of 'global' football.

The girls in the research recognised how consistently hegemonic images of football were played out through the media. Few newspapers carry reports and feature articles on women's football, and even fewer display photographs of female players (e.g. Thompson, 2002). In accordance with Althusser's (1971) theory of representation, the media thus sustains the dominant understanding of football as an exclusively male sport through the production of images from which women's football is simply absent. More fundamentally, feminist cultural studies recognises sport as a whole as a significant site for creating ideologies confirming male dominance, within which images, beliefs and practices of masculine power are continually replayed and reproduced. Male power, particularly within football, relies upon maintaining these beliefs and producing continuous images of male physical strength and sports superiority alongside those that denigrate femininity, women and sporting activities. The research demonstrates that the media are capable of undertaking this role and producing the 'correct' images. The girls reported that football as a masculine sport was continually replayed to them at both a global and a local level, thus affirming to them that 'real' football was not something they could access. The media are therefore significant in sustaining male hegemonic control of football despite the large numbers of females now participating in the sport.

The research suggests that the girls believed little was changing in men's control over football. Although by playing football the girls were challenging at a very basic level the belief that girls could not play, their discussions of football participation in the wider local environment suggested hegemonic discourses were prevalent. Wearing (1998) discusses how cultural theorising can allow us to understand how females can use leisure space to deconstruct gendered boundaries, moving beyond the restrictions of cultural stereotypes. Whilst the girls did redefine football within their space, the wider game still retained all of its masculine connotations and associations with masculine superiority. Reflecting Scraton *et al.*'s conclusions, structures of power within football still remain in the hands of men (1999: p. 108).

In postmodern culture it is possible for meanings to shift and for contexts where meanings develop to diversify (Butler, 1993). This is useful for understanding how the context of football has altered in this setting into something that has become accessible and valuable to the girls, but is extremely personal to them. Within their personal environment, they reshaped dominant discourses to create their own meaning for football. This remoulded football as a non masculine, 'non sporty' accessible activity. However, this redefinition of football was not taken up by any community outside of the girls' sessions. It had no impact on altering the prevalent football ideology. The potential for multiple discourses discussed in post modernist thinking (Hall, 1990) is demonstrated by the girls accessing alternative football discourses. They are able to achieve this because of the different context the sport has been placed in. They could not, however, access football outside the 'safe' environment of the sessions.

The subordination the girls experience when attempting to participate outside of this environment is contextualised using cultural theory as being created by the interaction between ideology and hegemony. In the research setting, the global ideology of football creates an extremely restrictive local hegemony that the girls have been unable to break down when attempting to compete equally with the boys on what has been defined by global and local discourses as 'their territory'. The ideology of football, constructed through the mass media, secures football as male and a symbol of normal masculinity. Hegemony involves a powerful group exercising social authority over a subordinated group, drawing on an ideology to achieve this (Connell, 1995). This has occurred in the current situation and ensured that the girls have had extremely negative experiences of football in male settings and have been unable to break down any of the dominant hegemonic practices associated with this space.

Birrell and Theberge (1994) maintain that, within cultural theorising, resistance alone is not transformative. The girls playing football can be understood as a form of resistance but, for changes in the structure of power and transformation to occur, resistance needs to be a conscious act. It does not appear that the girls consciously played football to alter gender assumptions and beliefs. Consciousness in cultural theory is defined as the recognition of the social relations that constrain individuals. Whilst the girls were aware of these, they did not necessarily see their own football setting as linking to the constraints they identified in the wider football environment. As a result their participation did little to challenge dominant assumptions of football at either material, structural or ideological level.

Cultural theorising also maintains that for an act of resistance to be transformative it must be 'public'. The girls' sessions were removed from the public setting. To transform football ideologies the sessions would have had to enter the consciousness of the dominant groups (Barker, 2000). The sessions did not achieve this: their experiences when they did play football away from the sessions, and their perceptions regarding the national profile of football, illustrated that little has changed to alter their belief that football was a male sport or a sport that females 'should not' participate in. Unlike the girls in the research work of Coakley and White (1999) they, at least, were aware of the structural and ideological barriers they faced, when attempting to play football and did not accept that it was simply that they could not play. However, whilst the girls did not necessarily feel these ideological and structural constraints were acceptable, and were very vocal about considering them unjust, they were relatively powerless to change these perceptions amongst their male peers within the school environment and even less so at a wider level. It has been evident that despite growing up within the huge expansion of female participation, these girls are still experiencing the same attitudes and issues presented in previous research work (Harris, 2002; Renold, 1997; Skelton, 2000; Swain, 2000) when attempting to access football within its normalised male domain.

Conclusion

Girls are participating in football more and this must be recognised as a very valuable first step to reconstructing football as a gender neutral sport and giving girls the opportunities to play. Whilst the increase in participation is important, the girls in this study can be viewed as playing 'their' football rather than 'the' football, and as such it was very difficult to present any real challenge to the prevalent views of football as a symbol of masculinity and female participation being inappropriate and subordinate to men's. Cole and Birrell (1986) suggest that participation in itself is evidence of a 'leaky hegemony' (p. 26). Positioning this understanding within the current female football context would suggest the dominant hegemony has been 'leaky' for nearly two decades, but as yet this participation has not managed to make significant alterations at an ideological level, despite the relatively high number of girls and women now involved in football as both participants and spectators. The factors contributing to maintaining the dominant hegemony are the lack of any real media profile, society continuing to perpetuate the belief that football is a male sport and one that girls cannot play, the continued education of young people that this is the reality, and finally the marginalisation of girls who do wish to play to alternative spaces as occurred with these sessions. Until these issues are addressed it is unlikely that girls' participation can have any significant influence on breaking down dominant discourses and redefining football or gender identities at a structural and ideological level.

References

Althusser, L. (1971) *Lenin and philosophy and other essays*. London: New Left Books.

Barker, C. (2000) *Cultural studies: Theory and practice*. London: Sage.

Baudrillard, J. (1983) *In the shadow of the silent majorities*. New York: Semiotext(e).

Birrell, S. and Theberge, N. (1994) 'Feminist resistance and transformation in sport', in D. M. Costa and S.Guthrie (eds) *Women and sport: Interdisciplinary perspectives*. Champaign: Human Kinetics, pp.360–378.

Bordo, S. (1993) *Unbearable weight: Feminism, western culture and the body*. Berkeley: University of California Press.

Butler, J. (1990) *Gender trouble*. New York and London: Routledge.

——— (1993) *Bodies that matter*. London and New York: Routledge.

Cahn, S. K. (1994) *Coming on strong: Gender and sexuality in 20th Century women's sport*. Cambridge, MA: Harvard University Press.

Coakley, J. and White, A. (1999) 'Making decisions: How young people become involved and stay involved in sports' in J. Coakley and P. Donnellly (eds) *Inside sport*. London: Routledge, pp. 77–85.

Cockburn, C. and Clarke, G. (2002) '"Everybody's looking at you!": Girls negotiating the "femininity deficit" they incur in physical education', *Women's Studies International Forum* Vol. 25, Issue 6: pp. 651–665.

Cole, C. (1994) "Resisting the Canon: Feminist cultural studies, sport and technologies of the body". in Birrell, S and Cole, C (eds) *Women, sport and culture.* Champaign, Windsor, Leeds, Auckland: Human Kinetics pp. 5–27.

Cole, C. and Birrell, S. (1986 Nov) Resisting the canon: Feminist cultural studies. Paper presented at North American Society for the Sociology of Sport, Edmonton, AB.

Connell, R. W. (1995). *Masculinities*. Champaign Ill: Polity Press.

Davies, B. (1993) *Shards of glass*. St Leonards: Allen and Unwin.

Derrida, J. (1982) *Positions*. London: Athlone Press.

Donnelly, P. (1988) 'Sport as a site for popular resistance', in Gruneau, R. (ed) *Popular cultures and political practices.* Toronto: Garamond pp.69–82.

Fine, G. A. and Sandstrom, K. L. (1988) *Knowing children: Participant observation with minors*. Newbury Park, Beverley Hills, London, New Dehli: Sage.

The Football Association (2001) *The football development strategy 2001–2006*. London: Football Association.

Foucault, M. (1972) *The archeology of knowledge*. London: Tavistock.

Gramsci, A. (1971) *Selections from the prison notebooks*. Eds Q. Hoare and G. Nowell-Smith. London: Lawrence and Wishart.

Hall, M.A. (1996) *Feminism and sporting bodies: Essays on theory and practice*. Champaign IL: Human Kinetics.

Hall, S. (1990) 'Cultural identity and diaspora', in J. Rutherford (ed) *Identity: Community, culture, difference*. London: Lawrence and Wishart pp. 222–237.

——— (1992) 'The question of cultural identity' in S. Hall, D. Held and T McGrew (eds) *Modernity and its future*. Cambridge: Polity Press pp. 273–327.

Hargreaves, J. (1990) 'Gender on the sports agenda', *International Review for the Sociology of Sport* Vol. 25, No. 4: pp. 287–305.

Harris, J. (2002) '"No you can't play you're a girl": Some primary school recollections of female football players', *The Bulletin of Physical Education* Vol. 38 No 3: pp.161–178.

Humberstone, B. (2002) 'Femininity, masculinity and difference: what's wrong with a sarong?', in A. Laker (ed) *The sociology of sport and physical education: An introductory reader*. London and New York: Routledge pp. 58–78).

Irigaray, L. (1985) *Speculum of the other woman*. Ithaca, NY: Cornell University Press.

James, A., Jenks, C., and Prout, A. 1998. *Theorizing childhood*. New York: Teachers College Press.

Krane, V. (2001) 'We can be athletic and feminine but do we want to? Challenging hegemonic femininity in women's sport', *Quest* 53 pp.115–133.

Krane, V., Choi, P.Y.L, Baird, S.M., Aimar, C.M and Kauer, K.J (2004) 'Living the paradox: Female athletes negotiate femininity and muscularity', *Sex Roles* Vol. 50, No 5/6: pp. 315–329.

Lowe, K. (1998) 'Gender maps', in N. Yelland (ed) *Gender in early childhood*. New York: Routledge, pp. 38–47.

McNay, L. (1992) *Foucault and feminism*. Boston: Northeastern University Press.

Renold, E. (1997) "'All they've got on their brains is football', Sport, masculinity and the gendered practice of playground relations", *Sport, Education and Society* Vol. 2, No. 1: pp. 5–23.

Salih, S. (2002) *Judith Butler*. London and New York: Routledge.

Sawicki, J. (1991) *Disciplining Foucault: Feminism, power and the body*. New York: Routledge.

Scraton, S., Fasting, K., Pfister, G. and Bunuel, A. *et al.* (1999) 'It's still a man's game?', *International Review for the Sociology of Sport* Vol. 34, No. 2: pp. 99–111.

Skelton, C. (2000) '"A passion for football": Dominant masculinities and primary schooling', *Sport, Education and Society* Vol. 5, No.1: pp. 5–18.

Smith, D. (1988). 'Femininity as a discourse', in L. G. Roman, L. K. Christian-Smith and E. Ellsworth (eds) *Becoming feminine*. London: Falmer Press, pp. 37–59.

Swain, J. (2000) '"The money's good, the fame's good, the girls are good": The role of playground football in the construction of masculinities', *British Journal of Sociology of Education* Vol. 21, No. 1: pp. 95–108.

Thomas, N. and Kane, C. O. (2000) 'Discovering what children think: Connections between research and practice', *British Journal of Social Work* Vol. 30: pp. 819–835.

Thompson, S. (2002) 'Sport, gender, feminism', in J. Maguire and K. Young (eds) *Theory, sport and society*. London, JAI Press, pp. 105–128.

Wearing, B. (1998) *Leisure and feminist theory*. London: Sage.

Whannel, G. (1992) *Fields in vision: Television sport and culture*. London: Routledge.

HOW IS FOOTBALL TAUGHT AND LEARNED IN PE CLASSES IN SPAIN? GIRLS' LEARNING ATTITUDES IN FOOTBALL PE CLASSES

Susanna Soler-Prat

INEFC Barcelona

Introduction

Physical Education (PE) at school in Spain has been mixed since the 1970 Education Law. Boys and girls follow the same PE classes, in the same place, at the same time and with the same content. The current curriculum for primary school (6–12 years old) is: The Body: Image and Perception; Abilities and Skills; Expression and Communication; Body Health; and Games. The games taught include several gender-stereotyped activities, with football being one of them. But what happens when the teacher introduces football exercises and games: can football provide a teaching/learning space in which it is possible to transform the traditional gender models associated with sports?

From a sociological point of view, we can observe that, parallel to the reproduction processes of traditional gender models, a process of 'individualisation' of gender is being developed. For Bette (1995), the individualization process gives greater autonomy to the person in the face of the social institutions' influence. Each social system has different norms that change according to the situation and the people, with differentiated behaviours that interact in them. These changes mean that individuals must define themselves progressively, beyond the values and norms fixed traditionally by the social institutions (family, social context).

Consequently, as Ortega (1996) emphasizes, gender is more and more perceived as an individual quality, a relational concept, being continuously transformed, generating a process of individualisation of gender. This process is also visible in sport, where hegemonic masculinity has come to be highly criticized, and new values in post-industrial society have been developed opposed to masculine stereotypes (Puig, 2000). Martin (1999) also indicates how women who practise traditionally 'masculine sports' are not reproducing the typical masculine or feminine world, they are just constructing their own gender identity. Are these changes reflected in PE classes and, if so, how?

In this context, to understand gender relations in sport and PE, as Wright (1995) and Puig (2000) propose, it is not enough to theorise in relation to the social and cultural reproduction through the institutions of the society (Hargreaves, 1994). It is necessary to combine this broad theory with other perspectives, such as poststructuralist theory, which allow for explanations around the multiple and contradictory situations that boys, girls and teachers experience in PE.

On the one hand, inequality and the reproduction of traditional gender stereotypes remain prevalent. Subirats and Brullet (1988) clearly show how the simple implementation of mixed education in Spain has not been enough to enough to redress such issues. With regard to PE in Spain, as in other countries (Brown, 1999; Fasting, 1990, 1993; Griffin, 1989; Scraton, 1992, 1995; Wright, 1997), studies show how at the beginning of the 21st century, the behaviour of the pupils and the beliefs of the teachers are still very much stereotyped (Fernández, 1996, 2003; Makazaga, Llorente and Kortabitarte, 2001; Martínez and García, 2002; Vázquez, Fernández and Ferro, 2000). The traditional stereotypes and the inequalities between boys and girls are reproduced through the hidden curriculum (Kirk and Tinning, 1990; Kirk, 1990; Tinning, 1992). Teacher language, space distribution, didactic strategies, or the kind and number of teacher interactions with boys and girls, are all factors that contribute to the continuing reproduction of the traditional gender stereotypes, as several studies in Catalonia and Spain have shown (Asins, 1992; Bonal, 1998; Bonal and Tomé, 1997; García and Asins, 1995; Tomé and Ruiz, 1996; Vázquez and Alvarez, 1991).

However, an analysis of sexism that continues to occur in PE, the school and sport not enough to understand and explain a reality that is increasingly complex and diverse. Moving beyond studies centred on the reproduction of gender relations in sport (Hargreaves, 1994), in which women are seen to be subordinated, it is necessary to look at the idea of sport as a space of resistance and transformation (Birrell and Theberge, 1994; Hall, 1996). From the educational field, Flintoff and Scraton (2001) assert that PE, apart from being a mechanism that contributes to the reproduction of gender relations, can also be a powerful instrument to challenge and resist these relations, and contribute to the physical and political empowerment of girls and young women. The school not only has a deterministic structure, but also each situation in which the teacher and pupils interact can contribute to the development of change as well as to the maintenance of rules, conventions, and so on. As Ronholt (2002) points out, learning is not determined only by the didactic approach of the teachers, as there are many factors that influence it. The attitudes and relations of the pupils also play an important role: boys and girls are not just passive recipients of the teaching (Scraton, Fasting, Pfister, Vázquez and Buñuel, 2000).

This chapter therefore considers within the Spanish education system: What attitudes do girls show in PE football classes? What are the relationships between boys and girls? Do these relationships favour interest among the girls in an activity that is not typical of the female sex, or promote their rejection and resistance?

The attitudes and relations of boys and girls: What role do they play?

On entering school PE, boys and girls already have a sports culture that must also be taken into account (Vázquez and Álvarez, 1991). In primary socialisation (in the family, between groups of friends, etc.) the bases of traditional stereotypes are already established, so that what their environment expects of them can inhibit behaviour which does not adapt to the traditional model. This is reflected in the beliefs and attitudes that they adopt in doing physical activity, seen in comments among the girls such as: "Sport is a boys' thing" or "I'm not playing with them because they are rough"; and "That's a girls' thing" or "I don't want to play with girls because they are clumsy" among the boys. These attitudes also contribute to the reproduction of traditional gender stereotypes and to the perpetuation of hierarchical relations between boys and girls. Furthermore, they can lead children to adopting attitudes and behaviours of resistance to those proposals of the teachers that — for boys and/or girls, depending on the activity — imply breaking with the traditional gender models, for example, in sessions that involve football tasks or dance. In these cases, a situation of tension is created between the culture of the boy or girl and that which is taught to them in PE. For this, as pointed out by Brullet (1996), we have to bear in mind that cultural habits are not modified simply by the fact that we can change them. It is necessary to overcome the resistance of individuals to any transformation of the models and processes already learned.

As pointed out by Kinchin and O'Sullivan (2003), research in the field of education indicates that pupils show resistance towards activities that they do not like, that are too difficult, that they regard as boring or not very useful, or that have little to do with what they are interested in. This lack of relevance of the activity can lead boys and girls to become frustrated and to oppose or 'refrain' from doing the task. Thus their dissatisfaction with their experience of PE leads some of the pupils to absent themselves from or avoid some activities while the less skilful pupils choose not to take part at all (Bain, 1990; Bramham, 2003; Carlson, 1995; Ennis, 1999; Flintoff and Scraton, 2001). However, we have to bear in mind that the process of individualisation that we observe in the sports system can also be reflected in the culture of the individual boy or girl (Martín, 2003; Puig, 2000; Puig and Soler, 2004). So for him or her the fact of playing football or performing dance perhaps no longer involves breaking stereotypes and he/she may accept participation in these activities, even showing enthusiasm for them, thus 'resisting the canon' (Cole, 1994). As Chepyator-Thomson and Ennis's (1997) study showed, "students reproduced and resisted gender-patterned life configurations in physical educationclasses" (p. 92) at the same time. In this work, these ambivalent or even contra-dictory circumstances between pupils, and teachers themselves, are described below.

Methodology

Studies of gender in PE in Spain during the 1990s were carried out primarily through the systematic observation of classes and were centred on quantitative aspects (Vázquez, Fernández and Ferro, 2000). International research has turned to qualitative methodologies and this type of research is also beginning to be carried out in Spain (Humberstone, 1993; Martínez and García, 2002; Sparkes, 1992; Wright, 1995). This study uses a qualitative approach in order to study the attitudes of teachers and pupils in their natural scenario. Therefore, a case study methodology has been used (Latorre, Del Rincón and Arnal, 1996; Heinemann, 2003).

Participants and context

The research was carried out analysing twelve PE football sessions taught by 4 female teachers and 4 male teachers from different schools (one or two sessions of each teacher). For this chapter, two schools have been selected from the broader project[1] as representative of the variety of situations that were found. These two schools are in Sabadell and Terrassa (medium-sized cities near Barcelona with 50,000–70,000 inhabitants), and are both located in districts of middle-low economic status.

Case A is a 5th year group (10–11 years old), whose specialist teacher is Fina, aged 35, who has been taking classes in this area at this school for six years and who is also a graduate in Sociology. The group was made up of nine girls and seven boys, among whom there were two girls and one boy of South American origin who had started that same year. The session that is described, lasting 90 minutes, took place in a gymnasium measuring 20 metres wide by 50 metres long. At one end was a small stage, under which were the boys' and girls' changing rooms.

Case B is a 6th year group (11–12 years old), whose specialist teacher is Fernando, aged 40, who has been taking PE classes at the same school for more than ten years. The group was made up of eleven boys and ten girls, all from families of different cultural and geographical origins (Arabic, South American, eastern countries or other areas of Spain). From this case, two 60-minute sessions are described, which were held on an outdoor five-a-side pitch (40m x 20m)[2].

Data collection

Following Latorre, Del Rincón and Arnal's (1996) research proposal, each session was observed and video-recorded, so that we have been able to combine the information gathered in situ by the researcher and the information extracted from the videos[3]. The videos were transcribed and described starting from my own experience as an observer, analysing in each task: the organisation (groups that were formed, use and distribution of space and material); the ways the pupils related with one another; the interaction between the pupils and the teacher; and the response of the pupils to the task (taking in elements of the previous aspects). Adhering to the recent rules about filming pupils in schools, all of the parents gave their consent for their children to be filmed, but neither the teacher nor the pupils knew exactly why we were there and filming.

Characteristics of the sessions observed

In case A, the first session (session A1) began with an initial talk from the teacher in which she explained the tasks that they were going to do. In order to start the practice, she suggested a game where the objective was to regain the ball from classmates who were in possession of the ball Next, they organised four groups and a circuit of different tasks typical of football were set up: a 'two against two'; dribbling between cones; a round; and the 'fast one' game, shooting at goal. Once all the groups had done all the activities, a final game was organised in which all the boys and girls Participated. Finally, before going to the changing rooms to get changed, the teacher brought the group together and raised a series of questions about what had happened in class.

In case B, the first session (session B1) began with an initial talk by the teacher in which he explained that the next four sessions were going to be about football. Next, the boys and girls did a short warm-up doing laps around the pitch, each at his/her own pace, for five minutes. After drinking water at a fountain near the pitch, the teacher explained the next game: football with four goals and two balls. After the explanation, which lasted 6 minutes and in which the teacher formed two mixed teams, both boys and girls got into position to play. After about seven minutes of play, the teacher brought the entire group together in a circle in the middle of the pitch in order to analyse what had happened in the game. This reflection and dialogue between the pupils and teacher lasted 20 minutes, after which Fernando proposed a game of 'pass the currant' to end the class.

The second session of case B (session B2) was much more practical. It began quickly with a game of football with a rugby ball between two mixed teams formed by the teacher. After this short warm-up, the teacher explained how games of 3 against 3 are played with the goals of each team located in the middle. This arrangement of the goals meant that if one team scored a goal, shooting very hard and straight, the ball could cross his/her own goal, meaning a goal to the opposing team. After playing for 15 minutes, the teacher once again seated the group in a circle in order to analyse how the session had gone, and if the girls had participated more than in the previous session. Finally, he allowed five minutes in order for the boys and girls to change shirts and return to class.

Girls' learning attitudes and relations with boys in football PE classes

The qualitative analysis of the football classes has allowed us to describe those attitudes, gestures, comments, etc. of the male and female pupils that suppose a difficulty for the normal accomplishment of the task, as well as to detect and describe those situations and attitudes in which boys and girls are favourable to the task.

Negative attitudes to the task

Sometimes, there was an active, direct and public rejection. In case A, when the teacher ordered Aida to drive the ball around the court because she had been the last one to arrive at the point the teacher had indicated, the girl said "No! I don't want to do it!". But this kind of direct rejection is not usual. Usually, we find situations in which some girls resist doing exercises or games by avoiding them. We could say that these girls show a passive, indirect and silent resistance. Several behaviours like this have been observed:

- Wasting time before beginning the task, taking the jackets out for example.
- Not paying attention: talking or looking somewhere else while the teacher is speaking or during the games.
- Adopting an inadequate posture during the game.
- Showing they are interested in other activities or in finishing the task with comments such as: 'How long is this task?', 'How long does it take to finish?'
- Showing insecurity for the task, with comments such as: "I don't know how to play", "As I don't play well I don't move".

Dewar (1991) sees this situation as an opportunity to improve behaviour through PE. However, the passive attitude of the girls is often regarded as a mere lack of interest or ability for the activity and the real reason for this situation is not analysed (Scott, 1985). This is observed for example, in case A, in which at the end of the session the teacher suggests analysing what has happened during the class. The dialogue is transcribed below (Session 1A):

> Fina (to the whole group): What has happened today?
> Aida: I don't know how to kick the ball!
> Fina: Aida says that she doesn't know, ok.

There are other interventions, but finally the teacher goes back to this idea.

> Fina: Why in this pre-sport is there someone who says that she doesn't know [how to play/kick etc.]?
> Aida: Because football is very boring, and I don't know...
> Maria: Because we don't practice.
> Fina: Probably, the problem is that we have different levels... But, are we interested in who plays very well or who doesn't?

Everyone: No.
Fina: The problem "I don't know", if we don't practice, is going to be worse. If we don't know something it's not a problem: we are here to learn.

Here we can see how the teacher does not give importance to the technique, but feels that the key is for girls to increase their practice and participation in games, simply that. Girls themselves feel that they are problematic, and girls are seen as problematic by the teacher when she says: "if we don't practice...". The teacher insists on promoting the girls' participation under a narrative of liberal individualism whereby the execution of the skill is secondary to the experience of performing it (Rich, 2004). Neither the girls nor the teacher analyse the boys' involvement in this situation, but, as we see, the relations between boys and girls are very important.

Problematic relations between boys and girls

As Flintoff and Scraton (2001) have already pointed out, relations between boys and girls, and between girls, sometimes promote negative attitudes towards the practice of PE. The passive behaviour of some girls, and also some boys, may be conditioned not only by their technical ignorance of the action but also by the type of relations that are established during the practice of the exercise.

In several scenes, in both Case A and Case B, boys or girls make fun of a team-mate. For example:

> In a circuit station where a group with two boys and two girls has to take a penalty, it is Roberto's turn as goalkeeper and Raquel is the one who has to take the penalty. Then, Roberto stretches out on the ground and says to Raquel: Come on, kick the ball!
> Raquel sees how the boy is lying on the ground and waits for a moment, but when the boy insists, she kicks the ball at ground level and finally, despite the boy's position, she doesn't score. Roberto laughs at her, and Raquel is left resigned....

In other situations, we can also see *requests* or hard corrective feedback between boys and girls with comments such as:

> 'Come on, pass the ball!! Quickly!'
> 'What are you doing? You have to go there!'
> 'They have scored because of you! Stupid.'

And we can also see how boys or girls completely ignore the ideas of some team-mates or directly exclude some team-mates from the game. There are also games where there is a complex situation of exclusion and self-exclusion at the same time. In case B, the first task was a football game with four goals and two mixed teams. During this game, a seven minute period ensued where the boys dominated the game and girls only touched the ball 'by accident'. As we have seen in this scene, we also observe situations in which some boys make gestures of intimidation towards the girls or even signs of aggressiveness that keep them away from the area of action. In case A, Miguel annoys his classmates on several occasions:

> During the pause, Miguel approaches the station where Rosa is doing a zigzag, and rudely kicks the ball, sending it to the other end of the gymnasium. Rosa goes to get it and he goes back to his match, without further ado.

The distribution of the circuit and working in small groups should facilitate interactions between boys and girls, but despite this, many situations are created that could even be regarded as violent. Although on many occasions accidental — in both Case A and Case B situations of unwanted hits are observed, caused by collisions or impacts of the ball. In this context it is likely that some girls convince themselves that they do not know how to play, even thinking that the best thing for the team, and for them, is not to intervene too much, excluding themselves, as they are convinced they do not know how to play. As Martínez and García (2002) suggest, it is not only a question of ability, but also confidence. These circumstances lead them to avoid direct conflict by instead remaining on the sidelines in areas where there is not much action, taking an interest in other things or watching the game.

However, the conflict exists and on many occasions the girls are fully aware of what is happening and the discrimination that they experience. While in case A we have seen how the low participation of girls is attributed to their 'lack of ability' (both by the girls themselves as well as the teacher), in case B the question is analysed for quite a while and different conclusions are reached. In session B1, after an intense debate between boys and girls and the teacher about why it is necessary to follow rules even though there is no referee, one of the girls asks to speak and expresses her problems:

> Carmen (to Fernando and the whole group): During playtime, when we are playing, some people think that they can order us about.

Fernando (to Carmen, after asking for the attention of a boy): Who are they? Who gives orders?
Carmen (to Fernando and the whole group): The boys.

In this dialogue, Carmen goes openly to the teacher to protest about the conduct of her class-mates and denounces the fact that her male companions give orders to the girls. Thus she rebels against one of the traditional stereotypes, that of submission of women in front of men.

On the other hand, Carmen's protest denotes a feeling of shared identity of the girls as opposed to the boys: 'they [the boys] can order us [the girls] about'. The teacher takes advantage of this protest to analyse in depth what is happening (Session B1):

Fernando (to the whole group): The boys give orders, why? Because football is a boys' game, right?
Several children: Nooo / It's for everyone...
Dani (to Fernando, and the whole group): There is also women's football.
Fernando (to the whole group): There is also women's football that is not on television, or not so much. What happens is that in your class there are girls that play...
Damián (to Fernando and the whole group): And nothing happens — Implying that for him it is not an inconvenience for them to play...

This speech denotes that for boys the existence of women's football is well known and that the belief that football is only 'a game of boys' is already disregarded. It seems, then, that the traditional stereotypes assigned to this activity are already surpassed. Nevertheless, this is one of the false beliefs held by the pupils, and also by the teachers. The problem is that this belief restrains the action for change: if someone thinks that the traditional gender stereotypes are no longer present, then it is no longer necessary to try to surpass and to change them.

However, as we see in the following debate, it is necessary to show not only that women's football exists, but also that there are more aspects to be considered.In this instance, the teacher focuses the debate on the girls' feelings while they are playing, unmasking a hidden conflict (Session B1):

Fernando (to the whole group): No, no, nothing happens, they play....
The problem is that they feel very bad, right?
Dani (to Fernando): Why? — Surprised.

> Fernando (to Dani): Ah! Ask the girls. Ask Carmen why they feel so bad...
> Dani (to Carmen): Why?
> Carmen (to Dani and the whole group): Because boys think that we don't know how to play, that we are bad and make fouls, and some boys, if we pass the ball to someone, they moan, insult us and things like that...
> Ester (to the whole group): It has happened to Sandra. Without meaning to, sometimes,... she has scored an own goal and they start: Eh! and whatever... Don't you know how to play?...

The girls report the unpleasant sensation of receiving insults and feeling that their male classmates think that they do not know how to play or that they foul the opposition. The answers of Carmen and Ester are very explicit, giving their view about why during playtime and the games that are proposed in PE, most of the boys are in the middle of the playground and most of the girls at the side. It is not a 'natural' attitude and as Carmen warns, it is not a situation that girls have chosen freely. The circumstances and the relations that girls experience during the game have sent them to this marginal and passive situation. Therefore, the difficulties are not as much in relation to the stereotypes assigned to the activity but in the type of interactions produced during the practice.

However, this explanation goes unnoticed'day in day out and the boys, defending themselves from the reproaches of the teacher for not passing the ball to the girls, express their point of view and the beliefs that lead them to act in this way (Session B1):

> Hassan (to Fernando and the whole group): During playtime, for example, Laura has the ball and always shoots, because the other girls don't move and don't try to get the ball, but Laura does.
> Fernando (to Hassan and the rest of the boys): How many times have we passed the ball to Laura?
> Hassan (to Fernando, quickly): None.
> Fernando (to Hassan and the whole group): So, we should think about that: How many times do I pass the ball to Laura? Why do I think that maybe Laura plays badly?... Maybe Laura plays badly because as nobody passes the ball to her she doesn't have the chance to play...

> Because, how do we learn?
> Several children: Playing.
> Dani (to Fernando, and the whole group): But the girls are always kicking... like this... thump, thump — moving his legs.
> Fernando (to Dani and the whole group): Well as far as I can see, the worst kicks during playtime are not from the girls...

In this dialogue, Hassan acknowledges girls' capabilities in football but at the same time he clearly expresses some of the more common prejudices in the area of PE and sport. It is understood that whoever wants to play can already play and if they don't take part in the game it is because they really don't want to. The situation comes to be regarded as normal and fair, as it is what each boy or girl 'wants'. These are beliefs that are not only present among boys and girls but also among teachers. According to Bonal (1998) and Rich (2004), this idea of individual freedom to choose, as well as the idea that traditional stereotypes no longer exist, legitimises the inequality that exists during playtime as the teachers think that the girls find space for their activities. However, it is not considered that it may be the other way round, that is to say, that they adapt their activities to the available space.

Girls themselves also denounce any conflict after the intervention of their male classmates (Session B1):

> Carmen (to Fernando and the whole group): The girls don't move because as we know that the boys don't pass the ball to us, why should we run...
> Ester (to Fernando and the whole group): The boys think that they never make a mistake or a foul or anything, and so the girls have to be on another side and if we don't try to get the ball, the boys always have the ball, and we are there at the side (she makes a gesture with her hand simulating that she is separating something) getting bored, because they never pass the ball to us, only if we go and get it.

Faced with this situation, the teacher insists to the boys that they have to pass the ball and let everyone learn. Makazaga, Llorente and Kortabitate (2001) point out that this approach is one of the habitual strategies of teachers to make up for inequalities and in this way get the girls to obtain specific results. However, these strategies are established under androcentric models of action: to master the technique and tactics of the game, score goals or get points, etc. The teachers, therefore, imply that the most important thing is to master these abilities so that it is basically the shortages of the girls that have to be 'resolved', ignoring the rest of the aspects to work on with regard to the potential of the individual.

In session B1, however, and after the protests of the girls, the teacher is very sensitive to the discriminatory situation that is produced in football and even floats the idea of forbidding it (Session B1).

> Fernando (to the whole group): Good, so.... what I am seeing, from what you're telling me, is that football during playtime is a wonderful sport, that we have a very good time, we enjoy ourselves a lot, both boys and girls. Those that like it and those who don't, and so as we don't have anything else to do in playtime apart from playing football, how lucky we are to be able to play such a fun sport! [*There are some comments, but Fernando continues*]... Only when on some occasions we have punished you, without playing football and you play basketball, and then it's the same people. Because you hit and push more when you play basketball than when you play football. Maybe we should forbid it...
> Several children: No, no...
> Fernando (to the whole group): No.... because it is a lot of fun — in an ironic tone of voice — Fun for who..., for three, four, six...

The banishing of football in PE is one of the measures that is often taken to avoid gender conflicts. However, does including football not solve the problem? If the pedagogical challenge in relation to football in PE is not confronted, the problematic remains and can even be increased since boys and girls continue maintaining these problematic relations in their free time. In this case, the omission of the teachers could be more problematic than their own action.

The girls follow with their protest, talking about teacher behaviour (Session B1).

> Ester (to Fernando): Fernando, you always choose boys to be captains, you always choose boys first....

Despite his critical speech, it seems that the teacher also contributes to the girls' discrimination. Faced with this awkward criticism, and more so taking into account that a researcher and a camera were there, Fernando denies the accusation and redirects Ester's accusations to the boys, concluding the discussion.

In order to resolve the low participation of girls, in the session B2 the teacher proposes a game of 3 against 3 in which boys and girls are encouraged to participate equally and the number of shots on goal and the number of passes are reduced (as the space is much smaller). Indeed, in this activity the participation of girls is much higher and much more favourable interactions are observed. However, the teacher makes it very clear whom he regards as 'good' and who is not when he organises the teams (Session B2).

> Fernando: Damián, come here. Manuel, come here, Carlos, come here. Hassan. Jaime. Five, one more. Dani.
> The 6 boys stand up and then Ester exclaims: This team? They will always win!
> Fernando (to Ester, in an irritated tone of voice): You don't know what I'm going to do now, do you? They are boys because I am choosing those that are the ugliest. Do you want to come here? No, right? — and he continues to organise the teams.
> Fernando (to the rest of the group): Let's see... Yeray, behind Manuel; Ana, behind Carlos; Laura behind Damián; Montse behind Dani; Carmen behind Jaime; Carolina behind Hassan; David behind Montse. Let's see, David, Martín and Jose, here.
> Fernando (to Ester): Are you happy now Ester? Do you see why we have done this?
> The girl nods her head.
> Fernando (to the whole group): I've arranged you so that you are more or less balanced.

And so, the six boys take on the role of captains of their respective teams and are given a higher status than the rest. As Bonal (1997) and Barbero (1996) point out, despite the fact that the teacher — in this case Fernando — is sensitive to the discriminatory situation that the girls and some boys experience, and finds it quite easy to give a critical speech in front of the class, he finds it much more difficult to find solutions and change his beliefs. As Sparkes (1992a, 1992b) proposes, for a really profound change, after changes in speech and in the methodological and didactic resources, it is also necessary to have a change in the beliefs of the teachers.

Favourable attitudes towards the task and positive relations between boys and girls

The protests that we have just described with regard to the inequality and discrimination that girls experience during games show that they are interested in increasing their participation. We also find other attitudes that suggest that some girls are also interested in football and participating in the game.

We observed favourable attitudes towards the task when some girls, as with the majority of boys, are ready quickly (in the space, with the material, looking for the team, etc.); looking to have everything correct; practice with high intensity and intervene many times; or practice during the transitory moments. Sometimes, there are girls, even those who have not participated with high intensity during the game, who when it finishes, get the ball and practice. It is an example of how it is often not about girls not wanting to play but instead about girls not finding their chance during the game and having to take advantage of the pauses in order to get the ball and play.

On the other hand, when the teacher organises a task modifying the rules so that participation is encouraged and the aggressiveness of the game is reduced, interactions between boys and girls clearly improve. In case B (session B2), in the games of 3 against 3, we can see several situations of collaboration (boys and girls help each other to do the exercises) and positive feedback (boys and girls give positive feedback and show interest in the action of the other). For example, Sara, who usually stays in the middle of the pitch without touching the ball in the big games, scores a goal and Hassan and Carolina congratulate her clearly, even clapping: "Very good Ester!", "Good shot!". Later, Hassan insists on congratulating Ester: "Good, good, Ester!". When the game is over, Ester and Carolina are talking and boasting about the goals they have scored. Both the boys and girls demonstrate a positive reaction to more equal participation.

Concluding comments

As we have seen in these two cases, in the classes of PE devoted to football in mixed groups of boys and girls between 10 and 12 years old, a series of circumstances are created that are both ambivalent and contradictory. As the study of Chepyator-Thomson and Ennis (1997: p. 90) indicates, "traditionally dominant forms of femininity and masculinity may be reproduced, resisted, or restructured, to produce transformative types of action or behaviour". Furthermore, a complex network of situations and interactions appears in which the pupils and the teacher interact. The different circumstances that may result from this complex network, although apparently opposed, may occur simultaneously, as follows:

1. *Contradiction between the beliefs, speeches and actions of the teacher* — The teacher verbally shows a favourable stance with regard to co-educational approaches, of equal opportunities between boys and girls, and the breaking of traditional stereotypes, but his/her daily practice and his/her beliefs (hidden curriculum) are not consonant with with the expressed positive stance. For example, in case B, we have seen the contradictions between the speech and the unconscious action of the teacher. As Vázquez, Fernández and Ferro (2000) indicate, although most teachers consider that it is necessary to encourage equality of opportunities between girls and boys, their beliefs continue reproducing the traditional models of femininity and masculinity.
2. *Behaviour and interactions of the different boys and girls* — Within the group-class they are subject to very different way of acting and relating, in some cases showing attitudes and behaviours that are favourable to change, and in others opposing or reproducing traditional models of masculinity and femininity. As we have seen in the dialogue in session B1, the relations between girls and boys are very significant. (Flintoff and Scraton, 2001; Martínez and García, 2002).
3. *Resistance to changing the traditional model: conflict T–P (Teacher–Pupil)* — The situation in which the teacher tries to favour change but most of the class has a tendency towards reproduction, resisting a change from the traditional model of that practice. This resistance involves a conflict between the teacher and pupils because, as Brullet (1996) indicates, cultural habits are not modified solely by creating opportunities. It is necessary to overcome the resistance of individuals to the desired transformations of the models being taught.
4. *Resistance to accepting the traditional model: conflict T–P* —The situation in which some of the pupils resist adopting the traditional model of practice in question. This resistance also involves a conflict between the pupils and teacher if the teacher reproduces the traditional model. As Chepyator-Thomson and Ennis (1997) indicate, while some students reproduce the generally accepted behaviour others contest the status quo. In the present study, girls show different forms of contesting behaviour: direct rejection, indirect and silent resistance, protests about boys' discriminatory

behaviours, protests about teacher's discriminatory actions, and finally, playing fully, challenging the generally accepted behaviour for a girl.

5. *Situation that is unfavourable to change* — in which both the teacher and pupils uniformly reproduce the traditional gender cultural models.
6. *Situation that is favourable to change* — in which both the teacher and pupils tend to overcome and change the traditional gender cultural models.

Faced with this complex network, in order to understand gender relations in PE it is necessary to analyse it from two perspectives simultaneously (Giroux, 1983; Chepyator-Thomson and Ennis, 1997): as a space of reproduction and perpetuation of the traditional gender models, and also as spaces of resistance and change to these hegemonic models.

Notes

1 In this broader project twelve football PE sessions and twelve dance (or expression/theatre) PE sessions were analysed. These sessions were taught by four female and four male teachers providing a small purposive sample (Heinemann, 2003). The eight cases of the study gather an heterogeneous sample which includes a variety of aspects considered to influence gender relations in PE: about the teacher (sex, age, experience teaching PE, and formation on PE didactics) and about the school (socio-economic level, immigration pupils percentage, and administrative type [public, subsidized religious, and subsidized non religious]).

2 In case B the first session is identified as "session B1", and the second session"is identified as "session B2".

3 In the broader project techniques have been mixed: participant observation, systematic observation, teacher interviews, teacher documents analysis, and pupil surveys. In this chapter there are only references to the observation data to focus on girls' attitudes.

References

Asins, C. (1992) 'L'ocupació diferencial de l'espai en educació física', in Institut Valencià de la dona (ed) *L'ensenyament de l'educació física. Ponències de les IV Jornades Internacionals de coeducació.* València: Institut Valencià de la Dona — U. de València, pp. 183–193.

Bain, L. (1990) 'A critical analysis of the hidden curriculum in physical education', in D. Kirk and R. Tinning (eds) *Physical education, curriculum and culture: Critical issues in the contemporary crisis*. Lewes: Falmer Press.

Barbero, J. I. (1996) 'Cultura profesional y currículum (oculto) en educación física. Reflexiones sobre las (im)posibilidades del cambio', *Revista de educación* Vol. 311: pp. 13–49.

Bette, H. D. (1995) 'Deporte e individualización', in'*Actas del Congreso Científico Olímpico 1992*, Málaga: Unisport, pp. 327–336.

Birrell, S. and Theberge, N. (1994) 'Feminine resistance and transformation in sport', in M. Costa and S. Guthrie (eds) *Women and sport: Interdisciplinary perspectives*. Champaign, IL: Human Kinetics, pp. 361–376.

Bonal, X. (1997) *Las actitudes del profesorado ante la coeducación. Propuestas de intervención*. Barcelona: Graó.

——— (1998) *Canviar l'escola: la coeducació al pati de jocs*. Barcelona: Institut de Ciències de l'Educació de la U. Autònoma de Barcelona.

Bonal, X. and Tomé, A. (1997) *Construir l'escola coeducativa: la sensibilització del professorat*. Barcelona: Institut de Ciències de l'Educació — Universitat Autònoma de Barcelona.

Bramham, P. (2003) 'Boys, masculinities and PE', *Sport, Education and Society* No. 8: pp. 57–71.

Brown, D. (1999) 'Complicity and reproduction in teaching in PE', *Sport, Education and Society* Vol. 4, No. 2: pp. 143–160.

Brullet, C. (1996) 'Roles e identidades de género: una construcción social', in M. A. García de León, M. García de Cortázar and F. Ortega (eds) *Sociología de las mujeres españolas*. Madrid: Ed. Complutense.

Carlson, T.B. (1995) 'We hate gym:'Student alienation from PE', *Journal of Teaching in Phisical Education* Vol.14: pp. 467–477.

Chepyator-Thomson, J. R. and Ennis, C. D. (1997) 'Reproduction and resistance to the culture of femininity and masculinity in secondary school physical education', *Research Quarterly for Exercise and Sport* Vol. 68: pp. 89–99.

Cole, C. (1994) 'Resisting the canon: 'Feminist cultural studies, sport, and technologies of the body', in S. Birrell and C. Cole (eds) *Women, sport and culture*. Champaign, IL: Human Kinetics, pp. 5–29.

Dewar, A. (1991) 'Incorporation or resistance? Towards an analysis of women's response to sexual oppression in sport', *International Review of Sociology of Sport* Vol. 26: pp. 15–23.

Ennis, C. D. (1999) 'Creating a culturally relevant curriculum for disengaged girls', *Sport, Education and Society* Vol. 4: pp. 31–49.

Fasting, K. (1990) 'Nuevas estrategias para una coeducación en la educación física', in VV.AA. (ed.) *El ejercicio físico y la práctica deportiva de las mujeres. Seminario 'Mujer y deporte'*. Madrid: Consejo Superior de Deportes–MEC, pp. 45— 51.

——— (1993) 'El género como perspectiva importante en el estudio de la sociología del deporte', *Investigación alternativa en educación física. Unisport* Vol. 275: pp. 51–60.

Fernández, E. (1996) 'Representaciones diferenciadas sobre actividad física y género en el futuro profesorado de educación primaria', in F. Del Villar (ed) *La investigación en la enseñanza de la educación física*. Cáceres: Universidad de Extremadura.

Fernández, E. (2003) 'Educación física y género: la trasmisión de estereotipos de género en la enseñanza de la educación física', in *Actas del V Congreso Internacional sobre la enseñanza de la Educación Física y el Deporte Escolar*. Valladolid: U. Miguel de Cervantes.

Flintoff, A. and Scraton, S. (2001) 'Stepping into active leisure? Young women's perceptions of active lifestyles and their experiences of school PE', *Sport, Education and Society* Vol. 6: pp. 5–21.

García, M. and Asins, C: (1995) *La coeducació en l'educació física*. Barcelona: Institut de Ciències de l'Educació de la U. Autònoma de Barcelona.

Giroux, H. A. (1983) 'Theories of reproduction and resistance in the new sociology of education: a critical analysis', *Harvard Educational Review* Vol. 53: pp. 257–293.

Griffin, P. (1989) 'Gender as socialising agent in Physical Education', in T. Templin and P. G. Schempp (eds) *Socialization into physical education: Learning to teach.* Dubuque: Brown and Benchmark, pp. 219–234.

Hall, A. (1996) *Feminism and sporting bodies.* Champaign, IL: Human Kinetics.

Hargreaves, J. (1994) *Sporting females: Critical issues in the history and sociology of women's sports*. London: Routledge.

Heinemann, K. (2003) *Introducción a la metodología de la investigación empírica en las ciencias del deporte.* Barcelona: Paidotribo.

Humberstone, B. (1993) 'El puesto y la importancia de la investigación etnográfica en el examen de aspectos relacionados con el género, la identidad y el poder en la Educación Física y al aire libre: ¿puede haber una etnografía feminista?', *Investigación Alternativa en Educación Física II.* Málaga: Unisport.

Kinchin, G. and O'Sullivan, M. (2003) 'Incidences of student support for and resistance to a curricular innovation in high school PE', *Journal of Teaching of Physical Education* Vol. 22: pp. 245–260.

Kirk, D. (1990) *Educación Física y currículum*. València: U. de València.

Kirk, D. and Tinning, R. (1990) *Physical education, curriculum and culture: Critical issues in the contemporary crisis.* Lewes: The Falmer Press.

Latorre, A., Del Rincón, D. and Arnal, J. (1996) *Bases metodológicas de la investigación educativa*. Barcelona: GR92.

Makazaga, A., Llorente, B. and Kortabitarte, B. (2001) 'La coeducación en el deporte en edad escolar', in'*Actas del Congreso Mujer y Deporte.* Bilbao: Emakunde.

Martín, M. (1999) *Making sense of the first stage in the history of women's rugby in England (1978–1985): Difference and multiplicity in gender and rugby.* Roehampton Institute London: M.A. in Sport, Culture and Development (non published).

——— (2003) 'El deporte en las sociedades postmodernas', in M. Mosquera and others (eds) *Deporte y postmodernidad*. Madrid: AEISAD–Librerías deportivas Estevan Sanz s.l.

Martínez Álvarez, L. and García Monje, A. (2002) 'Reflexionar sobre el gènere des d'escenes de pràctica escolar', *Apunts. Educació Física i Esport* Vol. 69: pp.118–123.

Ortega, F. (1996) 'La esquiva igualdad: el género y sus representaciones sociales', in M. A. García de León, M. García de Cortázar and F. Ortega (eds) *Sociología de las mujeres españolas*. Madrid: Ed. Complutense, pp. 309–323.

Puig, N. (2000) 'Procés d'individualització, gènere i esport', *Apunts d'educació física*, Vol. 59: pp. 99–102.

Puig, N. and Soler, S. (2004) 'Gènere i esport a Espanya. Un model interpretatiu', *Apunts. Educació Física i Esport*, vol. 76: pp. 71–78.

Rich, E. (2004) 'Exploring teacher' biographies and perceptions of girls' participation in physical education', *European Physical Education Review*, Vol. 10, No. 2: pp. 215–240.

Ronholt, H. (2002) '"It's only the sissies...". Analysis of teaching and learning processes in physical education: A contribution to the hidden curriculum', *Sport, Education and Society* Vol. 6: pp. 25–36.

Scott, J. (1985) *Weapons of the weak: Everyday forms of peasant resistance*. New Haven, CT: Yale University Press.

Scraton, S. (1992) 'Implicacions per a les xiques de l'educació física mixta', in Institut Valencià de la Dona (ed) *L'ensenyament de l'educació física — IV Jornades Internacionals de coeducació*. València: Universitat de València — Institut Valencià de la Dona, pp. 69–76.

——— (1995) *Educación física de las niñas: un enfoque feminista*. Madrid: Morata.

Scraton, S., Fasting, K., Pfister, G., Vázquez, B. and Buñuel, A. (2000) *Experiencia y significado del ejercicio físico en la vida de las mujeres de algunos países europeos*. Madrid: Instituto de la Mujer.

Sparkes, A. (ed) (1992a) *Research in physical education and sport: Exploring alternative visions*. London: Falmer.

Sparkes, A. (1992b) 'Breve introducción a los paradigmas de investigación alternativos en EF', *Perspectivas de la actividad física y el deporte* Vol. 11: pp. 30–33.

Subirats, M. and Brullet, C. (1988) *Rosa y azul. La transmisión de los géneros en la escuela mixta*. Madrid: Instituto de la Mujer.

Tinning, R. (1992) 'Sexismo y educación física', in R. Tinnng (ed)'*Educación Física: La escuela y sus profesores*. València: U. de València.

Tomé, A. and Ruiz, R.A. (1996) 'El espacio de juego: escenario de relaciones de poder', *Aula* Vol. 52–53: pp. 37–41.

Vázquez, B. and Álvarez, A. (ed) (1991) *Guía para una Educación Física no sexista*. Madrid: Ministerio de Educación y Ciencia.

Vázquez, B., Fernández, E. and Ferro, S. (2000) *Educación física y género*. Madrid: Gymnos.

Wright, J. (1995) 'A feminist poststructuralist methodology for the study of gender construction in physical education:'Description of a study', *Journal of teaching in physical education* Vol. 15: pp. 1–24.

——— (1997) 'The construction of gendered contexts in single sex and co-educational physical education: Description of a case study', *Sport, Education and Society* Vol. 2: pp. 55–72.

NEGOTIATING BARRIERS TO ENTERING AND PARTICIPATING IN FOOTBALL: STRATEGIES EMPLOYED BY FEMALE FOOTBALLERS IN THE UNITED KINGDOM

Jo Welford and Tess Kay

Loughborough University

Introduction

Historically, sport is a setting in which masculinity and maleness have dominated, and where women have been admitted it is on restricted terms that conform to the view of women as weak or fragile (Therberge, 1997). This 'male terrain' has been constructed through the exclusion of women, and as a result, masculine values are firmly invested in dominant sport (Young and White, 1995). Yet today sport, and in particular combative sports, is one of the few areas where force and intimidation are still allowed to triumph in an area that is seen to be beyond women's capacities (Wright and Clark, 1999) to the point where it is considered as the last true male preserve (Carle and Nauright, 1999).

The movement of women into body contact sport is a particularly significant site of shifting gendered terrain (Therberge, 1997), and is unsurprisingly met with resistance. Women's participation in what have traditionally been all-male enclaves challenges the validity of such sites for confirming those characteristics of masculinity that are considered the prerogative of boys and men. Accordingly, Carle and Nauright argue that "the determination of males to preserve sport as a male activity and privilege has affected every stage of the development of sport for women" (1999: p. 129).

Football is one of the most popular sports in the world (see for example Brown, 1998), that embodies, symbolises, maintains and reinforces masculinity as a male domain. The strong traditional ties between football and masculinity historically made football inaccessible for females, with the

Football Association (FA) in England going so far as to ban women from playing on football league grounds in 1921 on the premise "that the game of football is quite unsuitable for females and should not be encouraged" (cited in Williams and Woodhouse, 1991: p. 93). Even though the ban was lifted in 1971, women footballers today still face problems associated with the cultural and social expectations concerned with being a 'sporting female' (Lopez, 1997). This is a key underlying theme of this chapter.

The close association between football and masculinity works to marginalise girls and women of all ages and abilities. Both boys and girls are aware from a young age that football is a powerful signifier of masculine status (Epstein, Kehily, Mac an Ghaill and Redman, 1997). It is well established how unorganised boys football games dominate the primary school playground, excluding girls and helping to define gender-appropriate behaviour (see for example Swain, 2000). This continues into secondary school, where notions of femininity become even more prominent (Kay, 1995) and sport becomes far less important in the lives of adolescent girls due to its continued association with masculinity (Hargreaves, 1994).

Despite these issues,women's football has grown rapidly in the last ten years. An official audit from the FA provides data to show that women's football is the fastest growing sport in the country and that the number of girls playing football is rising (www.thefa.com/Womens/, accessed 26 June 2006). Williams (2003) attempts to view these rapidly-increasing figures in their male context by stating that this recent expansion is unthreatening to male football authorities because it fails to alter the "essentially amateur nature" of the female game (p. 23). However, behind the official figures lies a complex situation facing women and girls who play football. Fundamental is how, as participants, women and girls struggle to be accepted as footballers and face obstacles resulting from societal pressures and tensions surrounding gender, femininity and athleticism (see for example Hargreaves, 1994; Cox and Thompson, 2000).

The lack of a professionalised structure for women's football confirms the essentially amateur nature of the sport, and provides the background for this study which features a group (n=8) of women footballers at a university club. The aims of the research were two-fold: firstly, to explore the experiences of female football players at a university club to assess how gender ideologies influenced their access to and participation in football; secondly, to ascertain if gender ideologies created any obstacles to participation in and enjoyment of football for this group.

Theoretical context

As the research aimed to discover and analyse the experiences of women, feminist theory is used to provide a framework to enable the voices of women to be expressed and understood away from the constraints of mainstream male-dominated research (see for example Nielsen, 1990). This permitted the patriarchal nature of society to be acknowledged and, more specifically, the male-dominated structure of sport in general and football in particular to be recognised. Dominant assumptions of feminism in relation to sport focus on biologically-related inequalities and highlight how women are oppressed due to assumptions that explain their 'natural' inferiority in sport. In football, its strong historical ties with masculinity makes it particularly difficult for women to challenge this 'natural' inferiority, an inferiority further cemented by the notion that women lack the necessary physical strength to fully participate in sport (see for example Sabo, 1988; Hargreaves, 1994; Williams, 2003). Assumptions of biological difference between the sexes leads to claims that men are 'naturally' more aggressive, more competitive, and therefore better at sports than women (Hargreaves, 1994). Such assumptions therefore serve to maintain male domination of sport and limit women's opportunities to participate in and enjoy contact sports like football.

Methodology

This study was set in a leading sports university in the UK, which currently has 56 student-run sports clubs for both men and women. The women's football club had approximately seventy registered players spread over three teams at the time of the data collection (it has since grown and is currently at its maximum of ninety). One of the researchers was a member of the club at the time and this permitted access to be granted to conduct in-depth semi-structured interviews with eight members in February and March 2003. The selection of participants was based on access and convenience.

Feminists acknowledge that the presence of the researcher cannot be ignored and pre-judgements and bias are inherent in the research process (Cook and Fonow, 1990). Stanley and Wise (1993) emphasise that the researcher's part in the process cannot be simply 'omitted' so should be embraced and fully utilised. The research thus adopted an 'attached' method of enquiry that requires the researcher's personal involvement (Nielsen, 1990). This 'subjective' approach is consistent with feminist calls for researchers to 'submerge' themselves in their study so as to enable access to open and full accounts of women's experiences (see for example Reinharz, 1992). Researching as an 'insider' benefited the research greatly as rapport was quickly developed with the subjects and the familiarity between the researcher and the subjects encouraged in-depth discussions of their experiences.

Influenced by the feminist notion that woman-centred studies should draw on a range of research techniques, including modifying existing methods where necessary (Maynard, 1994), the analysis also encompassed some pictorial data from the participants as well as the interview transcripts. The use of pictorial data was adapted from Mason (2001) who states that it "can be a very creative way of accessing aspects of your interviewees' lives or experiences which are non-verbalised, or difficult to verbalise" (p. 77). After a pilot interview with an ex-member of the football club, it was found that identity was one of the more difficult subjects aound which to instigate a discussion. In order to overcome this difficulty, participants were asked to make two sketches of themselves — firstly playing football, and secondly socialising after a match. This allowed them to describe their identity (or identities) more comfortably and prompted a discussion around female identity in general, and how cultural definitions can influence–female identity.

Whilst the chapter deals with the experiences of a group of women footballers at a university club it is acknowledged that the findings are not reflective of the experiences of all women footballers at university. However the chapter offers personal insights into the experiences of a sample group that adds to the emerging base of literature on the experiences of women footballers. Even though anonyminity was not a feature of the data collection, pseudonyms have been used when referring to participants.

Research findings

Early experiences: access to formal opportunities

Entering the male-dominated world of football can be problematic for females, as even at a young age, football is associated with masculinity and is perceived by both boys and girls as being in opposition to femininity. School is a significant institutional setting for experiencing new activities, yet Harris (2002: p. 163) states that "many girls in schools today find that opportunities to play sports such as football are limited". In a comparative cross-county study on elite female footballers by Scraton"*et al.* (1999), it was reported that at primary school most of the English players interviewed were either denied opportunities completely or had to battle hard for them. Similarly, no players in this study recalled playing organised football at primary school, a time when boys and girls are physically similar in their development, underlined by the fact that restrictions on mixed-sex football in the UK are not enforced until the age of eleven (Williams, 2003). When moving into secondary school, opportunities to play football continue to be limited. Four of the eight players in this study recalled playing football in Physical Education (PE) lessons but this did not necessarily create a positive experience:

> We had it usually at Christmas so it was really rubbish outside. We had a couple of lessons, but often they'd just get missed out, the girls usually wanted to do netball or something instead. (Brenda)

For this player, PE activities were divided along gender lines, and other players also recalled having to choose between playing football and activities more associated with femininity. Eve commented that "I just used to play hockey and netball instead".

Sports provisions for the girls in this research were often based on traditional perceptions concerning the gender-appropriateness of certain sports. In both primary and secondary school, teachers' attitudes were often cited as problematic or discouraging, and these opinions were not exclusively from male teachers:

> The [female] teachers weren't too keen on it, except for the PE ones, I used to have one form tutor who just didn't like me playing football for some reason. (Carla)

> The bloke who ran the boys [team], the teacher, he was a bit sexist really... a couple of the women teachers, they were always really interested... bloke teachers, they'd make sarcastic comments about the standard. (Eve)

These stereotypical attitudes impacted the opportunities these girls had to play football at school, with players encouraged into sports more traditionally aligned with femininity: "I played hockey, and I did actually used to get forced to go and play for the team when I didn't want to" (Heidi). Wanting organised opportunities to play football but not getting them can be frustrating for girls, particularly if boys are being offered those opportunities.

Early experiences: access to informal opportunities

The lack of formal opportunities for girls to play football meant a reliance on informal opportunities that emerged both inside and outside of school. All players reported being introduced to the game by fathers or brothers, which correlates with findings by Cox and Thompson (2000) and Scraton *et al.* (1999) that describes how girls are encouraged by male family members to step into 'male space'. The predominantly male culture of football requires an insider (male) approval for girls to gain entry. Also, girls can have very few female sporting role models in the family that would encourage participation and involvement (Harris, 2002). Acceptance by male family members could however also be problematic — two players indicated that moving into this 'male space' was not met with instant approval. One described how she had to overcome gender-based opinion by her father to be accepted into the male culture of football:

> He [dad] took me to my first football match when I was six...he bought a ticket for my brother, cos he didn't think I'd be interested in going, because I was a girl obviously, and I kicked up a bit of a fuss so he got me a ticket as well. (Heidi)

Heidi was exposed to gender-based ideologies through the family unit at a very young age, and had to fight to gain acceptance as an equal with her brother. Another player described how it was the support of her mum that was influential in continued participation, rather than her father:

> When I first started playing football my dad wouldn't come and watch me play. I don't know why...It was just after the first season, when I won player of the year, he was like 'oh, maybe she's pretty good, I'll go and watch' and it was only then that he started coming to watch. (Carla)

For Carla, it was more difficult to be accepted by her father into the male football culture and, as is often the case with male peers (Harris, 2002), approval was dependant on proof of ability. Constraints related to acceptance are clearly not just manifested in schools or peer groups but can also occur at the home. Generally, family support was seen as vital to both entering and continued participation in football, by providing emotional support and encouragement alongside opportunities.

As well as the family, male peers also provided an entry route into football for these subjects. All players reported positive experiences with male friends both in and out of school and most had fond memories of 'kicking around' in the neighbourhood when they were younger. There were recollections of being good friends with male footballers and being accepted with few problems.

> They [boys] were like 'come and join in'. (Carla)
>
> I was quite well-known in the school for playing football... I hung around mostly with the boys, they liked me. (Heidi)
>
> Having my big brother, he respected how good I was, and my little brother did, out of them I got respect from their friends. (Frances)

Subsequently it is suggested that both gaining access to football and continuing participation at a young age required acceptance from male peers, and as the last quote highlights, is particularly strong when this acceptance is alongside support from male family members. However the common perception by children that football is solely a male activity (Harris, 2002) means that girls can be required to display their competence when playing this 'male activity' in order to even be eligible for acceptance into this culture, a point reinforced by Heidi.

Discussions around the earliest football experiences of these girls demonstrated that a potentially strong barrier to participation was access — access not only to the opportunities to play the sport but also access to the almost exclusively male culture that surrounds football. Negotiating this barrier required a great deal of male support, in particular from male family members and male peers, to provide an entrance route. This was most notably described by one player, who felt safer using a male link to gain access to an informal game:

> We went to the field, and we never used to want to ask or anything, so we used to send my brother up to go and ask if we could join in. (Gina)

Even at this informal, amateur level negotiating access into football was a difficult issue.

Early experiences: continued participation

Discouraging and negative attitudes, such as those described previously, not only provide obstacles to girls entering football but can also impact upon continuing participation in the game if they persist. This is particularly true of girls and women seeking to maintain membership in the male-dominated football culture. The support of male friends and family members is critical in keeping the female footballer in touch with the football world:

> I think as a child, I continued to play cos my friends were boys, perhaps if they had of had a different attitude towards me playing then maybe I wouldn't have played, but they didn't seem to mind. In fact when I was little they probably thought it was quite cool that I played. (Andrea)

As well as belonging to a male peer group, the support of female peers became more important for these girls as their participation in football continued. During adolescence, peer groups can strongly influence behavioural choices (Coleman and Hendry, 1999), and some players did recall experiencing tensions at this time between femininity and athleticism, two elements of female identity that are often perceived as incompatible (Krane, 2001).

> Gina: The girls would stand in a group and play football a little bit and just stand there talking, not playing. And the rest [boys] would play football.
>
> Interviewer: Which group were you in?
>
> Gina: Probably sort of in between, I'd probably be talking as well.
>
> Debbie: When I went to secondary school, I thought I'd try and be a bit of a girl instead of a 'boy', but then I made friends with the boys, and they were playing football, so I'd play sometimes...some of the girls used to think I was a bit odd.

Here, two players experienced the tension between athleticism and femininity, which is particularly influential during adolescence when both boys and girls are often pressured to cement their identity with either masculinity or femininity. In this case, participation in football is constrained by the need to conform to feminine-appropriate behaviour. Having support from their female peer group encouraged their continued participation in football and helped them to deal with any negative treatment they received:

> I used to have pretty good mates who I used to get to stand out with me whilst playing football. (Carla)

> I would go play with the boys, and my friends would just stand and watch. Giggle at the boys' legs, that sort of thing. (Frances)

'Giggling at the boys' legs' is a means of the female peer group assigning the activity (watching football) as feminine-appropriate behaviour and therefore identifying their position as spectators. The female football player is perhaps important here in her role of connecting the two gender-divided peer groups, a role that encourages her behaviour to be accepted. Without acceptance, participation in an activity that is not deemed feminine-appropriate can be problematic and can constitute a barrier that can be difficult to overcome.

Early experiences: identity formation

It is evident from the discussion so far that a lack of opportunities based on traditional gender-role expectations, and the attitudes of others that stem from these expectations, can constitute obstacles that females have to negotiate if they wish to participate in football at a young age. However for girls, developing their own gendered identity can also be affected by the close cultural association between football and masculinity. It was understood for this analysis that gender is socially constructed (Hargreaves, 1994) and is 'acquired' rather than 'given'. Also, it is not fixed or innate but is actively constructed in group life, and develops in social contexts such as schools where gender formally and informally saturates the structure at all levels (Thorne, 1993). In accepting that identity is developed both consciously and unconsciously by an individual from birth, deviance from feminine-appropriate norms can influence gendered identities from a very young age, as highlighted by one player:

> I wanted to be a boy. I got asked in primary school, when I was five, what I wanted to be when I grew up, and I said a boy! I've been killed for that for the rest of my life. (Frances)

This player underwent extreme gender conflict at a very young age and the close association between football and masculinity is particularly evident here. This deviance from traditional gender norms is incomprehensible to a young child. Yet as with previous research in the area (e.g. Scraton *et al.*, 1999), players in this study generally had fond memories of being a 'tomboy' at a young age. Deviating from traditional gender norms was not always accepted by peers, even as a child:

> I got the odd bit of abuse ... just kind of like 'you want to be a boy' ... it was mainly the boys. (Frances)
>
> You'd get other girls who'd want to play basketball, and we used to get a bit of abuse off them, like 'tomboy' and all that sort of stuff. (Carla)

For these players, gender-role conflict not only caused problems in terms of accepting that through playing football they had different identities from their friends, but also the attitudes of others towards girls displaying the masculine qualities associated with these differences could be harmful. In negotiating this problem, the notion of having different identities for different contexts was effective for one player:

> I was never a tomboy... I think I was more sort of when I was at home...but at school, with my friends, I was more sort of 'girly'. (Gina)

Here, Gina describes how she successfully manages her identity in different situations. This player is actively 'doing gender', though this is not ever entirely voluntary[1], as the previous quotes describe how there are social retributions for not performing gender 'correctly' (Butler, 1990). Pressure to conform to gender norms appears to have been greater in school where this player was more compliant with femininity, and she felt safer displaying a more 'masculine' identity outside school.

In summary, early experiences of football found in this study are similar to those explored in the few other studies that analyse the early encounters girls have with football (e.g. Cox and Thompson, 1999; Epstein *et al.*, 2001; Harris, 2002; Scraton *et al.*, 1999). Barriers to participation are generally a direct (lack of opportunity) or indirect (attitudes of others) result of their non-conformity to gender stereotypical behaviours. Girls in this study negotiated these barriers through gaining male — and to a lesser extent, female

— support and acceptance when both beginning and continuing their participation in the sport.

Adult experiences: stereotyping

In this context, current opportunities for the players to play football were not a problem, as the university club structure is in place to provide women of all abilities the chance to experience organised football. It was therefore expected that identity and perception issues would be of greater significance. Research has shown how the strong cultural associations between sport and masculinity have linked female athleticism with the lesbian stereotype (Cahn, 1995), associations that are particularly strong for women in traditionally male sports such as football (Caudwell, 1999).

However the effect of this stereotype was not as influential on the experiences of the players in this study as might have been suggested by previous research in this area. When asked, all players described the stereotype of women who play football to be butch, lesbian, or both, yet this seemed to cause few problems beyond annoyance amongst the players. When asked whether the stereotype of women's football bothered them, replies generally suggested that they did not:

> No...well it does and it doesn't, I think you get used to it, you either let it bother you or you don't. (Andrea)
>
> I'd just laugh at them, it's funny the way people think things totally different to the way it is. (Debbie)
>
> It doesn't bother me...[but] I think some people are a bit concerned about the whole sexuality thing. I would say some girls are probably put off. (Brenda)
>
> Not really, cos the type of people who come out with those kind of things aren't really worth bothering with anyway. (Eve)

These players appeared to be comfortable enough in their own identities to not allow stereotyping to affect their experiences of football, even though it was suggested that it could affect some women. However despite players being apparently unaffected by stereotyping, some tensions did emerge throughout the discussions:

> Sometimes I hesitate before I tell people [I play football], in case they think I might be crap…and I don't like people to think I'm a lesbian. (Heidi)

> We have had arguments, with boys, about their perceptions of girls who play football… He [male football player] assumed that all girls are gay, if they play football. (Andrea)

The effect of stereotyping on individual experiences is clearly a complex and often contradictory situation and responses were varied even from this small group of players. However although it was seen as an issue, and was therefore understood to impact experiences, throughout the discussions these players appeared much more concerned about being taken seriously as footballers.

Adult experiences: achieving serious recognition

By violating dominant notions of femininity, female athletes in traditionally male sports suffer from not being taken seriously whilst others marginalise their sporting credibility to maintain sport as a male preserve (Therberge, 1997). Players in this study expressed particular annoyance at how others found it difficult to accept them as footballers:

> I think men just don't watch women's football cos they think it's crap…some people have a very stereotypical view of women's football, because they've been brought up with that. (Gina)

> Sometimes you get really stupid questions, like 'do you play for 45 minutes?', 'do you play with a smaller ball?', 'do you play offsides?'…it really winds me up when people get the wrong impression about women's football…I hate it when people don't think you know anything about football. (Carla)

> The first thing boys usually do is laugh, and say 'oh god, women trying to play football', or say something like they don't mind if all the girls have short shorts on. It's never taken very seriously. (Andrea)

From the discussions, it was apparent that these subjects did not often feel accepted as footballers, an issue that appeared to be their main concern regarding their current participation at university, more influential than stereotyping. The above comments highlight two main techniques that can be used to degrade women's football and contribute to its lack of acceptance as a 'real' sport. Firstly, the game can be trivialised by suggesting that women play by different rules so women can't play the game in the same manner as men. Secondly, it can be sexualised by promoting the female body as an object of the male gaze (Obel, 1996) rather than as an athletic one. Both of these techniques to trivialise women's football work to protect football as a 'male' sport. Some players were also concerned that they were not taken seriously as footballers by those within football as well as those outside it. Referees were the subject of particular annoyance:

> Referees drive me mad...you'll find, in a match, you can get really bad tackles, and challenges, and they won't give a yellow card or anything. But if you swear on a pitch, it'll be like 'oh, ladies shouldn't be swearing' ... it's just because they don't think women should swear. (Carla)

> They [referees] don't let you get away with as much as they should do...they maybe see us as a bit more weak, and they think they've got to stop play. (Heidi)

The issue here appears to derive again from the lack of consistency between 'ideal' femininity and the attributes displayed by those participating in football. The two referees described clearly held deeply rooted opinions on the appropriateness of football for women, and let this affect their control of the game and as a result, the experiences of these players. The opinion that it's 'only women's football' can be experienced at all levels of the game (Davies, 1997) and for these players in particular that stereotyping became a common obstacle to be overcome.

Adult experiences: identity management

In negotiating problems, particularly issues relating to stereotyping and homophobia, identity management was occasionally used, either intentionally or unintentionally. This has been documented in studies of female footballers when analysing how players use visible strategies to counteract negative images associated with football (Caudwell, 1999; Cox and Thompson, 2000). The players in this study, although all seemingly comfortable with their identity, did indicate some strategies of identity management, at times 'performing femininity' (Butler, 1990):

> If I was out with people who were dressed up nicer I would probably try and make more of an effort...I think it becomes more difficult as you get older, you worry about things more, about looking right. (Andrea)

> Compared to what I was in first year, now I think I dress more feminine. Before I'd wear baggy shirts and baggy tops, I sort of show myself off a bit more than I used to do. (Frances)

> The stereotype's disappeared a little bit...I've noticed the way people have changed, so I think even here [university], players are a lot more feminine looking than they were when I started. (Heidi)

One player also stated how she wore make-up whilst playing, which could be understood as a conscious effort to retain her femininity whilst being required to display attributes more associated with masculinity. The pictorial data was useful here in demonstrating how players perceived themselves to have differing identities whilst both playing compared to whilst not playing football. In particular, players highlighted increased conformity to feminine ideals in their sketches of themselves after a game, as all players with long hair drew themselves wearing it down outside of football participation, which is considered a significant visible indicator of femininity (Cox and Thompson, 2000). The comment by Heidi even suggests that this kind of identity management may be happening on a larger scale, changing this player's perception of female footballers at the university. Alongside maintaining a feminine appearance, proving their heterosexuality was described by one player as the other way to avoid any negative treatment: "the only way to avoid the stereotype is to be girly, or be clearly with a bloke" (Frances).

Do women pose a challenge to the culture of football?

Even though at times they conformed to societal expectations, these players also suggested that they were attempting to challenge both the gendered norms that affected their experiences and the close association between football and masculinity. Miller and Penz (1991) explored this with female bodybuilders, highlighting how they were working to redefine their activity with their own values, and Scraton *et al.* (1999) found that female footballers can incorporate their own positive values into their sporting experiences. Similarly in this study, players described how they celebrated the beneficial differences women's football can give them in comparison to how they perceived men's football:

> I think women play football cos they enjoy it and they want to play, whereas a lot of the time men play football just because of the whole aggressive thing. Just to get their aggression out, just to go out and start a fight with someone. (Gina)

> I just think that with women players, they play because they love the game. For example our team, everyone plays because they want to play, you don't get paid for it...it shows that people really want to play, even if they're not that good...it's the basis of the game really. (Carla)

These women are redefining their sporting experiences, and enjoyment is regarded as the basis of their participation. Other benefits include "feeling happier, and more confident" (Andrea); "you all work together to achieve stuff" (Brenda); and helping their physical condition "you are just fitter all round, stronger, more stamina" (Heidi). Friendship and socialising are also considered major benefits, enhanced by the university environment, yet only one player reported that winning was a benefit, even though the club is very successful. Redefining experiences away from the dominant (male) model of sport can however be difficult for women — no meaningful alternative discourses are available (Young and White, 1995). For these players, the social aspect of the university context appears to provide a potentially empowering framework.

At this club, the support of team-mates appeared to be particularly significant in negotiating any barriers they might experience. The team environment assisted with countering any negative treatment:

> You're with people on the pitch and off the pitch, and you never go through anything on your own. (Frances)

> It's good to try and get your point across...I think you'd have a go [at somebody who was being negative towards women's football], round everyone up with their social shirts on! (Eve)

> I think that we do go out a lot as a team, and it's good because I think it helps the team, with bonding and that as well. Everyone's friends as well as team-mates, perhaps more so in a uni[versity] team. (Andrea)

This last comment not only highlights the importance of the team spirit these players gained from their involvement in the football club but also coincides with research concluding that the social aspect of sports participation is of a priority to women (see for example Lenskyj, 1994). Bonding appears to be an important benefit of this football club that may not be as significant in a different context.

> Everyone here is the same age, and similar people in a way...you've got people who are all together in a small space, and everyone goes out on a Wednesday, it's a routine more than anything. And I think that helps you on the pitch, it's something that is different. (Frances)

Discussion and conclusions

The discussions with this group of eight women demonstrated how female footballers can face various barriers when choosing to play football and can use varying techniques to negotiate these barriers. As with other studies in this area (Harris, 2002; Scraton *et al.*, 1999), these players found that organised opportunities to play football at a young age were limited. One problem may be that the majority of primary school teachers are female, with little experience of football (Lopez, 1997) and so the 'gendered positioning'[2] of teachers can clearly impact the type and quality of provision. The players in this study were lucky that they were able to gain acceptance from male peers and family members (although to varying extents) in order to be given informal opportunities to firstly try out football, and then continue their participation into adulthood.

It is significant that most of these girls were accepted into male playground football as this is a setting in which boys construct, negotiate and perform their masculinity (Swain, 2000) and which results in the exclusion of the majority of girls on the basis of their sex (Epstein *et al.*, 2001). However to achieve acceptance from male peers, girls were required to prove their ability, indicative of the different assumptions made about boys and girls regarding innate sporting ability. Gender dynamics were particularly salient here, even at such a young age, as sport in general and football in particular is strongly considered a male preserve (Therberge, 1997). Studies have shown that children believe football to be a solely male activity (Harris, 2002; Epstein *et al.*, 1997), an attitude that forms the basis of female exclusion. The fact that these players were generally accepted into the culture of playground football with few problems was an unexpected finding of the analysis. It seems that being able to prove their ability and display the required masculine attributes (being a 'tomboy') created an entry route into this male dominated enclave.

Issues with gendered identities, identity management and 'performing gender' were noticeable throughout the discussions, though not to the extent that was expected considering previous research in the area (see for example Caudwell, 1999; Cox and Thompson, 2000). The notion that being a 'tomboy' is acceptable so long as the child grows out of it (Comer, 1974, cited in Harris, 2002) is a result of the social retributions that can be associated with deviating from societal norms. As the players in this study grew up as female footballers, the need to conform to societal notions of gender-appropriate behaviour became more salient, and there was some evidence of individuals constructing different identities for different situations to negotiate their 'deviance'. Historically, professional experts and casual observers alike have linked female athleticism with lesbianism, due to the strong cultural associations between sport and masculinity (Cahn, 1995), and this stereotyping can mark all players' sexuality indiscriminately (Caudwell, 1999). Women who display characteristics that challenge male power can be dismissed by branding them 'lesbian' and therefore not 'real' women (Wright and Clarke, 1999). The stereotype surrounding women's football did not appear to impact heavily on the experiences of this group of players, and it was even suggested that the 'butch' stereotype may be diminishing. If this is the case, the cause of this is difficult (and perhaps impossible) to ascertain — is women's football becoming more popular because the stereotype is diminishing, or is the stereotype diminishing because the game is becoming more popular and more women and girls are involved? This discussion is beyond the scope of this study, but the situation is complex and is unlikely to be as clear-cut as either of these causal explanations.

In the western world there exists a dominant notion, reinforced by the media, of an ideal female body as thin, slender, toned and (hetero)sexually attractive (Krane, 2001). As a result, women who are subject to stereotyping due to their involvement in sports more associated with masculinity can 'manage' their identity and perform learned behaviours considered consistent with their gender (Butler, 1990). This can be done through the use of feminine clothing (Halbert, 1997), jewellery and make up (Obel, 1996), perfume (Wright and Clarke, 1999) or feminine hairstyles (Cox and Thompson, 2000). However, conforming to such notions of gender-appropriate behaviour merely reinforces this form of femininity as the dominant form — in this way, women can be seen to be contributing to their own oppression. This creates a paradox whereby women are colonising male spaces in sport (Young and White, 1995) yet simultaneously limiting this challenge by conforming to and therefore reinforcing ideal notions of femininity. The discussions with players in this study did suggest that practices of identity management were utilised at times, though not to a great extent, which is consistent with the suggestion that stereotyping did not appear to impact their experiences in any significant way.

A major and potentially valuable conclusion to the study was the relevance of the context within which these eight female footballers experienced football at the time of the interviews. The university environment within which this study takes place is particularly significant in impacting how these women experience football, assisting in negotiating any barriers they face, and encouraging them to attach their own meanings to their experiences. This context allows a collective experience, which has been shown to be effective in challenging sexist structures and exclusionary practices in sport (Pelak, 1997). In this environment, support, participation and friendship are promoted over achievement, allowing women to experience sport in a different (and potentially more empowering) way, and the importance of social aspects of participation was a major benefit to players of this club. The lack of negative treatment experienced by these players in comparison to those in the study by Caudwell (1999) could be explained to some extent by this environment — a successful and highly regarded sporting university with a variety of student-run opportunities on offer to both men and women.

This study therefore suggests that university clubs should be considered an important site for female experiences of sport, and in particular those sports or activities not traditionally associated with femininity. Not only are women provided with the opportunity to try new sports, but the university setting appears to produce a safer environment that limits the negative treatment that can surround female athletes, and encourages women to attach their own values to their sporting experiences. Players are of a similar age, live in close proximity to each other and have limited work commitments or responsibilities. The combination of these factors appears to provide a strong social support network that can encourage players to be more comfortable with their own identities. In this context, one that combines higher education and varying sporting opportunities, this group of women found that they were accepted as female athletes — though notably, still not treated seriously as footballers.

Notes

1 The extent to which individuals consciously 'do gender' is continuously under debate, and there is not the space to discuss here. For this study it was understood that both structure and agency are involved in the process of acting out gendered behaviours that can vary in different social contexts.

2 'Gendered positioning' is the process of defining teachers' positions in a school structure on the basis of their gender, usually teaching gender-stereotyped activities (Brown and Rich, 2002) but also the positioning of women as predominantly primary school teachers as a result of their assumed maternal and caring qualities (Measor and Sikes, 1992).

References Numerous incomplete references

Brown, A. (1998) (ed) Fanatics: Power, identity and fandom in football. London: Routledge.

Brown, D. and Rich, E. (2002) 'Gender positioning as pedagogical practice in teaching physical education' in D. Penney (ed) *Gender and physical education: Contemporary issues and future directions.* London: Routledge, pp. 80–101.

Butler, J. (1990) *Gender trouble: Feminism and the subversion of identity.* London: Routledge.

Carle, A. and Nauright, J. (1999) 'Crossing the line: Women playing rugby union', in T. J. L Chandler and J. Nauright (eds) *Making the Rugby world: Race, gender and commerce.* London: Frank Cass, pp. 128–148.

Cahn, S. (1995) *Coming on strong: Gender and sexuality in women's 20th century sport.* Harvard University Press: Macmillan.

Caudwell, J. (1999) 'Women's football in the UK: Theorising gender and unpacking the butch lesbian image', *Journal of Sport and Social Issues* Vol. 23, No. 4: pp. 390–402.

Coleman, J. C. and Hendry, L. B. (1999) *The nature of adolescence* (3rd ed). London: Routledge.

Cook, J. A. and Fonow, M. M. (1990) 'Knowledge and women's interests: Issues of epistemology and methodology in feminist sociological research, in J. M. Nielson (ed) *Feminist research methods.* Colorado: Westview Press, pp. 69–93.

Cox, B. and Thompson, S. (2000) 'Multiple bodies: Sportswomen, soccer and sexuality', *International Review for the Sociology of Sport* Vol. 35, No. 1: pp. 5–20.

Davies, P. (1997) *I lost my heart to the Belles.* London: Mandarin Paperbacks.

Epstein, D., Kehily, M., Mac an Ghaill., M. and Redman, P. (2001) 'Boys and girls come out to play: Making masculinities and femininities in school playgrounds', *Men and Masculinities* Vol. 4, No. 2: pp. 158–172.

Hargreaves, J. (1994) *Sporting females: Critical issues in the history and sociology of women's sports.* London: Routledge.

Halbert, C. (1997) 'Tough enough and woman enough: Stereotypes, discrimination and impression management among women professional boxers', *Journal of Sport and Social Issues* Vol. 21, No. 1: pp. 7–36.

Harris, J. (2002) '"No you can't play, you're a girl": Some primary school recollections of female football players', *The Bulletin of Physical Education* Vol. 38, No. 3: pp. 161–178.

Kay, T. (1995) *Women and sport: A review of research.* The Sports Council.

Krane, V. (2001) 'We can be athletic and feminine, but do we want to? Challenging hegemonic femininity in women's sport', *Quest* Vol. 53: pp. 115–133.

Lenskyj, H. (1994) 'Sexuality and femininity in sport contexts: Issues and alternatives', *Journal of Sport and Social Issues* Vol. 18, No. 4: pp. 356–376.

Lopez, S. (1997) *Women on the ball.* London: Scarlet Press.

Mason, J. (2001) *Qualitative researching* (2nd ed). London: Sage.

Measor, L. and Sikes, P. J. (1992) *Gender and schools.* London: Cassell.

Maynard, M. (1994) 'Methods, practice and epistemology: The debate about feminism and research',in M. Maynard and J. Purvis (eds) *Researching women's lives from a feminist perspective.* London: Taylor & Francis, pp. 9–21.

Miller, L. and Penz, O. (1991) 'Talking bodies: Female bodybuilders colonise a male preserve', *Quest* Vol. 43: pp. 148–163.

Nielsen, J. M. (ed) (1990) *Feminist research methods.* Colorado: Westview Press.

Obel, C. (1996) 'Collapsing gender in competitive bodybuilding: Researching contradictions and ambiguity in sport', *International Review for the Sociology of Sport* Vol. 31, No. 2: pp. 185–202.

Pelak, C. F. (2002) 'Women's collective identity formation in sports: A case study from women's ice hockey', *Gender and Society* Vol. 16, No. 1: pp. 93–114.

Reinharz, S. (1992) *Feminist methods in social research.* New York: Oxford University Press.

Sabo, D. (1988) 'Psychosocial impacts of athletic participation on American women: Facts and fables', *Journal of Sport and Social Issues* Vol. 12, No. 2: pp. 83–96.

Scraton, S., Fasting, K., Pfister, G., and Bunual, A. (1999) 'It's still a man's game? The experiences of top-level European women footballers', *International Review for the Sociology of Sport* Vol. 32, No. 4: pp. 99–111.

Stanley, L. and Wise, S. (1993) *Breaking out again: Feminist ontology and epistemology.* London: Routledge.

Swain, S. (2000) '"The money's good, the fame's good, the girls are good": The role of playground football in the construction of young boys' masculinity in a junior school', *British Journal of the Sociology of Education* Vol. 21, No. 1: pp. 95–109.

The Football Association. (2005) Accessed at *www.thefa.org.*

Therberge, N. (1997) 'It's part of the game: Physicality and the production of gender in women's hockey', *Gender and Society* Vol. 11: pp. 69–87.

Thorne, B. (1993) *Gender play: Girls and boys in school.* Buckingham: Open University Press.

www.thefa.com/Womens/, accessed 26 June 2006

Williams, J. (2003) *A game for rough girls? A history of women's football in Britain.* London: Routledge.

Williams, J. and Woodhouse, J. (1991) 'Can play, will play? Women and football in Britain', in John Williams and S. Wagg (eds) *British football and social change.* London: Leicester University Press, pp. 85–108.

Wright, G. and Clarke, G. (1999) 'Sport, the media and the construction of compulsory heterosexuality: A case study of women's rugby union', *International Review for the Sociology of Sport* Vol. 34, No. 3: pp. 227–243.

Young, K. and White, P. (1995) 'Sport, physical danger and injury: The experiences of elite women athletes', *Journal of Sport and Social Issues* Vol. 19, No. 1: pp. 45–61.

FEMALE FOOTBALL SUPPORTERS' COMMUNITIES IN SPAIN: A FOCUS ON WOMEN'S *PEÑAS*

Ramón Llopis Goig

University of Valencia (Spain)

Introduction

This chapter offers an introductory analysis of the relationship between football and women in contemporary Spain, with a focus on female football fans and their involvement in female football *peñas* — supporters' associations attached to Spanish clubs. *Peñas* are groups of friends and supporters that meet in order to watch matches of their football teams and also discuss the fortunes of their team when matches are not being played. Some *peñas* have an office in the club facilities but most are located in a bar that subsequently becomes their headquarters. *Peñas* meet regularly, sometimes three times a week, and are a well-established and important feature of Spanish football culture and Spanish football fandom. Considering the constitution of Spanish clubs and the importance of elected members to positions of power, it is possible for members of *peñas* to be elected to official positions within their respective clubs.

Traditionally, Spanish football has been a space for masculinity-building that kept women at a distance, in terms of their participation and consumption, as well as in its practice. Nowadays, sport interest and practice has increased among Spanish women, as has been shown by several pieces of research (Buñuel, 1996; Puig, 2000). In this context, in order to examine what happens in the relationship between football and women in Spain, in this chapter, I ask some questions such as: Have women become more interested in football? Do they watch football matches on television? Do they attend the stadiums? Do they play football? These questions are briefly dealt with in order to analyse the context of the relationship between football and women in Spain, since the main topic is the analysis of women's football *peñas*. In relation to this I ask: What are these female fan communities like? Why were they founded? What do women think about male peñas? What are the differences between male and female *peñas*?

I attempt to answer such questions by bringing together analysis of data from surveys and statistical registers and interview data collected from Spanish women (n=12) who were involved in *peñas*. Quantitative data contribute to shape a general overview of the position of women as fans and consumers in Spanish football. This data shows that, contrary to what happens in other sports, interest and consumption of football among women is reduced and is practiced by a minority. On the other hand, analysis of interview data reveals the fact that some women consider that football in Spain is 'taking off' as a sport for women. Nevertheless, football in Spain continues to be perceived as a space for masculinity building — something that alone could be regarded as a reason for the creation of separate women's *peñas*.

This chapter is divided into three parts. The first contains a very brief historical overview of the position of women in Spanish football during the twentieth-century. The second refers to women in football and aims at analysing the orientation of women towards professional and male football, considering some aspects such as interest in football, television audiences and attendance at matches. The third part offers evidence about their fans and associated activities, more exactly about their involvement in women's football *peñas*.

Historical overview of women's involvement in Spanish football

In Spain, football has been mainly 'men's business', a point clearly made in a famous brandy advert that was featured on football match radio broadcasts in the 1960s, 1970s, and 1980s. Spanish football culture has had a strong male component and the interest of females was exceptional. In these decades football, for many women at least, was a sort of torture that they had to endure on Sunday evenings. Either they did not enjoy football or, if they liked it, it was difficult for them to attend matches in stadiums defended as private arenas for their partners or husbands. For the Spanish people, football has always appeared as a masculine space. Historically, the small numbers of women who have attended matches have come from the higher social classes, and they went to the stadium, usually, as a simple companions or 'ornaments' of men. Fundamentally they were considered to be passive spectators. If they showed interest in being present at matches, their husbands were often suspicious of their motives. This was reflected in some popular Spanish songs early in the twentieth century, such as in 'Alirón!' composed by Álvaro Retana and Gaspar de Aquino, and premiered at Romea Theatre of Madrid in 1912:

> In Madrid it is in fashion / *En Madrid se ha puesto de moda*
> the song of 'Aliron' / *la canción del Alirón*
> Because it sings the *victory* / *porque canta las victorias*
> of the football aces / *de los ases del balón*
> And the sensible girl's / *Y a las niñas sensitivas*
> heart beats / *les palpita el corazón*
> for any of the eleven players / *por cualquiera de los once*
> from the winning team / *del equipo triunfador*
> (../...)
> and the same in Indochina / *y lo mismo en Indochina*
> than in other country / *que en cualquier otra nación*
> conquering a football player / *conquistar a un futbolista*
> is the hope of any girl / *de una chica es la ilusión*

The image of women in these songs is framed around two stereotypes prevalent at the time. Firstly, there is the stereotype of the 'football widow' — a woman who is alone at home and bored because she lacks the company of her husband or boyfriend. The image of a woman without life is particularly prominent as the stereotype depicts that this type of woman is a woman dependent on the company of a husband or boyfriend. The second stereotype is that of a generally younger woman who loses control when watching football matches and provides an image of a woman who is more irrational and more emotionally immature than was publicly acceptable in Spain at the time.

In terms of historical association, some Spanish clubs have attracted women as spectators, usually as companions of male fans, since the early 1900s. In the case of Real Madrid, for example, its President offered extra tickets to male fans in order that their wives or girlfriends or sisters could get free entry into the stadium in 1912. Football reports in the press started to make reference to these women 'fans' who were generally drawn from higher social classes. Their presence increased but in 1920 they accounted for not more than 5% of the total spectators at the Spanish football stadiums: such women came from the upper classes, a situation familiar to other Spanish sports at the time as sports event attendance was a privilege accorded only to women on the higher steps of the social pyramid (Bahamonde, 2000: p. 68).

From the establishment of the Second Republic in 1931, women consolidated their position as spectators in Chamartín, the new stadium of Real Madrid, but always as men's companions. There was still no penetration of the working-class market for female support but the really significant issue was the fact that the presence of women as fans reached a sustainable trend. Real Madrid issued its first *socia* (season ticket) to a woman in 1926 and in 1933 the census of the club showed 5,000 *socios* of which almost 20% were women. Significantly, women paid less for their *socia* than men, a strategy that lasted at Madrid until the 1950s. FC Barcelona already had 194 female *socios* in 1939 which accounted for 5% of its membership, whilst in the same year the first incorporation of women supporters occured in clubs such as UD Salamanca, RC of Santander and Real Zaragoza (Orúe and Gutiérrez, 2001: p. 20). In the mid-1970s, some Spanish clubs, such as Granada and Athlétic de Bilbao, relegated their female *socias* to the category of children where they were considered as powerless and voiceless and were not allowed to vote in the club elections and assemblies (Verdú, 1980). In General Franco's Spain of the 1960s a woman could not easily leave the country or open a bank account without the permission of her husband so the 'downgrading' of female football supporters is not surprising.

So, it is again no surprise that there are few references to women in Spanish books on football during these periods, nor is it strange that there are few references to women in the several books dedicated to historical aspects of the Spanish game. Those in which women are present depict them as a 'problem' for football and its players. For example, the only reference to a woman in a football book written by a famous author in Spain, Carlos F. Santander, is in the chapter which leaves little to the imagination, entitled: 'Skirt affairs' (Santander, 1997, pp. 27–36). Another book by the same author examines the relations between the Civil War, the Franco dictatorship and football, and in a chapter called 'Lola Flores, the femme fatale of players' (Santander, 1990: 125–130), a woman — Lola Flores — is considered a problem.

A brief overview of women's interest and audiences of male football in Spain

Contrary to what happens in countries such as England — where many scholars and institutes have carried out studies on women's interest in football (e.g. Wann, Melnick, Russell and Pease, 2001; Woodhouse and Williams, 1999; and, Woodhouse, 2001) — in Spain we know little about the attitude of women towards Spanish football. In this section I want to present some introductory figures on the issue in order to situate more clearly, within a social context, the research that I will expound in the next section. But first, I would like to say something about the existing material on female fans in England that could be useful to compare and thus understand better the Spanish case.

In England there are slightly conflicting accounts as to whether female attendance at football matches has increased significantly. Wann *et al.* (2001) suggest that women are now attending 'live' sport in higher numbers than in previous decades. In the same way Coddington (1997) has pointed out that up to 25% of football's new fans are female, and more women are watching football on television. But other pieces of research show that English football venues continue to attract mainly white, male, working-class audiences (Malcolm, Jones and Waddington, 2000). In contrast, for instance, 'live' British ice hockey tends to appeal to a more affluent supporter base which is made up of male and female fans almost in similar proportions (Crawford, 2001).

Some studies claim to demonstrate that the modernization of English football has increased female interest in the game: more of them are attracted to attend matches (SNCCFR, 1995: p. 14) or watch them on television (Williams and Woodhouse, 1991: p. 87). During the early 1980s, most surveys about football supporters showed that women made up between 5% and 15% of the live football audience, depending on the club involved. During that decade, the discussion about female football fans was often inextricably linked to debates about violence and disorder by young male spectators. In some accounts, the attendance of women was supposed to have had a 'civilising' effect on such behaviour (Woodhouse, 1991). A Football Association Fan Survey conducted by the University of Leicester in 1997 suggested that, on average, women constitute 12% of 'live' audiences at men's Premier League association football in England. In 2001 this figure rose to 15%, and in clubs such as Ipswich Town and Leicester City more than one in five of all season ticket holders were female. The message is that female interest in the game has been increasing in the last 15 years or so.

In Spain, recent data suggests gendered interest in sport as 72% of men and only 48% women are involved in some capacity or another. Of the population that is older than 15 years, 50.6% is interested in football and according to a survey carried out by Gallup Spain (March 2004), and men continue to be the main source of 'interested' fans for football in Spain with 70.9% in this category. However only 30.7% of Spanish women are interested in football, which means seven out of ten have no interest in football. Regarding the audiences for programmes related to football, on television and also on radio in Spain, differences between men and women are equally significant. A survey carried out by the Spanish Centre of Sociological Research (CIS) in 2003, 38% of men 'usually' watch television football programmes against just 6% of women,while 60% of men 'often' watch such programmes against just 12% of women. In the case of radio listening, 24% of men 'usually' tune in to football programmes compared to just 4% of women, while 44% of men and 9% of women listen 'often'. And finally, regarding attendance at matches, more than a quarter of the Spanish population (27.6%) have bought a ticket to attend a football match during the previous year (2002): of that figure, 41.7% were men but only 14% were women.

When analysing these statistics, it could be concluded that women have lately begun to be interested in football. Although the interest is certainly increasing, as has been seen above, these figures show that interest in football, attendances and audiences remain predominantly male, both in the UK and Spain. On the other hand, although figures between the two countries are not strictly comparable, it could be suggested that women's attendance at matches seems to be very similar in both.

The data shown above can be related to figures concerning the numbers of women in Spain playing football. Although it is not the main goal of this study, this information will allow us to go more deeply into the relationship between women and football today. In Spain, 26% of women practise at least one sport (Garcia Ferrando, 2001) and of these more than one-third play football, either in 11-a-side or five-a-side formats. However, interestingly enough, none of these versions of football is among the first ten sporting preferences for women (CIS, 2000). At the end of June 2004 there were 9,747 registered of female 'amateur' footballers and 2,329 'grass roots' female football players, representing 1.9% of the total number (646,812) of registered players in Spain.

The influence of the values and norms acquired during the socialisation process is important for understanding this difference (Diez Mintegui, 2003). Traditional sporting values such as competitiveness, physical power, potential and success are all associated with sports considered to be typically masculine in Spanish culture (Mosquera and Puig, 2002: p. 102). Traditionally those Spanish women who have not received a sporting education have not felt cheated by this fact and although this image is now changing, there are still a lot of Spanish women, mostly older and from disadvantaged classes, who do not readily see or place their own bodies in a sporting situation (Mosquera and Puig, 2002).

Fandom: the involvement of women in female football *peñas*

Even though there is data presented in the previous section it is difficult to draw conclusions about the development of female fandom and female support within football. Nonetheless, the data does show that some Spanish women do go to football stadiums and watch football on television. Only a few decades ago women tended to attend only as men's companions. Therefore, we should not ignore the fact that Spanish women have become more interested in footbal: these facts are closely linked to the deep transformation that Spanish society has undergone during the last thirty years as women have started to take the first steps on the path to equality, a path not trodden by previous generations.

However, those women interested in male football do not want to be seen as simple spectators of matches but seek to be regarded as active, committed and knowledgeable football fans. However this quest is not free from difficulties. Firstly, women sometimes feel uncomfortable among men who do not always accept them as football supporters. So, even in their role as spectators, women sometimes remain excluded as 'real' football supporters. Often they are seen to have the only legitimate female role, that is, to "spectate, support and admire" (Scraton, 1995: p. 122). Secondly, they would like to be involved in male football by joining *peñas* which would allow them to meet to watch away matches of their team among fellow supporters, and also to meet on other occasions to talk about their teams.

However women feel uncomfortable in traditional *peñas* due to the strong male ethos and masculine undertones associated with such *peñas*.

To give context to *peñas*, the numbers that are attached to individual clubs are impressive: Real Madrid has 1,605 *peñas*, FC Barcelona 1,508 and Valencia CF 716. However, the numbers of women in these associations is practically non-existent. Due to this, some Spanish women interested in football have formed their *peñas* exclusively for women. The first female *peña* to form was 'Peña Valencianista Luna de Valencia' in 1984, a *peña* attached to Valencia CF. After its successful establishment other *peñas* for females were formed at other Spanish clubs, and notable examples include 'Peña Izar' (Real Sociedad); 'Peña New Burguer' (Deportivo de la Coruña); 'Peña El Harén' (Extremadura); 'Peña La Tentación Blanca' (Real Madrid); 'Peña Juan Carlos Unzué' (Sevilla); 'Peña Juan Ureña' (Betis); and Peña La Regenta (Oviedo). This list demonstrates that not the interest in Spanish football from women but also their willingness to organise and formalise their interest as do their male counterparts.

In this section I shall examine twelve interviews carried out with Spanish women who were involved in *peñas* at Valencia CF, Villarreal CF, Real Madrid, FC Barcelona, Sevilla FC, and Athletic de Bilbao.

Justifying the reasons for the formation of these *peñas*, the women asserted that their role as a football spectator is not that of a simple 'companion' to men. Rather, they go to football matches because they like it, and one member affirmed that "we enjoy football as much as men". Another member commented that:

> Football has always been monopolised by men. Women who attended football matches were just as their husbands' companions. They would take them to the stadium so they would not be alone at home. Now we have shown that women go to a football stadium because we like football, we know about it, we enjoy it and we have things to say about it.

They state their interest in football as a sport and declare themselves as 'real' fans of their teams but note that this is something difficult for Spanish men to understand. It is a regular occurrence for men to reject the views of women on football matches and one female member remarked:

> We meet and we talk about football. If there are men with us, you know, at once, that they are going to say that you don't know about football, that you don't understand it.

The reluctance of some men to accept opinions and comments of women about football is, without doubt, one of the reasons that encourage women to find a space of their own in order to enjoy football. It came through the interviews that some men were willing to allow women to be present at football matches, whether in the ground or in a bar, but as soon as women dare to give an opinion about the match under way, a player's performance or the team's tactics they are derided by their male counterparts. This point was confirmed by one member:

> They [men] cannot bear it when we give our opinion about any aspect during the football match. I suppose that not all men are this way, but here [in Seville], it is something which they cannot help. They approve of us going to the stadiums and watching football matches, but only if our presence does not question their superior status. They have read about it all during the week in *As*, *Marca* or whatever sports magazine. And they know it all, so you make a comment and they look at you in such a way that makes it clear that you better remain silent.

These findings support the results Woodhouse and Williams (1999) obtained in their study in England which suggests that female followers of male mass sport events often find their patterns of support and 'authenticity' as 'real' fans questioned by other, mainly male, supporters. Since the development of a football fan's identity is primarily driven by social interaction, female fans of mass sport events such as football may find obstacles when trying to go up to the highest levels of the fan club structures (Crawford, 2004: p. 47). This perception of a limited 'career' as a football fan seems to be behind the reluctance to create or belong to a female *peña* in many of the interviewed women. Clearly, expressing views but not having them treated seriously by men is a frustration facing women with an interest in football and one of the key motivating factors for the emergence of female *peñas*.

Nonetheless, not all the women interviewed got involved in *peñas* for the same reasons. Some joined because their husbands, boyfriends or friends do not like football as they do and the *peña* provided an outlet for their interest. Others joined because they disliked the idea of being surrounded by so many men in the stadium. A further reason offered by some women was that they felt it unsafe to venture out alone to the stadium. Finally, some of the women did not feel at ease with their husbands regarding football because either they were not allowed to express themselves freely or they felt inhibited by their husband's presence in the stadium. The philosophy of the women-only *peña* was clearly expressed in one interviewee's comment:

> Being women alone, we can talk about whatever and we can do what we want. If [men] are with us, everything we do seems to be wrong. If we shout at the referee, they look at us out of the corner of their eyes trying to make us feel ashamed. If we give our opinion they tell us to shut up as we know nothing about football. Therefore, with women from peña it is fantastic, we have our own environment to enjoy the match.

This view stresses the importance of the sense of 'community' within female *peñas* where members are not faced with the overriding sense of masculinity that dominates male *peñas*. This sense of 'community' may be seen to influence the behaviour of women or their commitment to their club. Individuals may form football loyalties for many different reasons and it is increasingly common for fans to connect with each other on the basis of more 'individual' reasons. Further, supporters' communities are not just defined by a common sense of belonging but also by patterns of exclusion and even by opposition to others (Crawford, 2004: p. 53). In this sense, the creation of separate *peñas* for women could be considered an attempt to fight against the exclusion they suffer in the stadium as well as an attempt to oppose the strong male ethos which characterizes the world of football in Spain, and particularly male *peñas*.

Whilst male membership of female *peñas* is not wholly prohibited, most do not allow men to join, as explained by one member who said that "our *peña* is only for women. We have often talked about it and we are convinced that it is going to remain the way it is now". Traditional *peñas* do not formally prohibit access to women but there is an insurmountable cultural barrier that women do not dare to cross by joining. It is absolutely unthinkable, both for men and women, that a woman comes into a bar where the traditional *peña* meets and sits down to chat, as one member confirmed:

> A woman cannot go into a bar alone in which there is a men's peña. She can turn up with her husband, but not alone. She cannot turn up alone and take a coffee. This is why the women's *peñas* have appeared.

On the other hand, it should be made clear that their rejection of male membership does not make their *peñas* feminist. Most women interviewed rejected the word 'feminist' as a term that could describe the purpose of the *peñas* they belong to. The following comment shows the general opinion of the women who were interviewed on this matter:

> We are not a feminist *peña*. We founded a *peña* because of football and we still think that this *peña* has to be for women. We did not create the *peña* due to a feminist impulse. It is the same as a group of men founding a *peña* just for men, they do it because they like football and are supporters of a football team. We just do the same.

Therefore, the women interviewed insist on the fact that their *peñas* are just like men's — that is, they are centred on a deep passion for football, their club and generate a pleasant environment to enjoy football among like-minded people.

As well as men, teenage girls are also discouraged from joining women-only *peñas*. The reason for this is that such girls are not considered 'true' football fans as their interest is the men who play it rather than the sport itself. They are regarded as having merely changed their interest from male stars in music and film to those in football. To allow such girls to join would bring criticism that *peñas* permit 'hangers on' to join for superficial reasons. The following comment from one of the interviewees crystallises this:

> We wanted to create a female *peña*, for women. ... [not for] teen-agers who do not really like football and just want to come closer to famous football players.

A key issue for the women who join *peñas* is that their commitment has to be fitted around their domestic 'duties'. Female *peñas* simply cannot develop the same activities or schedules as the men's *peñas*:the women fans must accommodate their fandom within domestic constraints that simply do not apply to men. One member pointed out these aspects during the interview:

> Our *peña* cannot organise things in the same way as a men's *peña*. They finish at work and they have finished with their duties, they go to the bar and stay there as long as they want. They do not have to look after children, do the washing or make dinner. They arrive at home and have dinner. So, a women's *peña* cannot have the same role or be run in the same way.

It seems that even though *peñas* exist for women and point toward some form of equality, women are still restrained by traditional/domestic duties which affect their membership of and experience in their *peñas*.

Back, Crabbe and Solomos (2001) have pointed out in their work on football supporters' associations that an 'entry ticket' to a supporters' community always involves much more than a financial transaction. Boundaries of inclusion and exclusion within a given community are mediated through cultural terms and in this sense, possession of the right 'cultural ticket' may be achieved for those who can easily adapt to the norms of the existing community. However for those who have less 'flexible' differences, such as gender (and also, for instance, ethnicity), access and progress within the group may prove difficult to achieve (Crawford, 2004: p. 55). This is a key consideration regarding access to membership of *peñas* in Spain.

Some conclusions

Spanish women have had more access to sport in twentieth-century Spain and several studies have shown this (García Ferrando, 1990, 1997, 2001). It has even been said that the twentieth century was the century of the sporting revolution for Spanish women (García Bonafé, 2001). However, Spanish football has not experienced a huge increase in female involvement and, whilst this chapter has shown that interest exists, participation rates and attendance at matches are still male-dominated. Many women still perceive and experience football as being shaped by a strong male ethos that makes access for women difficult. As it has been pointed out in

England, football has traditionally been seen as a male domain and men "create barricades to protect their territory" from invasion by women (Whelehan, 1994: p. 127). Hence, though women may be attending football matches, they often remain excluded from football communities. Male supporters label female fans as 'uncommitted' in their support, and women see football as a forbidden territory (Woodhouse and Williams, 1999).

As other research has shown (Del Campo, 2002: p. 33) football in Spain can be characterised as a 'social performance' in which masculinity is recreated against other models of behaviour. As the main actors, football players are socialised into these patterns (Buñuel, 1996) but it is the same for football fans and for football that is played in the street. The impenetrability of football by women contributes to the difficulty of constituting a workable 'feminine' space within sport. Football does not appear among the ten first sports favoured by women as participants, and females make up less than 2% of total registrations in Spanish football. Moreover, the presence of men in women's football is high, both in coaching and organisational positions while the present structures for women's football are profoundly amateur and low status. This is an important area for future research as in Spain, like other European countries with a strong history in (men's) football, the female game in Spain still has a long road to travel.

In Spain those women who are 'interested' in football and follow their teams passionately are pressed to create strictly female *peñas* in order to engage with the professional male game. They find a space of liberation from masculine domination of football and the possibility there to develop a kind of 'gender individualization' (Ortega, 1996; Puig, 2000) in these *peñas*. Belonging to a *peña* lets women assert their particular interest in football and it allows them to create their own cultural spaces around football, spaces that cannot be found in the traditional peñas that are defined by the kind of strong masculine ethos that has become a barrier to the entry of women.

Women's *peñas* are 'sociability spaces' with a playful component that, in some cases, has emerged to 'gather' together women who otherwise would have nobody to go with to the stadium. Also there are those women for whom joining a female *peña* means that their husband will agree to their attendance at football without suspicion. Other women join *peñas* because they do not want to attend matches with their husband as they do not enjoy their partner's behaviour or feel restricted by their presence. These women experience their membership of the *peña* as something of a 'liberation' that allows them to enjoy their favourite sport on their own terms. Women *peñas* allow female fans to oppose the male stereotypes that define women fans in Spain as being incapable of understanding football. As Orúe and Gutierrez (2001: p. 46) have written:

> Women are driven to fight tirelessly against this absurd and persistent view that states that they do not understand football or are not able to understand it because they did not practice it when they were young. Nor do they have in their minds — or in their genetic heritage — this 'knowledge' that, as some man said, is the essential background needed to talk about sport and enjoy its performance.

This chapter has shown that women's *peñas* provide one such forum in which women can demonstrate their understanding of football and are allowed to express it without ridicule or derision.

Acknowledgements

I'd like to thank John Williams, Sheila Scraton and the editorial team for helping me in the improvement of this chapter.

References to be revised to housestyle

Back, L., Crabbe T. and Solomos, J. (2001) *The changing face of football: Racism, identity and multiculture in the english game*. Oxford: Berg.

Bahamonde, A. (2000) *El Real Madrid en la Historia de España*. Madrid, Editorial Taurus.

Buñuel, A. (1996) 'Mujer, machismo y deporte', *Temas para el Debate*, 23.

Coddington, A. (1997) *One of the lads: Women who follow football*. London: Harper Collins.

Crawford, G. (2001) 'Characteristics of a Britain ice hockey audience — major findings of the 1998 and 1999 Manchester Storm Ice Hockey Club Supporters Surveys', *International Review for the Sociology of Sport* Vol. 36, No. 1: pp. 71–81.

——— (2004) *Consuming sport: Fans, sport and culture*. London: Routledge.

Del Campo, A. (2002) 'Hacerse hombre, hacerse el hombre: La construcción de la masculinidad en el fútbol', I Congreso Internacional del Fútbol, Salamanca.

Diez Mintegui, C. (2003) 'Deporte, socialización y género', in Medina, F. X. y R. Sánchez (eds) *Culturas en juego: Ensayos de antropología del deporte en España*. Barcelona: Icaria.

García Bonafé, M. (2001) 'El siglo XX. La revolución deportiva de las mujeres', Apunts. *Educación Física y Deportes* 64: pp. 63–68.

García Ferrando, M. (1990) *Aspectos sociales del deporte: Una reflexión sociológica*. Madrid: Alianza Editorial

——— (2001) *Los españoles y el deporte: Prácticas y comportamientos en la última década del siglo XX*. Madrid: Consejo Superior de Deportes.

García Ferrando, M., Puig, N. y F Lagardera (eds) (1997) *Sociología del Deporte*. Madrid, Alianza Editorial.

Malcolm, D., Jones, I. and Waddington, I. (2000) 'The people's game? Football spectatorship and demographic change', in J. Garland, D. Malcolm and M. Rowe (eds) *The future of football: Challenges for the twenty-first century*. London: Frank Cass.

Mosquera, M. J. and N. Puig (2002) 'Género y edad en el deporte', in García Ferrando, M., Puig, N. y F Lagardera (eds) *Sociología del deporte*. Madrid: Alianza Editorial.

Ortega, F. (1996) 'La esquiva igualdad: El género y sus representaciones sociales', in M. A. García de León, M. García de Cortázar y F. Ortega, *Sociología de las mujeres españolas*. Madrid: Editorial Complutense, pp. 309–324.

Orúe, E. y S. Gutiérrez (2001) *Locas por el fútbol: De las gradas al vestuario*. Madrid: Temas de Hoy.

Puig, N. (2000) 'Proceso de individualización, género y deporte', *Apunts. Educación Física y Deportes* 59: pp. 99–102.

Santander, C. F. (1990) *El fútbol durante la guerra civil y el franquismo*. Madrid: Editorial San Martín.

——— (1997) *A bote pronto: El fútbol y sus historias*. Madrid: Temas de Hoy.

Scraton, S. (1995) 'boys muscle in where angels fear to tread: Girl's sub-culture and physical activities', in C. Critcher, P. Bramham and A. Tomlinson (eds) *Sociology of Leisure: A Reader*. London, E and FN Spon.

Sir Norman Chester Centre for Football Research (1989) *Football and Football Spectators after Hillsborough: A National Survey of members of the Football Supporters Association*. Leicester: University of Leicester.

——— (1995) *FA Premier League Fan Surveys: sample report*. Leicester: University of Leicester.

——— (2000) *FA Premier League Fan Surveys 1999: General Sample Report*. Leicester: University of Leicester.

——— (2001) *FA Premier League National Fan Survey: Worthington Fans Feedback*. University of Leicester

Verdú, V. (1980) *El fútbol: Mitos, ritos y símbolos*. Madrid, Alianza Editorial.

Wann, D. L., Melnick, M. J., Russell, G. W. and Pease, D. G. (2001) *Sport fans: The psychology and social impact of spectators*. New York: Routledge.

Whelehan, I. (1994) *Over loaded: Popular culture and the future of feminism*. London: The Women's Press.

Williams, J. and Woodhouse D. (1991) 'Can play, will play? Women and football in Britain', in J. Williams and S. Wagg (eds) *British football and social change*. Leicester: Leicester University Press.

Woodhouse, D. (2001) *A national survey of female football fans*. Sir Norman Chester Centre for Football Research, Leicester: University of Leicester.

Woodhouse, D. and Williams, J. (1999) *Offside? The position of women in football*. Reading: South Street.

INDEX